# The Novel
## in the
# Third
# World

BOOKS BY CHARLES R. LARSON

*The Emergence of African Fiction*
*African Short Stories (Editor)*
*Prejudice: Twenty Tales*
*of Oppression and Liberation (Editor)*
*Opaque Shadows (Editor)*

# The Novel
# in the
# Third
# World

Charles R. Larson

INSCAPE / Publishers / Washington, D. C.

**Library of Congress Catalog Card Number 75-42302**
**International Standard Book Number: ISBN 0-87953-402-8**

**Library of Congress Cataloging in Publication Data**
Larson, Charles R.
The Novel in the Third World

Bibliography: p.
1. Fiction—20th century—History and criticism.
I. Title
PN3503.L3     809.3'3
ISBN 0-87953-402-8

# Permissions

For permission to reprint copyrighted material, grateful acknowledgment is made to the following:

*Batouala*, by René Maran. Copyright 1972 by Black Orpheus Press, Inc., Washington, D.C.

*Bound to Violence*, by Yambo Ouologuem. Copyright 1971 by Harcourt Brace Jovanovich, Inc., New York, N.Y.

*The Crocodile*, by Vincent Eri. Copyright 1970 by The Jacaranda Press, Brisbane, Australia.

*In the Castle of My Skin*, by George Lamming. Copyright 1953 by McGraw-Hill Co., New York, N.Y. Selections are reprinted by the permission of Curtis Brown, Ltd., New York, N.Y.

*Cane*, by Jean Toomer. Copyright 1923 by Boni & Liveright, Inc. Copyright Renewed 1951 by Jean Toomer. Selections are reprinted with the permission of Liveright Publishing Corporation, New York, N.Y.

*Seven Arrows*, by Hyemeyohsts Storm. Excerpts from *Seven Arrows* Copyright 1972 by Hyemeyohsts Storm. Reprinted by permission of Harper & Row Publishers, Inc., New York, New York.

*Kanthapura*, by Raja Rao. Excerpts from Raja Rao, *Kanthapura*. Copyright 1963 by New Directions Publishing Corporation. Reprinted by permission.

*Two Virgins*, by Kamala Markandaya. Copyright 1973 by The John Day Co., New York, N.Y.

*Grateful to Life and Death*, by R. K. Narayan. Copyright 1963 by The Michigan State University Press, East Lansing, Michigan.

*A Question of Power*, by Bessie Head. Copyright 1973 by Pantheon Books, New York, N.Y.

To T. G. Rosenthal, Helen Wolff, Rosemary Daughton, and Eric Sellin for reprinting material from their letters quoted herein.

# Acknowledgments:

I would like to thank the following people for helping me in my research: Donald E. Herdeck, for supplying me with information about *Batouala*; Bernth Lindfors, Eric Sellin, T. G. Rosenthal, Paul Flamand, Helen Wolff, James Currey, and Rosemary Daughton, for answering questions about Yambo Ouologuem and helping me track down information about his novel, *Bound to Violence*; Kamala Markandaya, R. K. Narayan, and Bessie Head, for generously supplying information about themselves; Faye Kelly, Ezekiel Mphahlele, and Newton P. Stallknecht, for giving initial support for the project itself; the graduate students in my Theory of Literary Ideas seminar at American University, where some of these ideas were first generated; and, of course, my wife—my best critic—who is mentioned in a separate dedication. Lastly, I would like to express my appreciation to the National Endowment for the Humanities, for thinking me worthy (and young) enough to be awarded a Younger Humanist Fellowship for spring and summer of 1974, during which time I was able to write this work.

# Contents:

For Roberta

# Introduction

In an earlier book, *The Emergence of African Fiction,** I attempted to illustrate the relationship between the novel in the West and the birth of the novel in tropical Africa. By necessity, many of my comparisons were drawn from African and Western literary works. Out of related social conditions, somewhat similar literary works had emerged, though my essential argument was that the African novel had variously incorporated a number of defining characteristics from African oral tradition, traditional African life and culture.

The scope of this book is much broader, though my thesis is akin to that of the earlier study—namely, that culture frequently shapes literary form. But it is also based upon a second premise: novels from the Third World often share more similarities with one another than they do with those from the West. Hence, my approach is comparative. The works in this study have been chosen not only for what they reveal about themselves (and the cultures that produced them) but also for what they reveal about one another. The novels considered come from a wide variety of areas in the Third World: Africa, the Caribbean, India, the South Pacific; novels by Afro-American and Native American writers of the United States are also considered. The fact is that there are excellent studies of the novels from several of these areas, but they are limited because of their geographical approach. This study takes a different

*Indiana University Press, 1972.

approach, examining a group of works together in order to see what the similarities are, for example, between African and Afro-American novels, or any of the other combinations suggested by the areas within the Third World.

Instead of looking at the books in this study in relationship to novels from the West, I examine them in relationship to one another. Thus, my references to Western literary examples are few. Although I argue that René Maran's novel, *Batouala* (1921), is as technically innovative as Marcel Proust's *Remembrance of Things Past (A la recherche du temps perdu*, 1913-1927), my analysis of the novel is much more an attempt to place Maran's work within the total complex of black writing from Africa and the New World. Although I make reference to Waldo Frank, John Dos Passos, and William Faulkner in my examination of Jean Toomer's *Cane* (1923), my major concern is to place Toomer's work at the center of Afro-American writing, thus making it pivotal to our understanding of the novel in the Third World. My approach, then, is limited to a number of specific works which I feel best exemplify the other works from the geographical areas they represent; it is not a general survey of all Third World novels, an undertaking which would run to several volumes. My interpretations of these books are also intended to be cumulative—each chapter harkening back to earlier ones, comparing the novel or novels under examination to those already analyzed.

It is important to note at the outset that the very "form" of the novel from cultures within the Third World has often been strongly influenced by those cultures themselves, resulting in something contrary to our concept of the novel in the West. The "situational" novel is the most obvious example of this—ideally defined as a narrative in which the central character's importance is replaced by a collective group of people undergoing a commonly-shared experience. This situational trait is typical of most of the novels examined in this study, though there are a number of other important similarities that these works share.

One of these is "emergence," undoubtedly the most important word for indicating the similarity in time of development of these writings, for—since we will not be concerned with traditional oral literature—all of these literatures must be considered recent, newly written. For Africa, except for isolated examples which take us back to the beginning of this century, the emergence of the novel as a literary form has been mostly a post-World War II event.[1] The major flowering has been during the past twenty-five years.This tends to be true for the West Indies also (especially for the Anglophone and Francophone examples), with, once again, a few exceptions that go back prior to this time.[2] The first novel by an Afro-American writer, William Wells Brown's *Clotel*, was published in 1851. Again, this work is a kind of rarity, appearing some seventy years before the Harlem Renaissance when Jean Toomer's *Cane* was published.[3] Indo-Anglian fiction has its origins in the second half of the last century, but like Black American fiction, the major writing has been since World War I.[4] American Indian fiction has acquired a certain readership only in the 1960's and 1970's though there are a few isolated examples of earlier works before this.[5] Fiction from the South Pacific is just beginning.[6] Emergent, then, means "recent" in our context—with a few isolated works that may go back as far as 125 years, but with the vast majority since World War I.

The recent appearance of this fiction also implies something about the language each of these writers uses, for in all of these cases English or French is the language of transmission. A number of the novelists come from cultures that have been analphabetic until the most recent times. They have used the language of their colonial oppressors, though in some instances it may be the writer's second or third spoken language. We can see this pattern with Yambo Ouologuem, Vincent Eri, Hyemeyohsts Storm, Raja Rao, Kamala Markandaya, and R. K. Narayan. The other writers included here—René Maran, George Lamming, Jean Toomer, and Bessie Head—all use French or English as their first language, though their ancestors were all African. This is not the place to argue at length the problems of writing in a second language, since that subject has been thoroughly discussed elsewhere.[7] At the same time, one commentary—from Raja Rao's forward to *Kanthapura* (1938)—illustrates the concern many Third World writers have felt about the question of language:

> One has to convey in a language that is not one's own the spirit that is one's own. One has to convey the various shades and omissions of a certain thought-movement that looks maltreated in an alien language. I use the word "alien," yet English is not really an alien language to us. It is the language of our intellectual make-up—like Sanskrit or Persian was before—but not of our emotional make-up. We are all instinctively bilingual, many of us writing in our own language and in English. We cannot write like the English. We should not. We cannot write only as Indians. We have grown to look at the large world as part of us. Our method of expression therefore has to be a dialect which will some day prove to be as distinctive and colorful as the Irish or the American. Time alone will justify it.[8]

Besides using a "colonial" language, the novel as an art form in the Third World emerged during the period of the colonial presence. Thus, the contents of all of these works reflect a number of important similarities. In the widest sense we are dealing with protest literature, chronicling the lives of oppressed and exploited peoples; and, as one might expect, this writing is often addressed to the colonial power, attacking it, exposing it. Again and again, the theme of these works is the Third World culture exposed to the West, in all of its various stages and permutations. In the most extreme cases, the Third World culture may be facing a kind of cultural death, as in René Maran's *Batouala,* or undergoing racial genocide, as in Hyemeyohsts Storm's *Seven Arrows* (1972). These are novels dealing historically with the initial stages of exposure to the West. In the most subdued instances, they may be concerned with the final stages of colonialism, shortly before independence, such as George Lamming's *In the Castle of My Skin* (1953) or R. K. Narayan's *Grateful to Life and Death* (1945). In one or two cases, the writer may be concerned with those aspects of colonialism and racialism that have lived on, after independence, as in Kamala Markandaya's *Two Virgins* (1973), or, in a more ironic context, in Jean Toomer's *Cane.* In almost all of these instances, then, the Third World novel describes the clash of two or more cultures.

There is a progression in this clash of cultures, and this evolution is the basis of the arrangment of the works in this study. My analysis of René Maran's *Batouala* is given first place in this study because I feel it is a kind of archetypal Third World novel. Besides the fact that the work (written by a West Indian, but set in Africa) had a direct influence on a number of later black writers (in Africa, in the West Indies, and in the United States), many traits common to Maran's novel are found in later novels from other areas of the Third World: the situational plot, involving a group of people instead of an individual; the lack of a developing character; the cyclical use of time; the extensive use of the oral tradition for establishing milieu and character; and the use of anthropological materials for recording the death of a culture. Maran's *Batouala* not only establishes a pattern for examining the later works in this study, but it also depicts the early stages of the historical confrontation between the West and the Third World.

The second chapter is concerned with a novel from Africa (Yambo Ouologuem's *Bound to Violence* [*Le devoir de violence*], 1968), and one from the South Pacific, (Vincent Eri's *The Crocodile,* 1970). Ouologuem's novel is included because it illustrates a conscious attempt to pattern a work after a known Western literary example, because of his desire to write an historical novel. The result is not totally successful (though in no way limiting the novel's effect) because Ouologuem's own traditional concepts of time and space have made this imitative patterning impossible. Culture has dictated literary form. Eri's *The Crocodile* is included as a point of comparison: as a spontaneous example of a writer not concerned with writing an imitative work, yet achieving something similar to what Ouologuem intended. Both works show us that the historical perspective and the concept of time in the Third World may be treated differently than it is in Western fiction. In content, both works are again concerned with cultural chaos and destruction, with early stages in the Third World/Western confrontation.

The third chapter is an analysis of Hyemeyohsts Storm's *Seven Arrows*, a novel by a Native American. The diffuseness of the narrative has once again been brought about because of the chaos resulting from the threat of destruction from the West. The traditional central character has been eliminated in this hundred-year-saga which chronicles the story of the Plains Indians' confrontation with the white invaders. Storm shows us, however, that the clash of cultures may lead to something positive—growing out of a redefinition of the traditions of the past. Adaptability and change are necessary, Storm tells us, for the survival of any culture. These accommodations, he argues, should not automatically be regarded as negative aspects of cultural confrontation.

The next two chapters trace the manner in which certain traditional checks and balances within the cultures themselves begin to operate once the stage of initial exposure to the West has passed. In George Lamming's novel, *In the Castle of My Skin* (set in the author's country of birth, Barbados) the author illustrates the need for reasserting the collective consciousness of a people on the verge of political revolt. Jean Toomer's *Cane* illustrates a return to the past—to the black man's origins in slavery in the United States—and the need for exorcising this horror before true cultural renewal may begin. Both novels exemplify the negation of the main character (in favor of the group) so common to Third World novels as a whole.

The two Indo-Anglian novels discussed in the next chapter, Raja Rao's *Kanthapura* and Kamala Markandaya's *Two Virgins*, further illustrate the potential for cultural renewal—this time in large part from the age-old strengths of Hinduism. *Kanthapura* and *Two Virgins* also serve as a transition to the penultimate chapter in this study, since both herald the inward turning of the Third World novel. To illustrate that tendency toward introspection and the singular consciousness in contrast to the group consciousness, a third Indo-Anglian novel, R. K. Narayan's *Grateful to Life and Death,* and another African novel, Bessie Head's *A Question of Power* (1972), have been chosen. The focus in both of these works is upon the evolving individual consciousness, which moves us, thus, much closer to our own concept of the twentieth century novel in the West with its psychological focus.

Throughout this study, I have defined the Third World in literary rather than in political terms. In this view, it is limited to Africa, India, the West Indies, the South Pacific, and to the Afro-American and the Native American minorities in the United States. China and Latin America have been excluded, though many leaders in Latin America and the present leadership of the People's Republic of China conceive of their countries as being politically a part of the Third World. However, the novel form is not new in China as it is in all the areas discussed in this book, and the contemporary proletariat novels from China bear only a passing resemblance to the works discussed in this study.

Latin America is another matter, though here again the novel is not so recent an event. For that reason and because these writers use Spanish or Portuguese as their singular language, I have not included works from this geographical area in this study. For the present, it is only necessary to repeat that most of the writers included here have written in their second language—the language of the colonial power that subdued them—and the experience they record is most frequently colonial or neo-colonial. This is not an attempt, however, to deny a number of parallels that may exist between certain Latin American novels and the works interpreted here. Readers who are familiar with Gabriel García Márquez's *One Hundred Years of Solitude* (*Cien años de soledad*), for example, will immediately notice a number of similarities with two or three of the works discussed in this book.

One final note. In examining these novels, one often begins to wonder if peoples as unlike one another as those from the Third World and those from the West will ever be able to read each other's literature and fully appreciate it. The past critical responses that have been made to a number of the works treated here would seem to deny this possibility.* This is not, however, the problem I set out to solve. Literature is not so limiting that only one interpretation is possible. We cannot be African, Indian, Afro-American, West Indian, American Indian, South Sea Islander, and Western at the same time; but this should be no reason to deny these works their status in the canon of world literature or fail to read and enjoy them on our own. What is important, it seems to me, is that we realize when we read a work of non-Western literature that the interpretation we make of it may be somewhat different from what the artist intended, and contrarily, that we should not expect people who are not of our own culture and heritage to respond in the same way that we do to our own literature. For this reason, I would like to emphasize that many of the characteristics of the novel in the Third World that I identify are by necessity speculative. For better or worse, each of us was born into an ethnocentrically-sealed world. The purpose of any work of literature—no matter what culture it was produced in—is to show us something we were previously unaware of. Just as literature is a bridge connecting a life lived with a life not lived, so, too, all literature which is effective is a voyage into a world of previously untravelled experience.

---

*As we will shortly see, a number of these works have been denied the status of novels.

# 1
# The Death of a Culture
## René Maran's *Batouala*

In December of 1921, the Prix Goncourt was awarded to René Maran, for his novel, *Batouala,* which had been published earlier that year. A storm of protest broke out almost immediately—in large part, no doubt, because Maran was a black man. *Batouala,* subtitled "A True Black Novel" ("Véritable Roman Nègre"), was about Africa and the French colonial presence in French Equatorial Africa. But what was worse, Maran had prefaced his novel with a scathing attack on France's colonial policies in the tropics. The protests about the award were also triggered by another important factor: the year before, the Prix Goncourt had gone to Marcel Proust for *Remembrance of Things Past (A la recherche du temps perdu).* All of these factors were too much for the French literary community to accept.[1]

Maran was not an African, but a West Indian, born in Martinique in 1887 of parents from French Guiana. His father held a position in the colonial service and was transferred to French Equatorial Africa (Gabon) in 1890, when René was three years old. Undoubtedly these formative years in Africa had an important influence on Maran's later literary career. However, when he was seven, in 1894, his parents sent him to school in Bordeaux, since the climate in Africa did not agree with his health.[2] Fifteen years later, in 1909, after leaving the *lycée* in Bordeaux, he returned to Africa—to Ubangi Chari, a part of French Equatorial Africa, known today as the Central African Republic. For

17

someone of his education, there was little he could do but follow in his father's footsteps and join the civil service.

In his Preface to *Batouala*, Maran describes some of his reactions to life in Ubangi Chari, some of his feelings about becoming a part of the colonial machine. Of the latter he states, "If one could know on what continuous evil the great colonial life is based, it would be spoken of less—indeed, it would be spoken of no more. It degrades little by little" (p. 10; French, p. 13).* In vivid language, Maran showed that the colonial world degraded both his co-workers in the civil service and the Africans. Far from praising the "civilizing mission" of France, Maran irreverently charged that "civilization" in fact builds its kingdom on corpses. To prove his point, he describes an African village where over ninety percent of the population had died during only seven years of colonial rule. The exploitation of the Africans in the colonial ghettos was so severe "that in certain regions, some unfortunate Negroes [were] obliged to sell their wives at a price varying from twenty-five to seventy-five francs each to pay their poll tax" (p. 10; French, p. 13). Seared into Maran's consciousness was the sad spectacle of Africans searching for undigested grains of corn and millet in the dung of horses owned by the *colons*.

Maran's preface to *Batouala* was in fact an impassioned appeal for French intellectuals to stand up and take notice of what was happening in the colonies. By contrast, he noted that *Batouala* was "completely objective. It doesn't even try to explain; it states facts" (pp. 7–8; French, p. 10). Yet little happened to improve the situation in the colonies. The attack on Maran himself continued. Threats were made on his life.[3] Seven years later, according to Claude McKay, *Batouala* was still banned in all of the French African colonies.[4] Maran adds an addition to his preface, written seventeen years later for the definitive edition of his work, published in 1938:

> Only in 1927 did I receive the moral satisfactions owed me. It was in that year that André Gide published *Voyage au Congo* [*Voyage to the Congo*]. Denise Moran published *Tchad* [*Chad*] a little later. And the Chamber was shocked by the horrors which occurred during the construction of the Brazzaville-Océan railroad. (p. 14; French, p. 18)

The notoriety of *Batouala* was in large part due to the furor generated by the Prix Goncourt. Although the book was soon translated into several

*In the interests of readability, quotations from *Batouala* will be limited to the English translation of Maran's novel: Washington, D.C.: Black Orpheus Press, 1972; and London: Heinemann Educational Books, 1973. Both English editions have the same pagination. The page numbers of the French edition (Paris: Éditions Albin Michel, 1938), will be cited after the English version. All subsequent page numbers for these editions will appear in the text.

other languages—including English in 1922, in a highly bowdlerized edition which he abhorred—Maran's book has been for the most part neglected. Little has been written about Maran himself.* Critics, it seems, have hardly known what to do with him. Was he French? West Indian? African? One would expect that black American writers would have claimed him as a kindred soul, but they, too, have been almost unanimous in failing to recognize him. Given the recent interest in Black Studies, all this seems especially perplexing. Mercer Cook, perhaps his strongest supporter, has written, "When one re-reads the works of this pioneer . . . with their wealth of information on Africa, one realizes that subsequent French West Indian and American novelists are more indebted to René Maran than they themselves know."[5] Cook's way of explaining the obscurity that has always surrounded Maran is to suggest a kind of unconscious influence. Léopold Sédar Senghor, the President of Senegal and a prime exponent of *négritude,* has stated, "It is only with René Maran that the West Indian writers freed themselves from docile imitation of the Metropole and fear of their *négritude.*"[6] However, these are both statements by men who knew Maran.

Other less sympathetic readers were simply confused by *Batouala*'s form. The work was all the more confusing, perhaps, because it followed so closely after Proust's *Remembrance of Things Past*—clearly a landmark in the development of the Western novel, a turning point. When we examine *Batouala* carefully, however, we must conclude that Maran's work is as experimental a novel as Proust's. That factor has been a primary reason why *Batouala* has been ignored: it is an unconventional, innovative work, which does not fit into the stereotyped concepts many early readers had of what a novel should be. When the Prix Goncourt was awarded, the reaction of the press was one of shock that the award

*According to Mercer Cook, in one of the few studies written about Maran:

After leaving his beloved bush for Paris, he discovered that it was difficult for him to escape the public eye. *Batouala* had made him famous, but at the same time it had created a reaction that would motivate against him for many years to come. Though he would write novels definitely superior to that work, he would always be referred to as the author of *Batouala*. As late as 1938, there were Negroes living in Paris who did not know that he had ever published anything else. (*Five French Negro Authors,* p. 132).

Maran continued writing throughout most of the rest of his life, returning again and again in these works to Africa. In *Journal sans date,* a novel published in 1927, he built his conflict around an interracial love theme, involving an African and a European. In *Djouma, chien de brousse* (1927), he told the story of Batouala's dog. Another African novel with a romantic story, *Le livre de la brousse* (1934), Maran felt was his finest work, though like many of his works, it has never been translated into English. In 1947, he published an expanded version of *Journal sans date* called *Un homme pareil aux autres.* Other works include biographies of David Livingstone (1938) and Felix Eboué (1951). He died in relative obscurity in Paris in 1960.

could go to an "over-done work, obscene, poorly composed,"[7] as one journal referred to it. For many a French reader of the novel in 1921, *Batouala* was a first-time exposure to fiction from the Third World. If black writers have frequently accused Maran of being too French, his French readers found him too African. And that, too, has no doubt contributed to the confused reactions *Batouala* has almost always encountered, for Maran has been almost uniformily misunderstood by readers in each camp.

As recently as 1973, when a new translation of *Batouala* appeared in English, a certain reserve toward the novel on the part of Africans persisted. In a review of the newly-translated edition of the book which appeared in *West Africa*, Nicolas Godian begins,

> I am Batouala's countryman. At school in Oubangui-Chari... in a textbook called *Mamadou et Bineta Sont Devenus Grands* (known to us as "Mamadou gros"), we read and knew by heart an extract from René Maran's celebrated novel winner ef the Prix Goncourt.... To us Maran was one of many French writers featured in "Mamadou gros", alongside la Fontaine, de Vigny, Emile Zola, Chateaubriand. However, two passages by Maran—"Batouala mourant" (the death of Batouala), from *Batouala*, and "le petit Kossi" from *Le Livre de la Brousse* were more expressive for the pupils of the Catholic Boarding School, Krebedge (Fort Sibut) around 1956–7 than all the other French authors. From this text, we did not know that Maran, in spite of his French name, was a West Indian and a black like us, writing about his blood brothers and sisters.[8]

Although Godian notes a special affinity with him, his review is filled with comments about Maran's shortcomings: "Maran was too rationalist, too French to accept the Banda view of the world.... Maran in writing *Batouala* was not especially concerned with an African system of thought and belief.... Maran is not really known by the younger black intellectuals, except as one who accepted and worked within the colonial system."[9] Godian adds, "Maran sees himself as a representative of the moral values of his mother country, France."[10] These are rather strong statements. Yet Godian admits that what Maran is saying in *Batouala* "is vital, a summary of the reactions of Africans to the disruptive side of colonialism they so abruptly faced."[11]

Godian gives us another clue—related to the disruptive side of colonialism—to the reasons Maran has continued to be so misunderstood, so unappreciated: "Batouala was right. Before the coming of the whites he and his people were happy. Working a little, and only for themselves, drinking, eating, and sleeping, dancing, hunting and mounting their women."[12] Although the novel describes all of these activities, Batouala's people are no longer happy; they are no longer in control of their own destinies. *Batouala* is one of the most unromanticized accounts of African life ever written by a black man, and that fact in itself has made it impossible for many readers to embrace Maran the writer. Instead of describing the romantic days of the past, as numerous African writers have done, Maran has recorded a culture in decline, the collapse of a society—"an almost dead world," as Donald E. Herdeck has written.[13] Wilfred Cartey, another West Indian writer, has perhaps stated the case more succinctly: "Colonialism has done its work [in Batouala's village] for the native tradition has disintegrated internally and ends in debauchery and death."[14] *Batouala* is an account of the death of a culture.

At first glance, Maran's story of Batouala appears to be deceptively simple, almost plotless. As the novel begins, it is morning and Batouala is waking up. The elaborate rituals of his waking exercises are described in detail, followed by a number of vivid contrasts of African and Western life styles. Batouala's oldest wife, Yassigui'ndja, is characterized briefly —as is Bissibi'ngui, Batouala's young rival. Subsequent chapters are devoted to tribal customs—including the celebrated Ga'nza (circumcision) festival, after which Batouala's old father dies. After the funeral, Batouala plots Bissibi'ngui's murder since he fears the young upstart is about to usurp his chiefly position. The plan backfires, however. Batouala is wounded and dies alone—even his faithful dog, Djouma, disgusted by the smells of his putrid flesh.

Most of the innovations in Maran's novel can be identified in the opening chapter: Maran's concern with cyclical time, his personification of animals and natural events, his use of anthropological background materials for creating mood and atmosphere, his unorthodox treatment of character which results in the situational plot. In the opening paragraphs, Maran informs us that it is morning—the fire in Batouala's hut has burned down, the first rays of light are filtering through the porch. Under the hut, termites are working away, cautious, incessant—the natural world that continues no matter what happens to Batouala's villagers. Roosters are crowing; there are sounds of monkeys from the surrounding bush.

Suddenly Maran shifts and describes Batouala, the great chief, "the 'mokoundji' of so many villages" (p. 15; French, p. 19). He emphasizes the chief's physical attributes; we are told he is an excellent hunter, runner, and wrestler. Though the novel is told in the third person, Maran injects his reader into Batouala's mind almost immediately by the use of guided interior monologue, a technique he uses to show Batouala's views of the Europeans toward work:

In the language of white men [work] took on a strange meaning, signifying fatigue with no immediate or tangible result; and cares, disappointments, pain, exhaustion, and pursuit of elusive goals.

Aha! Men of white skin. What had they come to look for, so far from their homes, in the land of the Blacks? How much better they would all do to go back to their lands, never to leave again!

Life is short. Work only pleases those who will never understand it. Idleness cannot degrade anybody. It differs greatly from laziness. (p. 16; French, p. 21)

Here, almost at the beginning of the story, we can see Maran making us aware of the theme of his novel—the conflict of cultures—two ways of life, diametrically opposed to each other. The references to work and laziness are important because they illustrate two radically different concepts of time. The Europeans introduced something new: the passing of time, from the past, through the present, to the future. The Africans had always lived in the present. Work for the white man, the Africans were learning, was related to objectives in the future. To mark this contrast, Maran returns us to Batouala's thoughts: "To live from day to day, without remembering yesterday, without worrying about tomorrow, not anticipating; that is excellence, that is perfection" (p. 17; French, p. 21).

Batouala slowly gets up from his bed and contemplates rekindling the dying fire—a major image of the novel, a symbol of the dying culture of Batouala's people. Then he lies back down and listens to Yassigui'ndja's snoring nearby. Maran describes her briefly, then shifts to Djouma, Batouala's red dog, and to the other animals in the chief's hut—goats, chickens, ducks. As the light increases, many of the animals go outside. Then the narration returns to Djouma, whose mother "his masters had eaten on a day of famine" (p. 19; French, p. 25), one of the earliest references to the starvation that constantly plagued the Bandas. Maran places us inside of Djouma's mind; the dog is aware of the famine. He gets up because he is hungry, thinking of the possibilities of finding some food:

Didn't he know that at dawn it was pleasant to swallow goat's dung, which still smells like milk and even tastes like it? A succulent meal, which appears even more so to the dog who has nothing more substantial to sink his teeth into.

Dung? He would be sure to find a little of it everywhere. It was not possible that the dung-beetles had already gone to work. It was still too cool and foggy. It was even possible, if luck were with him, that he might find a few guinea-fowl eggs in the course of his morning wanderings. What joy that would bring! All the same, it would be better not to count too much on it. (p. 21; French, p. 27)

The passage ends as Djouma stands up, yawning and stretching, like Batouala, dreading to go outside.

Besides the personification of Batouala's dog, Maran makes the connection between the chief and his dog symbolic of another relationship developed throughout the novel: as Djouma is to Batouala, so the Bandas are to the whites—dogs. The fusion of the two, dog and master, becomes complete as Maran continues Djouma's thoughts:

> He had learned, by dint of necessity, to hide his slightest feelings and to fake at every turn the unending weariness of limitless boredom. He knew by experience that it was wise for him to act this way. Any dog's happiness attracts man's attention. He had only to make a show of good humor to have Batouala keep him in sight, and if need be, to follow him. (pp. 21–22; French, p. 28)

Batouala, of course, has learned to play a similar role with the whites.

Maran describes Batouala's waking up exercises, complete with scratching and grunting. The purpose is to focus our attention on the importance of custom and habits. Grunting "was an old habit with him. It came to him from his parents. His parents had inherited it from theirs. The old customs are always the best. For the most part, they are founded on the surest experience" (p. 23; French, p. 30). All of this was probably a bit too much for early readers of Maran's novel, hardly beyond the days of Mrs. Grundy.

The picture Maran creates of Batouala is that of a man slowly becoming aware that he is outside of his time, of his traditions. He is referred to as "a guardian of obsolete customs" (p. 23; French, p. 30), customs so weakened that they are no longer strong enough to hold back the whites. Maran makes a distinction between traditions and habits. Although Batouala still possesses the latter instinctively, his traditions are almost gone. Life is not as it was; the cyclical conception of Batouala's universe is changing.

As the chapter concludes, Batouala decides to go outside, but the cold is so biting that he immediately returns to his hut. The fog is so dense that he is not able to see "the houses where his eight other wives and the children they had given him were sleeping" (p. 24; French, p. 31). He warms himself before the fire. As he thinks of his first wife, his desire becomes so intense that he approaches her to fulfill his masculine duties. "As Yassigui'ndja has always been accustomed to these daily liberties, even though she was still asleep, there was no need at all to wake her up. She would wake up quite easily by herself" (p. 24; French, p. 32). The chapter concludes with a poetic interlude, describing the birds outside and the rising sun, again reiterating the cyclical nature of traditional life: "Day had come" (p. 25; French, p. 33).

There were no doubt numerous passages in this first chapter that offended many of Maran's earliest readers—the elaborate description of Batouala's morning toilette ("He got up scratching himself, after rubbing his eyes with the back of his hand and cleaning his nose with his fingers. He scratched his armpits. He scratched his thighs, his head, his buttocks, his back, his arms" p. 22; French, p. 29)—plus the elemental nature of Batouala's relationship with his wife. Batouala is, in fact, described in animalistic imagery—linking him closely to his dog, Djouma. Maran's characterization of his chief in the opening chapter is almost as extensive as it will be, for in many of the later sections, Batouala's presence is missing. While the elemental nature of his daily life continues briefly into the second chapter—where Yassigui'ndja prepares her husband's morning meal of cassava and white worms (food, then, following sleep and sex—the three drives of all men), Batouala's role in the narrative will henceforth be considerably reduced. Maran leaves him musing about the inconsistencies of the white man's world as he examines his feet for chiggers.

The narration in the second chapter shifts to Bissibi'ngui, Batouala's young rival who is also characterized as an elemental man. We first see him joking with Batouala's wives. Eight of them have already slept with the twenty-year-old upstart, and the ninth, Yassigui'ndja, looks forward to her encounter with him. Maran editorializes, "A woman should never refuse the desire of a man, especially when that man pleases her. That is a functional principle. The only law is instinct" (p. 36; French, p. 47). Although Maran mentions Batouala's jealousy of Bissibi'ngui, the scene is really the latter's: Bissibi'ngui tells Batouala's wives how Gato, the rooster (and a trickster) outwits the much larger animal, M'bala, the elephant, into believing that a chicken can eat more than an elephant. The implications are obvious: Bissibi'ngui, a trickster like Gato, has been outfoxing Batouala, who in old age has become slow like M'bala. The scene concludes with Bissibi'ngui smoking Batouala's pipe (symbolically usurping his role) as the chief's wives joke about the young man's promiscuous activities which they warn may lead to venereal disease. Bissibi'ngui's role is that of a foil to Batouala; Maran does not make much effort to develop his character. He will appear several more times, though we are never privy to his thoughts. Throughout, he is depicted as a man primarily motivated by his sexual instincts.

Yassigui'ndja is, of course, the third character in what we can now identify as a kind of triangular conflict. Although her characterization is somewhat sketchy, Maran also presents her as a person primarily driven by her sexual desires. Her interest to us is as a woman, an African woman. We have already noted the passage in the second chapter where Maran tells us that a woman should never refuse the desires of a man. Shortly after that comment, Maran places us inside of Yassigui'ndja's thoughts as she reflects upon her relationship with the old chief. There are ethnological details concerning marriage and sexual mores relating to pregnancy and childbirth, justifications of polygamy. Yassigui'ndja recalls the satisfactory nature of her union with Batouala, realizing, however, "The sad thing was that he was beginning to grow old and seemed eager only to smoke his pipe" (p. 45; French, pp. 56–57). Maran tells us, "The fire which devoured her could not be quenched by the one sexual experience her husband provided her each day" (p. 45; French, p. 57). She thinks of Bissibi'ngui and the passion he has already expressed for her. The night before, the two of them had made an agreement for a secret rendezvous. Her erotic thoughts then shift to white men as she wonders if they are as sexually active as Africans.

The erotic overtones of Maran's *Batouala* are an exception to almost all subsequent African fiction, as, indeed, is the triangular nature of the conflict of the story itself. In most African fiction, the relationship between men and women is utilitarian—the machinations of the plot tend to emanate from a masculine world in conflict with the encroaching forces from the West. *Batouala* does not belong to this pattern, and I suspect this is due in large part to the cosmopolitan nature of Maran's upbringing, though I would argue that the triangular affair here is subordinate to the main thrust of the book itself—the demise of a culture because of the coming of the West. The conflict here is also, however, an example of the instinctual nature of male/female relationships, untainted by any sense of Puritan morality.

The triangular nature of the story is constructed around three important scenes where Batouala, Yassigui'ndja, and Bissibi'ngui are brought together. In the first of these (at the end of the third chapter), Yassigui'ndja walks into the bush for a rendezvous with the younger man, but encounters instead both Batouala and her intended lover hunting together. The second is during the Ga'nza festival and leads to Batouala's determination to kill his young rival. The death scene at the end of the novel brings them together, ironically, once again; but this time with Bissibi'ngui as the victor, groping after Yassigui'ndja as the old chief dies.

The Ga'nza festival is the most important of these three scenes and the central episode of the novel because of its anthropological overtones in addition to a number of secondary themes and techniques it illustrates. References to the festival occur in the first chapter of the novel. Later, when Batouala beats his talking drums, making the announcement of the festival for his villagers, the drums reverberate throughout the countryside. Maran states, "The unseen was coming to life" (p. 32; French, p. 42). Maran makes it clear that these drums speak only to the Africans and not to the white man. The incident reminds us of a passage involving talking drums in Camara Laye's novel, *The Radiance of the King* (*Le regard du roi*, 1954), a work undoubtedly influenced by *Batouala*. In Laye's novel of African life, when the naive white man, Clarence, tells a beggar,

" 'I could have been a simple drummer boy,' "[15] the beggar replies,
" 'That is not a simple occupation. . . . The drummers are drawn from
a noble caste and their employment is hereditary. Even if you had been
allowed to beat a drum, your drumming would have had no meaning.
You have to know how . . . You see, you're a white man.' "[16] The implication is quite clear: the Western world is all surface; the African way
of life is mystical.

Much of Chapter Five is devoted to the preparations for the circumcision festival itself. The reader learns that Batouala has chosen the time
for the festival when the commandant will be away from the village
on an inspection of a neighboring region. The passages describing the
elaborate preparations for the festival become intermixed with Maran's
harshest comments about colonialism, reminding us that on one level
*Batouala* is a protest novel. As the women prepare the food for the
festival, the men hold a palaver about the "Boundjoudoulis," the whites.
There are references to the war in Europe between the French and
the Germans. Batouala's old father enters into the conversation also.
Who are worse—the French or the Germans? The consensus is that
they are the same. One African comments, " 'We should have massacred
the first one who came to our land' " (p. 70; French, p. 91). It is impossible
to read these conversations without realizing that the infiltration of the
West into Batouala's village has been total. Only the elders can think
back to the beautiful days before the onslaught of the whites.

As the Europeans encroached upon them, the Africans kept moving
their villages to get further away. But the whites kept advancing, until
they covered the entire territory, until there was no unspoiled area for
the Africans to retreat to. In the most polemical passage of the novel,
Batouala sums up the Africans' feelings about the colonial era:

"Our submission . . . did not even earn us their good will. And, at
first, not happy with trying to suppress our most cherished customs,
they didn't cease until they had imposed theirs on us.

"In the long run, they have succeeded only too well there. Result:
the gloomiest sadness reigns, henceforth, through all the black country.
Thus the whites have made the zest for living disappear in the places
where they have taken up residence.

"Since we have submitted to them, we have no more right to bet
any money at all at the 'patara.' We have no more right to get drunk
either. Our dances and our songs disturb their sleep. But dances
and songs are our whole life. We dance to celebrate Ipeu, the moon,
or to praise Lolo, the sun. We dance for everything, for nothing,
for pleasure. Nothing is done or happens, but we dance about it
forthwith. And our dances are innumerable. . . . Maybe it is better
to say that we danced them all not long ago. Because as far as these

times are concerned they allow us to do them only rarely. And still we have to pay a tithe to the government." (pp. 72–73; French, pp. 93–94)

The past is no more. The pre-colonial era has become little more than a memory.

Batouala and his contemporaries continue to harangue the Europeans. Then he adds, " 'I will never tire of telling... of the wickedness of the "boundjous." Until my last breath, I will reproach them for their cruelty, their duplicity, their greed' " (p. 75; French, p. 97). The profundity of Batouala's comments can only be understood when we remember that there is, in fact, very little evidence of any direct presence of the whites in Batouala's village. The corruption from the West has been almost totally indirect and because of that much more subtle. We have only to contrast *Batouala* with later African novels—such as those by Chinua Achebe, in which the European presence is shown much more directly—to understand how great the upheaval has been for Batouala's countrymen. Batouala's diatribe continues,

"Well, everybody knows that from the first day of the dry season to the last of the rainy season, our work only pays taxes, when it doesn't fill, at the same time, the pockets of our commandants.

"We are only taxable flesh. We are only beasts of burden. Beasts? Not even that. Dogs? They feed them, and they care for their horses. Us? We are for them less than those animals; we are lower than the lowest. They are slowly crushing us." (pp. 75–76; French, p. 98)

Maran editorializes in the next few paragraphs, bringing his attack on the whites to a crescendo: "At present, the blacks were no more than slaves. There was nothing to hope for from a heartless race. For the 'boundjous' didn't have any hearts. Didn't they abandon the children they had by black women?" (p. 76; French, p. 98). Maran's ideas here clearly make him a precursor of the *négritude* writers who followed him in a few short years—particularly his contrast of the emotionlessness (heartlessness) of the whites with the black man's sense of humanity. The leading exponents of *négritude* in the 1930's (Etienne Léro, Aimé Cesaire, Léopold Sédar Senghor, and Léon Damas) believed that Western man had become over-mechanized, too analytical, stripped of his humanity—in part because of World War I. As Ellen Kennedy and Paulette Trout have stated about these men,

The *témoins de la négritude*, as they dubbed themselves, become convinced that there were acutal differences in perception, in the fundamental apprehension of reality, between the white and black races. Their credo, and the new literature through which it was to be expressed, would find its sources in what they thought of as the Negro's "special" sensibility, his feeling for rhythm, myth, nature, the erotic and emotional life, group solidarity.[17]

All of these "sources" are, of course, found in *Batouala*.

It is Batouala's old father, however, who has the last word about the whites. He tells his companions that it is too late to change what has already happened. " 'We would do better to complain less about the whites and to drink more. You know as well as I that except for the bed, Pernod is the only important invention of the 'boundjous' " (p. 77; French, p. 100).

The festival itself—the sixth chapter of Maran's novel—draws us closer to the theme of the dying culture than any of the earlier sections of the book. An element of the forbidden is hinted at, since the commandant is away. Much of the chapter is descriptive, anthropological. The young novitiates (isolated into groups of males and females) dance naked, followed by other groups of youngsters and adults. Maran's image of the early part of the festival is one of intense happiness and joy: " . . . what cries, what laughs, what gestures! The presence of so many men and of so many women, the beer, the hemp, the activity, the joy pushed the quivering heat of desire little by little to its culmination" (p. 82; French, p. 105). And shortly thereafter,

> They bent down to the earth, touched it with their hands, and leaned on it while doing a few gyrations. And still bent over, they stamped their feet alternately to the right, then to the left, and then to the right again. They waved their hands in the air, and raised and lowered them like the wings of a large vulture who runs forth, takes flight, and hovers indolently over the thick brush of the jungle. (p. 82; French, pp. 105–106)

As the talking drums beat out a chant for the initiates, an old man and an old woman appear among them—the elders who perform the operations. The excisions are graphically described—perhaps too vividly for many of Maran's readers. It is clear that the Ga'nza festival is one section of the novel that led to much of the original attack on the novel as obscene, as Zolaesque naturalism. The descriptions of the circumcision are intermixed with the continuous flow of song:

> Ga'nza . . . ga'nza . . . ga'nza . . . ga'nza! . . .
> That only happens once in your life . . .
> Ours, women! . . . Ours, men!
> Now you are ga'nzas.
> Ga'nza . . . ga'nza . . . ga'nza . . . ga'nza! . . . (p. 85; French, p. 109)

Maran continues, dwelling on the reaction of the onlookers:

Each operator wiped his knife, then excised the last girl and circumcised the last man. The tumult now reached its height. All that had gone before was nothing by comparison. All those outcries and confused actions were only preparation for the event they were all anxiously awaiting: the great dance of love, the one which is never allowed except on the evening of the ga'nza.

And during this glorious dance all things are permitted, even perversions and sins against custom. (p. 85; French, p. 109)

After the last novitiate has been excised, Yassigui'ndja and a virgin female make their appearance amid the crowd of people, dressed only in jewels. Maran states, "Yassigui'ndja wore, besides these jewels, an enormous painted wooden phallus" (p. 86; French, p. 110). The two of them act out a symbolic defloration. The ceremony ends with an orgy of violence and passion:

A strange madness suddenly seized the confused human throng surrounding the dancers. The men tore off the pieces of fabric which served as loincloths; the women also removed the rest of their clothes.

The breasts of the women bounced. A heavy odor of genitals, urine, sweat, and alcohol pervaded the air, more acrid than the smoke. Couples paired off. They danced, as Yassigui'ndja and the girl had danced. There were fights and raucous cries. Bodies spread out at random on the ground and all the movements of the dance came to fruition. The children imitated the movements of their elders.

Sexual drunkenness, increased by alcoholic drunkenness. Immense natural joy, released from all control. Blood flowed freely from spendid abuse. Desire was the only master. (p. 87; Frenchn p. 111)

One suspects that in spite of the orgy at the end of the Ga'nza festival, Maran wants his reader to believe in the functional aspect of the ceremony, its positive side, rather than be disturbed by its erotic overtones. Besides being a collective event, participated in by all, the ceremony is of utmost importance in the cycle of life—a bridge in one's social position between childhood and adulthood, a symbolic rebirth. The impression Maran leaves his reader with is that this is the last time Batouala's people will know such happiness. Since they have realized this, the orgy becomes a kind of final release of their emotions. Already Batouala's villagers have been denied their adulthood, since the Europeans refuse to see them as anything other than wards.

The cyclical nature of traditional African life is of utmost importance for our understanding of Maran's novel. The Ga'nza festival (with its emphasis on rebirth and ritual cleansing) is perhaps the most obvious example of this in Batouala, though Maran's novel is replete with other examples. We have already noted the images of rebirth or daily renewal of the life cycle in the opening chapter plus Maran's references to Batouala's growing awareness of a major change in his life: the white man's work schedule which has made him aware of a new concept of time. In *Cosmos and History*, Mircea Eliade states, "the life of archaic man ... although it takes place in time, does not bear the burden of time, does not record time's irreversibility ... the primitive lives in a continual present ... he repeats the gestures of another and, through this repetition, lives always in an atemporal present."[18] Batouala's atemporal present has been threatened by the intrusion of the Europeans. He has become aware of a conflicting sense of time and, as a consequence, he makes one final attempt to restore the cyclical orientation of his existence by calling the Ga'nza festival which Eliade would see as

> the need of archaic societies to regenerate themselves periodically through the annulment of time. Collective or individual, periodic or spontaneous, regeneration rites always comprise, in their structure and meaning, an element of regeneration through repetition of an archetypal act, usually of the cosmogonic act. What is of chief importance to us in these archaic systems is the abolition of concrete time, and hence their antihistorical intent. This refusal to preserve the memory of the past, even of the immediate past, seems to us to betoken a particular anthropology.[19]

The sense of regeneration through daily acts is also typified in the numerous oral tales incorporated into the narrative itself and in ubiquitous references to nature's daily cycles: the sun and the moon. The tale that Bissibi'ngui tells Batouala's wives, for example, incorporates a number of stock conventions which Eliade would see as repeating the cosmogonic act: it begins "In the time when" (p. 38; French, p. 49), that is, "once upon a time," and concludes with the moral tag, "Since that time, M'bala the elephant lives in the brush, and Gato the chicken in the villages of man" (p. 39; French, p. 50). Eliade would interpret this tale as a further example of the cyclical nature of Batouala's time perspective, embodying a number of mythic overtones:

> Through repetition of the cosmogonic act, concrete time, in which the construction takes place, is projected into mythical time, *in illo tempore* when the foundation of the world occurred.... Any ritual whatever ... unfolds not only in a consecrated space ... but also in a "sacred time," "once upon a time" (*in illo tempore, ab origine*), that is, when the ritual was performed for the first time by a god, an ancestor, or a hero.[20]

There is no reason, of course, why this tale could not be removed from the text of the novel—with no excisions—and placed in an anthology of folktales and myths, except, of course, for the symbolic overtones of the story, illustrating Maran's genius for understanding primeval man's relationship to the organic world around him.

The beginnings and endings of so many of the individual chapters of *Batouala* also develop the concept of cyclical time, as does the overall structure of the novel itself. For example, at the end of the first day in the narrative (at the end of the second chapter) Maran highlights the "death of the sun," (p. 41; French, p. 53) and the re-birth of the moon, "Like a canoe stirring the water plants in its wake—oh! how slowly she slid across the clouds—here 'Ipeu' the moon appeared silently. She was already six nights old . . ." (p. 41; French, p. 53). Again, it is instructive to notice a statement made by Mircea Eliade: "If the moon in fact seems to 'measure' time, if the moon's phases—long before the solar year and far more concretely—reveal a unit of time (the month), the moon at the same time reveals the 'eternal return,' "[21] the cyclical rhythms of Batouala's world. Similar descriptive comments occur periodically throughout the rest of Maran's narrative.

Nature is, of course, an adjunct to Maran's treatment of time in *Batouala,* since so many incidents involve the repetition of the daily cycle—the return of the sun and the moon. Batouala's people, however, are constantly aware of the other ways in which nature controls their lives. In Chapters Three and Four, Donvorro, the tornado, is personified, lashing out his fury at them. At the beginning of the eighth chapter, Maran gives us a praise song (albeit in prose), in homage of Lolo, the sun, illustrating the harmony of the Bandas with their environment. We are told of Lolo's greatness, his function in the order of things:

> He's a good old man, the sun, and so equitable! He shines for all living people, from the greatest to the most humble. He knows neither rich nor poor, neither black nor white.
>
> Whatever may be their color, whatever may be their fortune, all men are his sons. He loves them all equally; favors their plantations; dispels, to please them, the cold and sullen fog; reabsorbs the rain; and drives out the shadow. (p. 101; French, p. 127)

In the eleventh chapter, the creatures of the African bush are described in tandem with the birth of a new day—in harmony with each other. And at the beginning of the hunt scene (when Batouala tries to kill Bissibi'ngui) nature's destructive side is described, again in a kind of traditional praise song—this time for fire.

> Ah! Who will sing of fire? Who will praise as is fitting, with words right in bounty and in fervor; who will praise that miniature sun which gleams, sometimes alone, more often innumerable, night and day, in spite of rain, in spite of wind? (p. 137; French, p. 173)

As one might expect, many of the examples of traditional oral literature that Maran has incorporated into his novel are drawn from the natural world, beginning with the tale that Bissibi'ngui tells to Batouala's wives. Batouala's old father frequently draws on the natural world when he speaks, as does Batouala himself the night before the hunt, when he tells Bissibi'ngui the sacred stories of his order. The first of these is, ironically, about fire and death—why men do not live forever. Bissibi'ngui fears that his own death is imminent unless he can find some way of escape. "Batouala was revealing to him mysteries which only the very old are allowed to know" (p. 120; French, p. 151). When the tale is over, Bissibi'ngui contradicts Batouala, by giving his own explanation for the origin of fire on earth. Then Batouala begins another tale—of Lolo, the sun, and Ipeu, the moon—of the hatred each has for the other. The implications are quite clear yet they backfire the next morning when Mourou, the panther, mortally lashes into Batouala as the latter's assegai (intended for Bissibi'ngui) flies astray.

The final chapter of *Batouala* draws most of Maran's narrative techniques together. The chapter begins, "Batouala gave a gentle death rattle. He had been like that for fifteen nights" (p. 143; French, p. 181). Maran continues,

> In a few more moments—at the most a night and a day—Batouala, the great mokoundji, will be no more than a traveler. He will leave, eyes closed forever, for that gloomy village which has no return road. There he will rejoin his "baba" and all the elders who have preceded him there. (p. 143; French, p. 182)

Maran reiterates an idea expressed earlier in his novel—things will be better in the afterworld than on earth. Batouala will not have to exert any energy despising the whites. "One doesn't have to obey them any more" (p. 144; French, p. 182). Life is short. "The songs and the dances do not last forever. After the dry season, the rainy season. Man lives only an instant.... It was all over for Batouala" (p. 144; French, p. 182). Maran's tone is matter-of-fact, impersonal. Death is simply one more stage in the cycle of life that Batouala fully accepts.

In a brief digression, Maran develops a double irony. Not only was it Batouala who felt the blow from the panther, but the hunters left him alone, wrapped in a blanket under a tree, so they could continue to chase wild cattle. The hunters thought he had received an insignificant wound. Batouala's sorcerers' attempts to exorcise his evil spirits are unsuccessful: "more and more from day to day, that chest spread out its rot. The fat carrion flies, blue, green and black, buzzed around, revelling in his swelling and oozing wound" (p. 146; French, p. 185). The stench becomes so unbearable that even Djouma stops licking his master's wound. When the commandant is finally asked to help, he replies that Batouala is "quite welcome to die and all the [other Africans] with him" (p. 146; French, p. 186).

Batouala is left alone to die. Maran writes:

> They [Batouala's people] have divided the millet of your granaries, raided your flocks, stolen your arms. It is only just if they have not yet stolen your women. But be reassured. Their fate is settled. They have been spoken for for a long time. All have already found takers. (p. 147; French, p. 186)

Maran's picture here is similar to the one Colin Turnbull gives of the Ik in his book, *The Mountain People,* in which the stronger steal food from the mouths of the weak and dying. As Turnbull states, "The Ik clearly show that society itself is not indispensable for man's survival, that man is not the social animal he has always thought himself to be, and that he is perfectly capable of associating for purposes of survival without being social."[22] In the case of the Ik, the alteration has been brought about by a cataclysmic change in life styles—the government movement of the Ik to a new land. Batouala's world has undergone a similar upheaval: colonialism. Turnbull concludes, "They have made of a world that was alive a world that is dead, a cold, dispassionate world. . . ."[23]

Except for Djouma, Yassigui'ndja, and Bissibi'ngui, Batouala is left alone, abandoned to his fate. In the last few moments of his life, suffering from delirium, he is unaware of his wife and Bissibi'ngui, locked in an embrace. Batouala utters a final reproach of the whites—for "untruths, cruelty, illogical thought, hypocrisy" (p. 147; French, p. 187). His monologue becomes incoherent to the others. Nicolas Godian has written about this episode as follows:

> when the dying Batouala stopped complaining about a constant fever which was gnawing at his bones, and just talked and talked and talked, we at once understood that he was talking with the souls of his dead ancestors who had gathered invisibly round him to wish him welcome. What the whites and Maran called incoherent delirium was a language of souls, of spirits, of ghosts. Batouala's words were not comprehensible to the living around him because they were a language of another world. Only the inhabitants of that world—the dead who are not dead—could understand it.[24]

Bissibi'ngui finally accomplishes his seduction of Yassigui'ndja in the room where the chief is dying.

Batouala makes one final lunge at the lovers, and then dies, falling to the ground with a heavy thud.

At that noise, the ducks quack, the chickens cluck and the goats run in all directions. By force of habit, Djouma grumbles without opening his eyes. And for a long, long time the termites fill their galleries of brown earth with a lasting vibration.

But Yassigui'ndja and Bissibi'ngui have already fled in the night . . .

Little by little the noises die down. Sleep overtakes the animals. There is only silence and solitude watching over you, Batouala. The great night is upon you. Sleep . . .

Sleep . . . (p. 149; French, pp. 189–190)

The world goes on. The termites continue their incessant chewing. Darkness and sleep reign supreme.

*Batouala* is not quite a perfect novel—not quite totally successful, but still of such importance that we must regard it as a seminal piece of black fiction, of Third World literature. We have only to recall the time of its original publication, 1921, to understand this significance. Maran paved the way for much of what was going to follow shortly thereafter: the Harlem Renaissance in the 1920's, *négritude* in Paris in the 1930's, the emergence of fiction on the African continent in the 1950's and 1960's. His influence cannot be denied. I suspect, too, that as a black writer, Maran will continue to exert an increasing influence over African writing in the 1970's. Now that his works are being seriously studied and some of his other novels are scheduled for translation into English this is especially true.

On the negative side, I think the major weakness of *Batouala* is Maran's talkiness—his tendency to editorialize. Much of the time the reader is aware that *Batouala* is a protest novel—but protest is, after all, one of the defining traits of most Third World writing. It is not simply the passages of protest that weaken *Batouala,* however, as much as Maran's consciousness within the novel itself. He is too often present as a voice within the story, manipulating and preaching. At times we cannot be certain if an opinion is Batouala's or Maran's. We are accustomed to reading novels in the twentieth century in which the novelist has taken great pains to disguise his presence. However, the opposite is true of *Batouala.* We are almost always certain where Maran stands.

A lesser weakness of *Batouala* is the confusing voice of Maran himself —not just his position as narrator. We are not always certain *for what* he stands. Does he take sides with the Africans? The answer can only be yes, but there are those (such as Nicolas Godian) who believe that Maran was too French to understand the Banda world view. He was, after all, not African, but West Indian and he was French as far as his educational background was concerned. This cultural confusion (Maran was a cultural half caste, to borrow a term from Senghor) has resulted in a number of perplexing attitudes toward specific incidents in his novel itself. How, for example, are we to interpret the violence and the perversions unleashed during the orgy that follows the Ga'nza festival? Are the excesses described there the result of too much drink —Pernod, introduced by the Europeans? Are they to be interpreted as a kind of backlash against the colonial oppressors—a final, abortive orgasm of happiness and joy? Is the orgy to be interpreted as a positive factor within the Banda life cycle—a purgation because of the release of excesses held in check the rest of the time? Perhaps these are not to be regarded as excesses at all, for Maran states, "and during this glorious dance all things are permitted, even perversions and sins against custom" (p. 85; French, p. 109). Both of these interpretations seem to be realistic possibilities interlocked, of course, as they are. There can be no doubt about the importance of the festival itself: it is a major stage in the lives of the participants themselves, the doorway from childhood to adulthood in the Banda cycle of life, a rebirth.*

The Ga'nza festival is perhaps the place where we should begin enumerating the strengths of Maran's novel, for it is undeniable that Maran has brilliantly recorded a way of life most of us in the West will never be exposed to, a way of life that even many Anricans today are unaware of. We can be grateful that Maran wrote his novel when he did—that he got down on paper some of the aspects of traditional Banda life before they were forgotten, for there were few people within Ubangui-Chari at that time who could have written what he did. That is exactly the novel's strength—Maran wrote *Batouala* at a time when hardly anyone else could have, but he wrote it, inevitably, as a partial outsider. It is still a remarkable achievement. I can think of no other novel that pays so much attention to the natural rhythms of men's lives, of the daily cycles: sunrise, sunset, the passing of each moment of the day and night—rhythms that are designed to show us that for Batouala's kinsmen there is no ontological gap. They are also illustrative of a kind of anti-history, a term used by Alberto Moravia in his recent book, *Which Tribe Do You Belong To?*: "As for the Africans, they . . . have known only anti-history, that is, nature, which itself too strong to be dominated, has in turn dominated them, outside any sort of history."[25] Few African novels (except for Chinua Achebe's *Things Fall Apart*) that follow *Batouala* illustrate the cycle of traditional village life quite as well as Maran's

---

*A further explanation for the orgy can be found if we return, once again, to *Cosmos and History* by Mircea Eliade. Eliade describes an orgy practiced by the Ewe tribe of West Africa, commenting, "All these orgiastic excesses find their justification, in one way or another, in a cosmic or biocosmic act: regeneration of the year, critical period of the harvest, and so forth." (pp. 26–27). *Batouala* is, of course, filled with examples of such regenerative events.

does, for he managed to record most of the important aspects of this cycle within his book: symbolic birth (rebirth) in the rites of passage, marriage, death, ritual purification. The only aspect of the cycle that is not presented directly is birth itself and that is due to the fact that *Batouala* is the story of a childless world—another trait which identifies it with a great number of Third World novels.

Although there is not quite the sense of community here that we will see in later works by African and other Third World writers, *Batouala* is closer to subsequent African fiction than to later West Indian writing. This de-emphasis of the communal is understandable, however, since *Batouala* depicts the end of a culture, the death of a culture. It is a world that has become quite sad, a world in which the traditional sense of group solidarity no longer exists, a world in which there is intense pain, reminding us of the words of Alberto Moravia: "There is no greater suffering for man than to feel his cultural foundations giving way beneath his feet."[26] Sadly that is what we see in *Batouala*: an entire population, stripped of its adulthood, becoming in the process a people tragically close to the Ik in Turnbull's *The Mountain People*.

There is, however, one aspect of the communal world that is so often a defining trait of Third World fiction: we do have a situational plot, that is, an event (the early stages of colonialism in Africa) that ultimately affects not just an individual character but everyone. At the end of the story when Batouala is dying, one thing is certain: colonialism will be with Batouala's countrymen for a long, long time. Their lives have all been altered by the common group-shared situation. Batouala, the chief, may be a symbol of this dying culture, but colonialism will not die out with his death. Rather, it will continue to hold his people in chains, since they have yet to evolve a political consciousness capable of thwarting the European rule. We have only to remember that Bissibi'ngui regards the Europeans as an option for escape, a way of releasing himself from Batouala's domain of authority. As he tells Yassigui'ndja, he can always get a job, working for the *colons*.*

As for Batouala himself, he is, I feel, very much a part of a pattern common to Third World fictional characters. If not quite passive, he is nevertheless a questionable hero, often more acted upon than active. He is essentially the same at the end of the novel as he was at the

---

*Bissibi'ngui has none of Batouala's stature or rigidity. He will bend; he will give into the new dispensation—even join forces with it if necessary. As a representative of the future generation, Bissibi'ngui plays much the same role that Okonkwo's son, Nwoye, does in Chinua Achebe's *Things Fall Apart*.

beginning (except, of course, that he is dead) *    There is no sense of his having discovered something about himself, of his knowing himself any better, though he may certainly have a greater understanding of colonialism than he had earlier in his life. In this sense, as a non-developing character, he belongs with a group of other protagonists we will shortly examine in later Third World novels: Jean Toomer's *Cane*, Hyemeyohsts Storm's *Seven Arrows*, Yambo Ouologuem's *Bound to Violence*—novels without heroes. Like these later examples, Batouala tends to rationalize little that happens to him, though there is, still, a certain amount of introspection here—the use of several points of view. As already noted, we occasionally enter into Batouala's thoughts and those of several other characters' including Batouala's dog, Djouma. A lack of character introspection, however, is often a defining trait of the novel in the Third World.

Djouma reminds us, too, of the originality of *Batouala*, of Maran's ability to give his novel form and pattern by incorporating African folk materials into its basic structure: folk tales, songs, proverbs—traditional oral literature. These are the aspects of the structure of *Batouala* that eluded many of its early readers and made them label the novel as formless, structureless, needlessly repetitive. But those are naive interpretations. Each and every section of the story in which folk materials are used plays an integral part in the novel itself—for foreshadowing, for characterization, for developing irony, and so on. Maran's use of animals in adult fiction is one of his major innovations, providing a storehouse of rich material for folklorists. Animals are personified; they become as important as human beings. His fascination with the quotidian aspects of daily life in an African village is also far ahead of his time. Natural cycles (the sun and the moon, the rainy season and the dry season) become lifegiving forces around which man constructs his life. He does not try to change his environment, he merges with it. These are the aspects of this novel (and his later works) that illustrate Maran's true brilliance.

There is another aspect of the novel that must be mentioned. While on the surface we have a quasi-revenge story growing out of a triangular love affair (which, as we have seen, is most untypical of subsequent African fiction), in *Batouala* there is also a mythological descent that must be considered pivotal to our understanding of the totality of Third World fiction. *Batouala* is too early in the history of Third World fiction to give us the entire sweep of experience—too early for Maran's chief

---

*In this sense, too, Maran's use of Batouala's name for his title is a misleading one, since his novel is not about a character but, rather, about a culture. Maran's title does not have the same implication as numerous Western novels in which an individual's name has been chosen for the title: *Moll Flanders*, *Tom Jones*, *Emma*, *Jane Eyre*, etc.

to recover from that descent, too early for Batouala's kinsmen to revolt. Rather, *Batouala* records the beginning of a descent into hell (the colonial period) from which there can be no return at that time in the history of African/Western relations. Like Chinua Achebe's *Things Fall Apart* and *Arrow of God* (1964), like James Ngugi's *The River Between* (1965), like Camara Laye's *The Radiance of the King* (in which the descent is reversed so that a European is exposed to Africa), Rene Maran's *Batouala* describes that confusing period of time when two cultures first come together—and one of them undergoes a symbolic death. *Batouala* sums up that experience, portraying it symbolically as the death of a culture. We will have to wait for a rebirth—which will not come until some time later.

# 2
# History without Time
Yambo Ouologuem's *Bound to Violence*
Vincent Eri's *The Crocodile*

In spite of the initial *cause célèbre* created by the Prix Goncourt, René Maran's *Batouala*, as we have seen, has largely been ignored during the more than fifty years since its original publication. For many black readers, it was not "African enough"; for some French readers, it helped reinforce certain stereotyped beliefs they held about darker peoples. How ironic that history would repeat itself nearly fifty years later with the publication of an almost equally misunderstood work: Yambo Ouologuem's *Bound to Violence* (*Le devoir de violence*). When the novel first appeared in France in 1968, it received immediate critical acclaim from the French press and was awarded the Prix Renaudot. The thesis of Ouologuem's bloody chronicle of Africa's past appeared to be that Africans had exploited each other, had done as much harm to each other before the arrival of the white man as the colonial system had since that time. The novel's graphic sensationalism—in the opening chapter alone there are descriptions of rape, castration, disembowelment, cannibalism, and ritual sacrifice—was received with a kind of perverse delight. For once the colonial system appeared in a better light; it was no worse than what Africans had done to each other in the earlier stages of their history. An African intellectual, it was felt, had set things right for the first time: Africa's past had never been romantic.

A number of African readers reacted to the novel somewhat less en-
thusiastically, though generally Africans acclaimed the book also —believing that the French colonialists came off worse in the story than the
Africans. If Ouologuem had not been an African, he would have been
accused of being a racist—as was William Styron when he published
*The Confessions of Nat Turner.* The reaction to Ouologuem's novel, then,
was similar to the reactions to René Maran's *Batouala* —ideologically,
European and African readers found themselves in different camps.
What this illustrates is the Third World writer's frequent problem of
a double audience—one often willing to accept him for what he is trying
to say from within his own culture, the other willing to accept him
if he can be placed into a Western framework. Granted, in both of
these cases, the issue is not that clear. In Maran's instance, the Africans,
by whom he wanted to be accepted, often turned out to be his harshest
critics. However, the problem of the dual audience is clearly the issue
with Malian novelist, Yambo Ouologuem, and Papuan writer, Vincent
Eri, the second novelist whose work will be discussed in this chapter.

Both are also examples of Third World novelists who have tried to
adapt their writing to a Western concept of history and time but have
been unsuccessful in escaping the dictates of their own cultural back-
grounds. Ouologuem's case has been well publicized in the press during
the last few years; Eri's fame has hardly extended beyond his own geographical area, Papua New Guinea, because European and American
publishers have not thought his novel significant enough to want to
reprint it.

Yambo Ouologuem was born in eastern Mali (of Dogon parentage)
in 1940. His early education was in local schools and in Bamako, the
country's capital. In 1964 he went to Paris for advanced studies in
philosophy, English literature, and sociology—marked influences on his
first novel, *Le devoir de violence* (1968). In 1971, the novel appeared
in an English translation, published simultaneously in London and New
York. British and American reviewers (of which I was one) were generally
ecstatic about the novel—heralding it as a great African novel, even
as "the first truly African novel,"[1] as the American publishers described
it in the cover blurb. The latter it was not, but his publishers were
most probably unfamiliar with an entire generation of earlier African
novelists who had written "truly African novels."[2] Ouologuem participated in a promotion tour for the book in the United States, paperback
rights were quickly gobbled up—and then Ouologuem's luck began to
change.

In an article in *Research in African Literatures* (Fall 1971), Eric Sellin
published a terse little exposé entitled "Ouologuem's Blueprint for *Le
devoir de violence*."[3] Although Sellin does not use the word "plagiarism,"

his article calls attention to a number of embarrassing similarities between Ouologuem's novel and André Schwarz-Bart's *Le Dernier des Justes* (*The Last of the Just*), published in 1959 by the same French publisher of Ouologuem's novel and winner of the Prix Goncourt.* Sellin goes so far as to speculate that Éditions du Seuil, the publisher of both books, may have "commissioned Ouologuem to write an African *Dernier des Justes.*"[4]

Sellin's revelations were followed by an even more cutting indictment in *The Times Literary Supplement* of May 5, 1972. An entire oversized page was devoted to an item headed "Something *New* Out of Africa?" Most of the page reproduces a number of paragraphs from the French edition of Ouologuem's book and a comparable number of paragraphs from Graham Greene's *It's a Battlefield* (1934). The extracts from the two novels are remarkably similar—except for obvious changes in names of characters and places and the fact that the passages from Greene are in English and the ones from Ouologuem are in French. *The Times Literary Supplement* quotes Ouologuem's statement that he "wrote [his] book in French but followed the traditional African rhythms and the spirit of the African past."[5] The editors of the publication continue, "It presumably says something for Graham Greene that, even before he went to a continent that later much concerned him, he was capable of effortlessly conveying its traditional rhythms."[6] The article also cites Eric Sellin's discoveries about Ouologuem's novel in *Research in African Literatures* and asks, "Is M Ouologuem on to something: a style of literary imperialism intended as a revenge for the much-chronicled sins of territorial imperialists?"[7]

On the same day of *The Times Literary Supplement* revelations, an article in the New York *Times* reported that the American publisher of Ouologuem's novel, Harcourt Brace Jovanovich, had stopped publication of the work in the United States and that "3,400 hardback copies still in the hands of the American publishers have been withdrawn."[8] William Jovanovich, chairman of the company, is quoted as saying, " 'Even if Mr. Greene were to say that he just wants an acknowledgment, we would still go ahead and destroy the copies. . . . If I can not warrant it, I can not publish it.' "[9] Jovanovich bemoans the loss of approximately $10,000 in publication costs and hopes that it will be recovered from the French publisher.**

*Schwarz-Bart's novel is a chronicle of the Jewish experience, beginning in 1185 and ending in the Nazi extermination camps in World War II. Ouologuem's novel follows the exploitation of black Africans, beginning in 1202 and ending in 1947.

**In a later query I made of Harcourt Brace Jovanovich about these decisions, Helen Wolff, Ouologuem's editor, stated, "A paperback contract with Avon had to be cancelled for the same reasons, though the book had already been set in type."

Since these initial revelations about Ouologuem's novel, insinuations and innuendoes have continued to flow from the pens of a number of academics and the editors of a number of journals. A letter to the editor of *The Times Literary Supplement* from Paul Flamand, Ouologuem's editor at Éditions du Seuil, states that Ouologuem's novel was not "commissioned" as Sellin speculated. Flamand goes on to explain that when Seuil noticed a "few echoes" of Schwarz-Bart's novel, they wrote him and received a reply which stated:

> I am in no way worried by the use that has been made of *Dernier des Justes* . . . . I have always looked on my books as appletrees, happy that my apples be eaten and happy if now and again one is taken and planted in a different soil.
>
> I am therefore deeply touched, overwhelmed even, that a black writer should have leant on *Dernier des Justes* in order to write such a book as *Le Devoir de Violence*. Thus it is not M Ouologuem who is in debt to me, but I to him.*[10]

As we will later see, there are more than just a "few echoes" in Ouologuem's work to Schwarz-Bart's novel. Robert McDonald (an Australian student of Graham Greene's novels who discovered the passages from *It's a Battlefield*) later published an article in *Transition* concerning his discovery.[11] McDonald refers to *Bound to Violence* as "straight-forward plagiarism," and adds to the fire, "the one thing of which we cannot be certain—that all of the rest of *Bound to Violence* is the unaided work of Yambo Ouologuem."[12] McDonald feels suspicious about other sections of Ouologuem's novel and concludes, "M. Ouologuem has no possible way of proving conclusively that he *did* write his book."[13]

What have Ouologuem's reactions been to all of these accusations? In a published reply that appeared in *Le Figaro Littéraire* in June 1972, he states that he never intended to disguise his borrowings, that he referred to them in numerous interviews:

> Precisely because of the explosive nature of the subject of my novel, *Bound to Violence* (scenes of torture, cannibalism, insanity, legendary and historical facts, with links at the *récit à clés* [sic], at racial disputes,) being objective meant causing to be heard when necessary several contradictory voices in the very image of contradictory things— prejudices, superstitions, and sensitive issues—which inevitably surround the problems of Blacks.

---

*Schwarz-Bart benefited in others ways also. His next novel—a chronicle of black life beginning in West Africa and ending in slavery in the New World—*La mulatresse Solitude* (*A Woman Named Solitude*, 1971) shares an unusual number of similarities with Ouologuem's work. Then Schwarz-Bart's wife, Simone, joined the act of dubious literary influences and published a similar novel, *Pluie et rent sur Télumée* (*The Bridge of Beyond*, 1972), about a woman of Guadeloupe, again, spanning the time of several generations.

In my manuscript, which is now deposited at my attorney's, the allegedly plagiarized passage from Mr. Graham Greene was in fact cited in quotation marks, just like several lines from Schwarz-Bart.... In using the text from Mr. Greene, between quotation marks, I was not doing the job of a plagiarist; by putting a fact of a legally actionable nature into a [purely] literary perspective, I was preventing myself from being disavowed by my own kind. The references to Graham Greene, to Kipling, and to others were given publicly by me to the New York *Times,* the *New Yorker,* and elsewhere, at the time of meetings both with professors and with various Black Studies Programs....[14]

Ouologuem also makes a number of vague references to racial descrimination blacks have experienced and concludes by attacking his publisher who he says has given him no support in the case. Ouologuem is in fact vague about his original intentions, and I suspect this is because we have seen only the tip of the iceberg. When I asked Eric Sellin about Ouologuem's reaction to these allegations, he replied, "I have heard indirectly that he thinks there is a Western conspiracy afoot to discredit him,"[15] implying that Ouologuem appeared somewhat paranoid about the entire thing. The idea of a conspiracy is also supported by Kaye Whiteman, former Deputy Editor of *West Africa* in the only published defense of Ouologuem that I have been able to locate. Ms. Whiteman states,

> First of all, *Le Devoir de Violence* is full of literary allusions and quotations, some long, some short, some attributed, others not. Yambo has never made any secret of this, as he says, and from the moment the book appeared, this aspect of it has been discussed.... When I saw Yambo in his Paris flat recently he was much pre-occupied by the new attacks, and was talking sombrely in terms of conspiracy. He was in particular very caustic about the whole relationship of white literary circles, especially publishers, with black writers.[16]

The article continues,

> To demonstrate the injustice of the charges against him, he spent some time taking me through his original hand-written manuscript (in an old exercise book) of *Le Devoir de Violence* showing me all the places where there had been quotation marks, if not actual mentions of his literary allusions and quotations. He gave me a fairly comprehensive run-down on all the other authors he might be accused of plagiarising, including the 16th century Portuguese explorer Lope di Pigafeta, and a modern detective story by John Macdonald (the basis of the sequence containing the asp killing), as well as traditional epic sources in Arabic, Bambara and Amharic, and even in French colonial documents that he says are still in secret archives. I saw, for instance,

where he had written "here ends The Last of The Just", a reference omitted like so many others, for whatever reason, from the published version.[17]

For whatever reason?

Kaye Whiteman is about as vague as Ouologuem himself, though she does help clarify a number of matters. She refers to Ouologuem's style as that of a collage, a new novel, "or even [like] the work of some modern film-makers in which clips from films of others are inserted."[18] She stresses that "the so-called plagiarism is a stylistic technique to further the purposes of the novel,"[19] adding that there are no reasons for Africans to feel embarrassed about what has happened. "And to those who say it is less of an 'African novel', one should note that the style of allusion and quotation is *par excellence,* as Yambo says, that of the griots."[20]

The reactions of Ouologuem's various publishers have been mixed. There is currently no American edition of the book (the rights have reverted to the French publisher), but two reprint editions are in print in English editions, one of them having appeared after the scandal broke out. In the Sphere paperbacked edition, the passages from Greene's *It's a Battlefield* have simply been excised, and the publisher told me, "The cuts in the book . . .were made by the hard-cover publishers, Secker & Warburg."[21] Correspondence from Martin Secker & Warburg Ltd. to me revealed that these cuts were made at Graham Greene's request. T. G. Rosenthal, Managing Director of the company, had this to add:

> I may say that Graham Greene throughout behaved with exemplary dignity, tact and dignity since he could well have sued all the publishers of this particular book for plagiarism but, on the understanding that full exposure would be given to the matter in the press, remained content to let things rest at that provided of course that the offending passages were removed.[22]

The Heinemann African Writers Series edition—for sale in Africa only—contains a note, inserted on a slip of paper: "The Publishers acknowledge the use of certain passages on pages 54-56 from *It's a Battlefield* by Graham Greene."[23] In a letter that he refused me permission to quote from, Paul Flamand, Ouologuem's editor at Éditions du Seuil, stated that there are numerous passages taken from André Schwarz-Bart and Graham Greene and from other writers as well (whose names he does not identify). He added that Ouologuem's original manuscript made no mention of these borrowings in footnotes or in any other way. The letter ends by stating that Éditions du Seuil will not permit the novel to be reprinted as long as Ouologuem does not amend his work—that is, presumably until he cuts all the borrowed passages. Flamand's implication is that what happens next will depend on what Ouologuem himself decides to do.

I have detailed these various allegations about Ouologuem's novel for a specific reason: almost uniformly, reviewers who praised his novel were shocked and embarrassed when they learned of his borrowings from other writers. Many of these reviewers (myself included) felt cheated. The Sierra Leonian literary critic, Eldred Jones, told me that the very passages he thought were *most* African, turned out to be the borrowed ones. Helen Wolff, Ouologuem's American editor, wrote to me in a letter, "I have nothing to add . . .other then my personal regret that so gifted an author who certainly did not need to make loans from other literatures, should have acted so unwisely."[24] Somehow I think many critics felt that Ouologuem's borrowings denied the book its authenticity, its Africanness. Yet many of the initial reviewers who praised the novel were not versed in African cultures or African literature, and their statements about the novel's blackness were made out of this ignorance. They had been impressed with Ouologuem's use of language, his dazzling rhetoric.

I suggest that Ouologuem's borrowings do not make the novel any less African than it ever was thought to be, that much of the supposed "authenticity" was never there in the first place, and that in *Bound to Violence* we have another literary hybrid like *Batouala*. For purposes of our analysis here—to identify some of the traits of the novel in the Third World—Ouologuem's book is ideal because he has relied on a number of known examples from the West, especially the Schwarz-Bart novel. The "Africanness" of Ouologuem's novel, however, is not made up of the bits and pieces that have been picked at by the critics but, rather, by its over-all structure as related to Ouologuem's concepts of character and historical events removed from any specific time warp. This is what I find so interesting in *Bound to Violence:* Ouologuem tried to use Western models for the shape of his novel, and although he succeeded in doing this in specific passages, he apparently was incapable of escaping his own ingrained cultural ways of looking at character and anti-history, to use Alberto Moravia's term once again. Expressed in another manner, Ouologuem's novel—unlike André Schwarz-Bart's *The Last of the Just,* which is a chronology of man *in* time within his own personal ethnic history—is a pastiche of man *outside* of time, devoid of any personal history as we tend to think of it in the West. This is why Ouologuem's reliance on Schwarz-Bart's novel is especially revealing.

There can be no denying that the first section of *Bound to Violence* has been heavily patterned after Schwarz-Bart's novel, patterned so closely that the whole idea of Ouologuem's creativity is seriously in question. Without *The Last of the Just* there would be no *Bound to Violence*. It is surprising that it took so long for the connection between the two novels to be pointed out. There are similarities in the opening paragraphs of the two novels, in the scope of the number of years (that is, the so-called "epic" nature of both narratives), in specific sentences (especially transitional phrases and concluding comments at the end of similar incidents), and in repeated references to a kind of vague authenticity, that is, "history tells us" in Schwarz-Bart and "the griots tell us" in Ouologuem. All of these are related—but that is all, because in almost every case, analysis shows that Ouologuem has shifted his emphasis, his point of focus.

Here are the opening paragraphs of the two novels:

> Our eyes register the light of dead stars. A biography of my friend Ernie could easily be set in the second quarter of the twentieth century, but the true history of Ernie Levy begins much earlier, toward the year 1000 of our era, in the old Anglican city of York. More precisely, on March 11, 1185.[25]

> (Schwarz-Bart)

> Our eyes drink the brightness of the sun and, overcome, marvel at their tears. *Mashallah! wa bismillah!* . . . To recount the bloody adventure of the niggertrash—shame to the worthless paupers!—there would be no need to go back beyond the present century; but the true history of the Blacks begins much earlier, with the Saifs, in the year 1202 of our era, in the African Empire of Nakem south of Fezzan, long after the conquests of Okba ben Nafi al-Fitri. (p. 3; French, p. 9).*

> (Ouologuem)

Both novels are told in the third person by the omniscient author. Schwarz-Bart's novel begins in 1185; Ouologuem's in 1202. The language is similar, but here the similarities end. Schwarz-Bart's novel is about an individual character, Ernie Levy, and his ancestors. Ouologuem's is ostensibly about a group of people—the African masses or "niggertrash" as he calls them. Ernie Levy becomes the "hero" of Schwarz-Bart's novel when that term is used in its conventional sense, that is, when the stress is on the individual. In Ouologuem's case, the emphasis is collective, on a group, the blacks of an entire continent. Though Ouologuem from time to time shifts his narration so that one specific character is central, ultimately the result is situational—an entire race of people is exploited for 750 years. In contrast, Ernie Levy ends up in the gas chambers at Auschwitz, as do hundreds of thousands of others;

---

*Ouologuem's French publisher, Éditions du Seuil, has denied me permission to quote from the French text of the novel. Quotations, therefore, are limited to the English translation of the novel (New York: Harcourt Brace Jovanovich, 1971 and London: Heinemann Educational Books, 1971). The pages for the French edition (Paris, 1968), however, will be listed after the page number for the English translation. Subsequent page numbers for these editions will appear in the text.

yet though Schwarz-Bart uses Ernie in an emblematic way to represent an entire race, the emphasis is on the individual horror.

In their over-all concerns with prejudice and exploitation, there is also a major difference in the novels. Schwarz-Bart's book is concerned with specific Jewish victims of Aryan atrocities down through the ages, culminating in Ernie Levy's singular ordeal. Ouologuem, on the other hand, places equal emphasis on the oppressors—the Saifs at the beginning and later the European slavers and colonial representatives—a colonial situation similar to the one Maran shows in *Batouala*. Significantly, Ouologuem eventually sides with the oppressors rather than the victims. Related to this is the specific nature of each of the victims. In Schwarz-Bart's novel, Ernie Levy's ancestors try to cope with the evils perpetrated on them; they try to break out of the pattern of racial victimization. When the novel shifts to Ernie himself, we see the portrait of a man acting, trying to control his own destiny. In Ouologuem's case we have no comparable portrait. By the end of the novel, nothing has changed for the African masses—they are the same. Ouologuem says quite early in his novel, "...the niggertrash...accepted whatever came their way" (p. 22; French, p. 29). Even their oppressors, the Saifs, are exactly as they were—using the same methods to keep the niggertrash down that they used centuries earlier, employing identical methods to kill off the invading whites. What is even more fascinating is that although Ouologuem mentions a dozen or more descendants of Saif Isaac al-Heit, by the time we complete our reading of *Bound to Violence*, they have become indistinguishable from one another, they have no singular identities. It is as if there is only one Saif—a sadistic butcher of the masses —who lives for 750 years.

There are two utterly different world views operating here, representing opposing concepts of history and time. Schwarz-Bart's novel goes back in time in order to discover the *reasons* why these atrocities have happened. Ouologuem's goes back to show how history repeats itself. Schwarz-Bart's characters, acting in time, try to learn from past experiences and events the means of escaping what is happeinng to them in the present; Ouologuem's Africans do not even try to break out of their pattern. Schwarz-Bart's concept of time is linear and causal; Ouologuem's is cyclical and static. Indeed, Ouologuem's view of time is precisely the same as the fictional Batouala's.* Ouologuem also changes historical events, places, and figures when it is necessary—since, after all, he is writing fiction, not history. The first two sections of his novel span the years from 1202 to 1901 as he chronicles the Saif dynasty —beginning with Saif Isaac al-Heit and ending with Saif ben Isaac al-Heit—in its quest for continuous exploitation and power over the Afri-

---

*There is a difference here, of course, in the totality of the time involved: the recorded time in *Batouala* is a few weeks; in *Bound to Violence*, 750 years.

cans. This family, Ouologuem tells us (part Arab, part Jew, part black African), controlled the African masses centuries before the first European explorers arrived in Africa.

Just as in Maran's *Batouala*, in Ouologuem's novel there is no romantic picture of an idealized Africa prior to the arrival of the white man.* For the African masses, colonialism was little different from what preceded it. Ouologuem's novel seems purposely designed to upset many of its readers, be they African or Western. As he says, "The destiny of Saif Isaac al-Heit stands out most illustriously, [endowing] the legend of the Saifs with the splendor in which the dreamers of African unity sun themselves to this day" (p. 5; French, p. 11). Ouologuem is especially relentless in his attacks on Pan-Africanism.

Althouth Ouologuem's colorful use of language impressed his early critics, his rhetorical tricks are often borrowed from Schwarz-Bart's novel. Schwarz-Bart's first chapter is titled "The Legend of the Just Men" ("La legende des Justes"); Ouologuem's is titled "The Legend of the Saifs" ("La legende des Saifs"). Ouologuem's use of understatement to play down an incident is straight from Schwarz-Bart. After describing a particularly unbelievable incident, Ouologuem states, "But there is nothing unusual in this story . . ." (p. 5; French, p. 10). Schwarz-Bart says, "This anecdote in itself offers nothing remarkable" (p. 4; French, p. 12). For historical authenticity, Schwarz-Bart notes that "exact details are lacking and the opinions of the chronicles are divergent" (p. 5; French, p. 13). Ouologuem renders this, "At this point tradition loses itself in legend, for there are few written accounts and the versions of the elders diverge from those of the griots, which differ in turn from those of the chroniclers" (p. 6; French, p. 11). A most revealing difference between the two in their regard for historical fact lies in the note that Schwarz-Bart places at the beginning of his novel:

> This book is a work of fiction. In making use of historical fact the author referred principally to the following sources: *Du Christ aux Juifs de Cour; Le Bréviaire de la Haine*, by Leon Poliakov; *Écrits des Condamnés à Mort*, by Michel Borwicz; *L'Univers Concentrationnaire*, by David Rousset; *De Drancy à Auschwitz*, by Georges Wellers; *Tragédie de la Déportation*, by Olga Wormser.

And in Ouologuem's novel,

> Since this book is a work of fiction, any resemblance to real persons would be fortuitous.

*Ouologuem is not the only African writer to have done this. Wole Soyinka, the Nigerian author, has often depicted an equally unromanticized African past. So has Ayi Kwei Armah in his fourth novel, *Two Thousand Seasons* (1973).

Over and over again, Ouologuem embellishes incidents borrowed from Schwarz-Bart's novel. Even Ouologuem's most telling put-down, used dozens of times throughout the narrative, is borrowed from *The Last of the Just*. In Schwarz-Bart's novel, after one of Ernie's ancestors is burned to death in a public execution, Schwarz-Bart says, "A tear for him" (p. 8; French, p. 15). Ouologuem renders this "A prayer for him," (p. 9; French, p. 15); "A hymn to it," (p. 11; French, p. 17); "A sob for her," (p. 16; French, p. 22); and "A tear for him," (p. 18; French, p. 24) in the first section alone.

Schwarz-Bart uses "A tear for him" once, to establish a particularly ironic tone. Ouologuem uses his variations over and over to establish a sarcastic tone that pervades the entire novel. The result is that we never know when to take him seriously. There is a strange brand of humor (black humor?) ringing throughout the entire narrative. It appears as early as page eight. Ouologuem appears to be saying, "I dare you to take me seriously!" This tone—often built from a kind of reversal which cancels out what he has said before—is intermixed with vindictiveness. After describing the dastardly acts of a particularly tyrannical Saif (Saif Moshe Gabbai), Ouologuem concludes, he died of a ruptured gall bladder. In another incident, Ouologuem informs us that the goodness of Saif Isaac al-Heit haunts black romanticism to this day: "Chroniclers draw on the oral tradition to enrich his cult and through him celebrate the glorious era of the first States with their wise philosopher-king, whose history has called not only archaeology, history, and numismatics but also the natural sciences and ethnology to their highest tasks" (p. 8; French, p. 14). Numismatics? It is the third item in the series that always surprises: "Yet amid this hideous hodgepodge of tribal custom, violence, and dilettantism . . ." (p. 21; French, p. 27), and so on. The mocking tone never ceases; at its most extreme it becomes a put-down, interrupting a sentence that is otherwise serious:

> Then, once peace was restored among the various tribes, for the war had failed to break out—hee-hee—the same notables promised the same subjects that after . . . hum . . . hum . . . a brief "apprenticeship" of forced labor, they would be rewarded with the Rights of Man . . . . As to civil rights, of them no mention was made. Hallelujah! (pp. 21-22; French, p. 28)

Much of *Bound to Violence* is in fact designed to shock the reader. The novel is constructed around a number of violent scenes, mostly described gratituously. Here again, it is revealing to draw a parallel with *The Last of the Just*. Schwarz-Bart also includes elements of violence in his novel—there is no way he can escape them because of his subject matter. But Ouologuem puts them in needlessly, seemingly bent on depicting the most violent matters he can imagine. Often—and this happens in Schwarz-Bart too—violence is related to religion, though religion is linked more directly to Ouologuem's depiction of the atrocities of slavery and colonialism. Violence, however, is not quite enough for Ouologuem; it has to be related to sex, something that Ouologuem never treats naturally, realistically. It is always in tandem with some other narrative element. Fortunately, one of these is humor:

> On April 20, 1532, on a night as soft as a cloak of moist satin, Saif al-Haram, performing his conjugal "duty" with his four step-mothers seriatim and all together, had the imprudent weakness to overindulge and in the very midst of his dutiful delights gave up the ghost.... (p. 16; French, p. 22)

Moreover, Ouologuem is often overly romantic, especially in the later sections of his novel; and he often links sex with violence or perversity. Hence, in the first section of the novel there are accounts of incest, bestiality, and homosexuality—mostly prefigurations of later sexual incidents in the story. Many readers have reacted to his novel as if it were pornography. I find this term inadequate for Ouologuem's work, though it is clear he has tried to be intentionally erotic; he has consciously attempted to write a commercial best seller. Perhaps that is Ouologuem's major downfall in *Bound to Violence*: in a way, it is formula fiction. Ouologuem figured out the kind of book that would be a commercial success and then he wrote it.*

What happens to Ouologuem's "history" of the African masses? By the time the major thrust of his story emerges (at the beginning of the third section, in the year 1901), Ouologuem has given us a bloody chronicle of seven hundred years of African misery under the hands of Saif Isaac al-Heit's descendants. Violence has bred more violence. When the Europeans arrive, the reader coming to this scene is jolted by the realization that it is Africans who have been exploiting Africans, Africans who have enslaved Africans until this time. Then the methods simply change a little.

> Having depopulated whole regions, the slave trade had long been unprofitable and seeped away like water in the hungry sand. It had become difficult to find good laborers, and all in all it seemed preferable to bleed the people with all manner of taxes, direct and indirect, drive them to the utmost in the fields and workshops of the notables at a meager wage for which the Hereafter would find means to compensate them. The religious gymnastics of the five daily prayers of Islam

*Seemingly believing he had not gone far enough, Ouologuem published an avowed pornographic novel in 1969, *Les mille et une bibles du sexe*, under the pseudonym Utto Rodolph (Editions du Dauphin). In that work, his erotic fantasies know no end.

were maintained as a safety valve; the poor in mind and spirit were kept busy searching and striving for Allah's Eternal Kingdom. Religion, whose soul had been vomited by the clergy of Nakem, became a deliberately confused mumbling about human dignity, a learned mystification; losing its mystical content, it became a means of action, a political weapon. (p. 23; French, pp. 29-30)

Religious exploitation of the Africans was paralleled by the European realization that Africa offered an almost inexhaustible raw material—the niggertrash. Saif ben Isaac al-Heit fights one final battle with the Europeans, in 1898, and then surrenders to the white invaders. After the signing of the peace treaty, Saif sends one of his sons, Madoubo, to Paris, as part of an official delegation. The second section concludes,

> Presents were heaped upon the son of Saif, who, now became a symbol of Franco-African co-operation, returned to his illustrious father.
> On his return to Nakem, Madoubo found that his father had not been idle; he had populated his palace with twenty-three newborn babes conceived by twenty of his twenty-seven wives.
> An unforeseen consequence: on Madoubo's return the popular imagination transformed defeat into genius and the dictatorship of a tyrannical dynasty into eternal glory; the defeated emperor was numbered among the cohorts of "those just men whose greatness quenches the thirst of the agonizing heart...."
> Twilight of the gods? Yes and no. More than one dream seemed to be fading; a turning point of civilization, or should one say a convulsion presaging its ultimate end? Presaging a new birth? Or merely a sempiternal agony, presaging nothing? A tear for the niggertrash, O Lord, in Thy compassion! ... (p. 33; French, pp. 43-44)

The central and longest section of *Bound to Violence* is called "The Night of the Giants." The influences of Schwarz-Bart's *The Last of the Just* are considerably fewer here than in the first two sections, though Ouologuem has made borrowings of a different kind. The years covered run from 1901 to 1947 and illustrate Saif ben Isaac al-Heit's total and unceasing control over both the African masses and the European invaders, that is, the official French representatives and members of the Catholic missionary delegation in Nakem. It is in this section that a major problem with credibility develops.

The section begins with a shift to the exploited Africans: "The sole vestige of those abortive dreams—the venom is in the tail!—was the serf whose days of hard labor closely resembled those of a convict" (p. 34; French, p. 47). Ouologuem dwells for a time upon the idyllic relationship of two of Saif's servants, Kassoumi and Tambira. It is a particularly sad affair—doomed to violence as are almost all other relationships in the novel. Ouologuem's description of their relationship shows him at the height of his imaginative powers, and yet once again illustrates the problem of the dual audience. Ouologuem appears to be writing for the non-African reader here. When Kassoumi sneaks up upon Tambira as she is bathing in the river, the description of her beauty seems far too erotic for its African context. Tambira is embarrassed when Kassoumi gets a glimpse of her naked breasts. The whole scene has a ring of falseness about it. Nakedness does not produce shame in an African, as Camara Laye has illustrated in *The Radiance of the King* (*Le regard du roi*). In that novel, when Clarence—the white man—is taken to court, it is suggested that he give his shirt and trousers to the plaintiff as restitution for a crime he has supposedly committed. " 'Can you see me walking naked in the streets?' " Clarence asks the judge. And the judge replies, " 'There is no law against that....' "[26] Ouologuem, on the other hand, appears to have included this scene in order to describe another erotic encounter.

Despite a certain poignancy in the scenes between Kassoumi and Tambira, there are other red herrings to confuse the issue. This mixture only serves to illustrate the obvious tendency in Ouologuem's attitude toward male/female relationships: women always come out the worse. Ouologuem builds a scene to an intense emotional pitch—Kassoumi realizes that even in his love for Tambira, his servitude comes first: "In his rage he shook with a sense of impotence, with impatience and irritation, because she did not belong to him" (p. 41; French, p. 54). Then, two paragraphs later Ouologuem ruins all of it by having Kassoumi say, " 'Look, Tambira....it can't go on like this' " (p. 41; French, p.55). It sounds like something from a 1940's Hollywood movie.*

Their victimization, however, is real enough. When Saif permits them to marry, we learn (though Kassoumi and Tambira do not) that once again the serfs have been manipulated: "Saif decided that only the sons of the servant class would be constrained to undergo French education, the masses of the missionaries, and the baptism of the White Fathers, to adopt French dress and shave their heads, while their parents would be obliged to make amends and swear secrecy" (p. 46; French, p. 60). In the same month that Kassoumi and Tambira are married, Saif arranges 1623 other weddings. And, in Tambira's case, Saif performs the ritual defloration on her wedding night. (All of this, of course, is rather graphically described.)

Ouologuem makes it quite clear that the French never really control Nakem. The representatives of the government are always in Saif's hands, because he controls the masses. The governors of the "colony" are killed off one by one—always in such a manner that their deaths appear to

*Perhaps it is.

be accidental. The first of these dies with his wife and daughter, because Saif has had vipers (asps) secreted into their sleeping chambers.

The next day life went back to normal: wires went out reporting the deaths, requesting replacements . . . . Since, thought the white man, Africa is and remains the savage continent, what wonder that thoughtless men, suddenly catapulted from the European cradle of civilization into the land of the Blacks, ignoring all advice and letting the grass grow too high around their houses, should fall victim to "poisonous snakes driven out of the woods by fire"? (p. 47; French, p. 61)

Jean Chevalier, the next governor, is killed in such a way that the whites believe an assassination plot was planned to eliminate Saif. It is in the scenes preceding this incident that Ouologuem has placed the borrowed passages from *It's a Battlefield*. Robert McDonald has already illustrated how the paragraphs from Greene seem out of place in this context,* but so do the passages that follow, describing a seduction involving Chevalier and Awa, an African woman spying for Saif. The seduction itself is ridiculous. Chevalier is aided by two dogs who tear off Awa's clothing, and that scene is followed by one of bestiality with Awa and the dogs—then a bible of sexual variations between Awa and Chevalier:

A flowing cup—Awa—a lavish board! An Eve with frantic loins, she cajoled the man, kissed him, bit him, scratched him, whipped him, sucked his nose ears throat, armpits navel and member so voluptuously that the administrator, discovering the ardent landscape of this feminine kingdom, kept her there day after day, and, his soul in ecstasy, lived a fanatical, panting, frenzied passion. (p. 57; French, p. 71)

African readers of the novel have told me that the scene is ludicrous—that no African woman would act this way. Again, Ouologuem has gotten his audiences mixed up. Pornotrash, as one of my students once called it.

The murder of the next governor, Vandame, is equally violent but gives us a remarkable insight into Ouologuem's intention. I am indebted here to James Olney's book, *Tell Me Africa*. Olney wrote to Ouologuem's translator, Ralph Manheim, and learned from him that Ouologuem rewrote a number of the passages in the English version of the novel.[27] The account of Vandame's death in the English translation differs from the original French version. Olney states,

. . .Ouologuem introduced into the translation a number of apparent allusions to English and American literature . . ."the awful daring of

---

*Among other things, the house is an anachorism for Africa at that time.

a moment's surrender . . . . Then blood shook his heart" (*Waste Land*); "There was no end, only addition" (*Four Quartets*); "because he could not stop for death" (Emily Dickinson).[28]

There are, however, more borrowings than Olney has noted. In the last three paragraphs describing Vandame's death, Ouologuem incorporates lines from two of Emily Dickinson's poems —#328 "A Bird Came Down the Walk" and #712 "Because I Could Not Stop for Death" —not just the one Olney pointed out:

> When he sensed danger, he groped at shapes and ran *because he could not stop for death*. Suddenly Wampoulo clasped his shoulders and shook them so frantically that Vandame's neck swung and broke.
> Quicker than speech, his arms waltzed above him, *then rowed him softlier home*, to the Artful Creator.
> Blood spurted from the nape of his neck like reluctant rubies grasped by a beetle. *His eyeballs like frightened beads*, Vandame *drank a dewdrop from a blade of grass*. He was a righteous man.
>
> (p. 115. Italics mine)

Ouologuem has begun to play an intellectual word game with his readers.

For the Western reader, one of the highlights of Ouologuem's novel is his parody of the German anthropologist, Leo Frobenius. Ouologuem begins this section as follows: "A year and three months later—July 13, 1910. Three foreigners, a family of Germans—Fritz Shrobenius, his wife Hildegard, and their daughter Sonia . . .arrived" (p. 85; French, p. 100). What follows is a passage of high comic relief—once again illustrating that Ouologuem is a man of great talent when he wants to use it. Shrobenius writes down the stories Saif makes up. Ouologuem says of him, "he was determined to find metaphysical meaning in everything," (p. 87; French, p. 102), continuing, "African life [Shrobenius] held, was pure art, intense religious symbolism, and a civilization once grandiose—but alas a victim of the white man's vicissitudes" (p. 87; French, p. 102). Shrobenius walks around, drooling, absorbing the mystical world around him, hoarding African carvings by the hundreds. When he returns to Europe, he is raised to a "lofty Sorbonnical chair, while on the other hand he exploited the sentimentality of the coons, only too pleased to hear from the mouth of a white man that Africa was 'the womb of the world and cradle of civilization' " (pp. 94-95; French, p. 111). Ouologuem concludes, of the school of Shrobeniusology:

> An Africanist school harnessed to the vapors of magico-religious, cosmological, and mythical symbolism had been born: with the result that for three years men flocked to Nakem—and what men!—middlemen, adventurers, apprentice bankers, politicians, salesmen, conspirators—supposedly "scientists," but in reality enslaved sentries

mounting guard before the "Shrobeniusological" monument of Negro pseudosymbolism.

Already it had become more than difficult to procure old masks, for Shrobenius and the missionaries had had the good fortune to snap them all up. And so Saif—and the practice is still current—had slapdash copies buried by the hundredweight, or sunk into ponds, lakes, marshes, and mud holes, to be exhumed later on and sold at exorbitant prices to unsuspecting curio hunters. These three-year-old masks were said to be *charged with the weight of four centuries of civilization*. To the credulous customer, the seller pointed out the ravages of time, the malignant worms that had gnawed at these master-pieces imperiled since time immemorial, witness their prefabricated poor condition. *Alif lam! Amba, koubo oumo agoum.* (pp. 95-96; French, p. 112)

A tear for Leo Frobenius.

Nothing significant happens to improve the lot of the niggertrash during this time. Ouologuem refers to them as idiots several times. Saif permits them to be converted to Christianity.

Let the white apes in helmets civilize the pickaninnies, the jigaboos, the niggertrash baboons, all those hopeless idiots who, fishing in the troubled waters of the "cultural mission," knocked themselves out licking the white man's boots and praying to his Christ, sucking the breast and bottle of Abbé Henry's sermons, the spirit of the sons of the Oratory of the Divine Love in Rome . . . . (pp. 66-67; French, p. 81)

The Arabs still sell many of them as slaves. Often, Saif has the unruly ones drugged, turned into helpless zombies, so they will work his land without complaint. Their exploitation continues down through the years, until World War I ("the anonymous niggertrash [were] dragged twenty thousand miles and fallen for unjustifiable ends" p. 123; French, p. 143). Then the emphasis shifts to Raymond-Spartacus Kassoumi—the eldest son of Tambira and Kassoumi and the future hope of the masses.

Raymond Kassoumi's years in Paris permit Ouologuem to strike out at still another sacred cow: French education. More specifically, Ouologuem illustrates what became an almost archetypal reaction to French education by many of the Africans who were first schooled in Europe, namely, rejection of their African heritage. Raymond is little different from dozens of African students in Europe. Saif is in complete control here, too; it is he who picks Raymond to go to Paris. An analogy should be made between Raymond and Ernie Levy in *The Last of the Just*. Raymond is Ernie's equivalent in the last fifty pages of Ouologuem's novel, but the connection can go no further than that. There is no introspection on Raymond's part; there is no introspection in the entire novel. Raymond never makes a single decisive act throughout the entire sequence; he always permits others (Saif, Lambert, his wife) to push him around. He is totally passive—he makes no attempts to understand his past (as Ernie Levy does) or to escape the roles that others have chosen for him to play. He lives in the present, devoid of a past and a future.

The scenes in Europe also permit Ouologuem to indulge in some of his most graphic descriptions of sex and violence, for the two are almost always linked together. There are a number of Henry Millerish scenes that take place in Paris. In one of especial importance, after an orgy with a number of other students and several prostitutes (the scene takes place in a hotel in Pigalle), Raymond discovers that the black prostitute with whom he has just made love is his younger sister, Kadidia. She reveals to him still more crimes committed by Saif back in Nakem before she escaped the tyrant's clutches. But apparently the element of incest is not quite enough. Ouologuem writes,

> A week later Raymond, taking advantage of Sunday to visit his sister, was told that a sadistic customer had concealed a razor blade in the soap on Kadidia's bidet and that in washing herself she had cut herself so deeply that the hemorrhage had drained her blood and killed her before help could come. (p. 147; French, p. 169)

Thereafter follows a lengthy description of Raymond's homosexual relationship with Lambert, replete with purple prose and corny dialogue, followed by Raymond's marriage to Suzanne after Lambert leaves him in the lurch. The sections devoted to Raymond continue until shortly after World War II (July 1947) when Saif (ever faithful puppeteer that he is) brings Raymond back home to lead the masses:

> a cult of the good nigger had arisen, a philistine Negromania without obligation or sanction, akin to those popular messianisms which appeal as much to the white soul enamored of niggerdom as Aunt Jemima's pancakes to the white mouth. (p. 165; French, p. 189)

Ouologuem sums up the relationship between Saif and Raymond:

> Kassoumi the shrewd calculator had miscalculated: armed with his degrees and the support of France, he had expected to become his old master's master, when in reality the slave owed his election exclusively to the torch of Saif, more radiant than ever after a momentary lapse. *Yérété! aou yo yédè?* (p. 167; French, p. 191)

Immediately before the last section of Ouologuem's novel, Bishop Henry (earlier Abbé Henry) encounters Raymond-Spartacus Kassoumi and tells him that he has discovered Saif's manner of killing off his enemies: asps concealed in cylinders of bamboo. The Bishop warns Raymond that he should be careful of Saif, that Raymond has never made his own choices: " 'You've had no choice since the day when you first sat down on a school bench' " (p. 171; French, p. 196). Henry says he is going to see Saif, referring to him as Machiavelli and Judas. This meeting and the subsequent dialogue between the two of them brings about the climax of the novel. Ouologuem's title for this last section is "Dawn", but a more accurate title might be "The Game of Chess."*

The scene begins with Bishop Henry telling Saif about a movie he saw the day before, a film " 'inspired by the history of Nakem...' " (p. 173; French, p. 199). Both are old men—probably in their eighties. Both have survived the changes in Nakem down through the years, beginning before Saif surrendered to the French. In the dialectic that follows, Saif represents Africa, secularism, servitude, might, the Devil, and power in general; Henry, the opposites: the West, religion, freedom, right, God, and love. The dialogue they have places them on an equal footing for the first time since they have known each other, and —although it is filled with meaningless platitudes—the overall effect of the scene is impressive, if somewhat cold. One finds here none of the emotional intensity of the last chapter of Schwarz-Bart's novel.

Henry describes a massacre in the movie he has seen. It appeared as if the hero had been shot, but that turned out to be incorrect—you cannot have a dead hero. Henry then comments about violence, self-perpetuating violence:

> "The crux of the matter is that violence, vibrant in its unconditional submission to the will to power, becomes a prophetic illumination, a manner of questioning and answering, a dialogue, a tension, an oscillation, which from murder to murder makes the possibilities respond to each other, complete or contradict each other." (p. 173; French, p. 199)

Violence has become a way of life, breeding on itself. For a moment, it appears as though Henry has adopted Saif's strategy, but then he says, " 'Men kill each other because they have been unable to communicate' " (p. 175; French, p. 201). He lets Saif know that he has discovered his method of killing his enemies. Then he suggests that they play a game of chess.

As they are about to begin their game, Saif places a bamboo cylinder on the floor near Henry, ironically stating, " 'I warn you. I don't know how to play' " (p. 176; French, p. 202). A number of puns follow, as

*There appear to be a number of internal references to the second part of T. S. Eliot's *The Waste Land* (Eliot: "And we shall play a game of chess"; Ouologuem: "Have you some game we could play? Chess?")

the players use the terminology of the chess game (" 'Can you hope to kill you adversary . . .?' " p. 177; French, p. 203). Henry develops the relationship of specific chess men with figures from Nakem's history (most of them now dead: Chevalier, Vandame, Kassoumi, and so on). The bamboo cylinder moves back and forth on the floor between them. Saif speaks the most revealing line: " 'Each player is a functional object, a plaything and at the same time the stake of the game' " (p. 179; French, p. 205). Such has been Saif's relationship with all other human beings; they are disposable, functional. When Henry calls Saif's bluff, stating that every game has to have its rules, Saif throws the cylinder into the fireplace and the asp crackles in the fire. The game ends as they each make their respective moves, killing off their opponents. Saif philosophizes, " 'Nakem was born generations ago, and only in the last fifteen minutes have men learned to discuss the state of its health' " (pp. 180–181; French, p. 206).

There is only a page and a half of text left and the reader assumes that the scene he has just read symbolizes a *rapprochment* between Africa and the West. For the first time in the history of colonialism in this area, both sides have come together and talked. But Ouologuem is not that optimistic. If the novel had ended with the dialogue between Saif and Bishop Henry, the result would have been inconsistent with everything that preceded it. Ouologuem twists things around once again, ending with things as they are, as they have always been. The niggertrash (the pawns) will continue to be kept in tow by the powers that have always been—they are far away from any sense of political consciousness. Nothing has happened. Nothing has changed. The history of Nakem has existed in a vacuum, outside of time:

> Often, it is true, the soul desires to dream the echo of happiness, an echo that has no past. But projected into the world, one cannot help recalling that Saif, mourned three million times, is forever reborn to history beneath the hot ashes of more than thirty African republics.
> . . . That night, as they sought one another until the terrace was soiled with the black summits of dawn, a dust fell on the chessboard; but in that hour when the eyes of Nakem take flight in search of memories, forest and coast were fertile and hot with compassion. And such was the earth of men that the balance between air, water, and fire was no more than a game.* (pp. 181-182; French, p. 207)

*The reader will notice a number of similarities here with the end of André Schwarz-Bart's *The Last of the Just:*

> Yes, at times one's heart could break in sorrow. But often too, preferably in the evening, I can't help thinking that Ernie Levy, dead six million times, is still alive somewhere, I don't know where . . . . Yesterday, as I stood in the street trembling in despair, rooted to the spot, a drop of pity fell from above upon my face. But there was no breeze in the air, no cloud in the sky . . . . There was only a presence.

Ouologuem's novel is a mosaic, a pastiche of borrowings from sources we may never be able to track down. Although the result is often a challenging intellectual word game, I am appalled by the method and the poverty of his borrowings. In a way, Ouologuem has used a technique similar to one René Maran used in *Batouala*. Maran incorporated passages from the oral tradition into the text of his novel; Ouologuem borrowed passages from other published works. My feeling is that Ouologuem did not know how to handle the incorporation of these borrowings. The Graham Greene passage is inexcusable; the several lines from Emily Dickinson are not. The first borrowing does not work, the second does. It is a difference of technique, of manner, of not balancing the mixture of satire and parody with the over-all seriousness of the novel in the way, for example, that John Barth parodies the history of the novel in *The Sot-Weed Factor*.

There are numerous other passages in the novel that seem out of joint—there are too many red herrings, too many places where Ouologuem has not been faithful to African life (if that was what he intended, and we can never be certain of that). There is, for example, a continual juxtaposition of romanticism and naturalism throughout the book. Ouologuem gushes about the beauty of African life and then destroys it all in the next minute. One moment he is manic (on top of his material); the next he is depressive. In a delightful scene between Sonia Shrobenius and Saif's son, Madoubo, the comic bawdiness changes to sado-masochism. In the midst of seducing Sonia, Madoubo plays a phonograph record of Spanish music. Sonia, in the throes of passion, asks him, " 'Is it functional?' " (p. 90; French, p. 105). Then the scene gets out of hand (like that razor blade in the bar of soap) and Sankolo, spying on them and masturbating at the same time, eviscerates his mistress, Awa. The hijinks of the early part of the scene have turned into something sick. I suggest Ouologuem's quasi-indebtedness to Jean Genet, de Sade, William Burroughs and *The Story of O*. Women are objects—to be used and then disposed of. I find the violence the most disturbing aspect of Ouologuem's novel.

The book is also too long, in spite of what some people have referred to as Ouologuem's economy. A scene describing Sankolo's drugging stretches on for page after page. In several places, Ouologuem's satire wears thin. Schwarz-Bart's *The Last of the Just* is more than twice the length of Ouologuem's *Bound to Violence*—a telling comparison. Yet Schwarz-Bart has learned to economize and Ouologuem has not. Ultimately, however, Ouologuem has come off better than his attackers, and I cannot help thinking that Ouologuem is going to have the last laugh. He is the only one who knows where all of the pieces in his puzzle come from. Like Fritz Shrobenius, peddling those faked pieces of African art all over Europe, Ouologuem has sold us exactly what we wanted to buy—an imitation instead of the original. That is why his novel is not the *tour de force* he wanted it to be. We have both gotten the short end of the stick. As Ouologuem would say, "A tear for both of us."

If Ouologuem's *Bound to Violence* may be said to deal with the public history of a group of people—the events that happen to them over a period of 750 years—Vincent Eri's lesser novel, *The Crocodile* (1970), ostensibly concerns itself with private history—what happens to an individual during the time span of a dozen or fifteen years. One novel focuses on a group of people, the other, essentially, on an individual. The recorded time is hundreds of years in the first case and part of an individual's lifetime in the other. Yet the treatment of those two periods is similar. In Eri's *The Crocodile*, we again see evidence of a non-evolving character, the opposite of a development novel or *bildungsroman*. Even less than in Ouologuem's *Bound to Violence* is there a sense of cause and effect. I stress this fact because I believe that a sense of causality is a prime concern in the Western novel, but not in the novel from the Third World—unless we include external causes, which shift the emphasis so that people are acted upon. Western novels which de-emphasize character development—and there are many, of course—still have a sense of causality. *Moll Flanders* is a good example of this: we can never be certain that a "moral conversion" has taken place in Moll's life. She is essentially the same at the end of her story as she was at the beginning, but she has made decisive acts throughout her entire life. If there is no comprehension on the part of the main character in literature as extreme as the New Novel (such as Alain Robbe-Grillet's *The Voyeur* [*Le Voyeur*]) there is still a sense of cause and effect —events caused because of choices the character makes.

Often the world does not operate in such a manner in Third World fiction. Batouala does not seem capable of changing his destiny, though we have to admit that Maran has endowed him with a sense of comprehension of what has happened to his culture and, by extension, to himself. Raymond in *Bound to Violence* is totally passive—the same at the end as he was when he first appeared, and he has not comprehended what has happened to him. (It is Bishop Henry, after all, who tells him that he has always been Saif's puppet.) Hoiri Sevese, Eri's main character, is an even more extreme example of the passive hero than the others. His story ends, as it began, in bewilderment.

There are probably a number of similarities shared by Hoiri and his creator, Vincent Eri. Eri was born in 1936 in the Gulf District of Papua, in a village named Moreave. He was educated at mission schools, eventually completing a teacher training course. In 1970, he was one of the first graduates from the newly-established University of Papua and New Guinea. Since then he has held various educational positions in the government, including Acting Superintendent of Primary Education in Papua New Guinea. *The Crocodile* is his first novel and also the first published novel by a Papuan.

At the beginning of *The Crocodile*—which is told in the third person—Hoiri Sevese is roughly seven years old, attending a Catholic school in Moreave. His mother has recently been killed by a crocodile and Hoiri's father believes that sorcery was involved. Some years later after Hoiri is married, his wife, Mitoro, is also the victim of a crocodile, and sorcery is once again suspected. When World War II begins, Hoiri is drafted by the Australians to work as a carrier. Although this experience exposes him to many things he has not seen before, the result is confusion more than anything else. His father dies before the war is over, and Hoiri believes he has seen his wife, possessed by the sorcerers. The most fascinating aspects of *The Crocodile* are the novel's use of time and of superstition, the unseen, the occult—that is, the unexplainable.

Much of the novel is spent describing daily life in a Papuan village. As is so typical of other Third World novels, the author explains many of the important stages in the traditional cycle of life: birth, marriage, death. The rituals behind all of these events are described in extensive detail, once again giving us that closed world we saw in *Batouala,* that self-renewing cycle of life based on repetition and ritual. Since there are few exact references to time (no specific dates are ever mentioned) we have to infer these dates from the story—such as the sections concerned with World War II. At the beginning of the novel, Eri describes a picture of King George II, hanging in the classroom of Hoiri's school. We can assume that the year is 1936 or later. Since the novel ends soon after the war, we might be led to conclude that Hoiri is sixteen years old. Possibly—but I strongly doubt this, because if that is so he would have been married at twelve or thirteen which would be unusual for Papuan society.

Rather, I suggest that the vagueness of time is something that exists only within the Western reader's mind—that for Eri and the Papuan reader these matters are of no concern. There are other periods of time that also elude close analysis. Mostly, however, time has simply been ignored in this novel as if it had no effect on the people involved—as indeed it does not—except for the external forces represented by the West, that is, Australia in this case. Occasionally, Eri refers to specific blocks of time—"two weeks ago" or "the great day came at last" or "three years"—but more often than not, changes in time are indicated by the word "now." "How very different life was now for Hoiri,"[29] Eri tells us early in the story. If we stop our reading at that sentence, we have no idea what is being referred to or what time period this is. We have to read on to determine what and when the "now" refers to. (In this specific case, it is the healing of a wound.)

A better example of the cyclical time frame of the book is a later passage where the word "now" occurs twice. Masoare is talking to her daughter, Mitoro, Hoiri's wife:

> "I can recall the day when Siarivita was clubbed to death near the spot where your father built our house. It was a pathetic affair, three to one. But now the married man who makes a girl pregnant is taken to court and the government puts him in jail for two or three months. After that the Government orders him to give food to the mother to maintain the child and that is all there is to it. Her parents or brothers won't dare to make the man marry her. Even now married men committing adultery get the same length of jail sentence and there is no fear of death." (pp. 69–70)

The past is what was, the present is now. Equally typical are a number of inconsistencies concerning other time blocks in the story. Although Hoiri is seven at the beginning, he is referred to as old enough to be married before we are aware of any time passing. In another place, when Hoiri is drafted to be a carrier before the outbreak of the war, a voyage in a small boat takes several days. Word comes from other villagers (who have been paddling similar boats) that Hoiri's wife died "two days ago"—in other words that the second group of paddlers had covered in two days what Hoiri had covered in several days. When Hoiri gets back to his village (presumably even several days later), it is still only two days since his wife's death. It is as if time has been slowed down to magnify the emotional aspect of the violent death.

Another example of the confusing use of time is an incident at the end of the war. Hoiri says to his friend, Meraveka, " 'Don't you feel sorry for a place where you've lived so long?' " (p. 165). Meraveka replies, shortly thereafter, " 'It is more than three years since we left our village ...' " (p. 167). All of this comes as quite a surprise to the reader who has no idea that such a span of time has passed. The impression, rather, is that of several days—a week or two at most. All of this is by way of saying that Eri's use of time in *The Crocodile* is perplexing because there are no transitions. The reader has to figure out the time relationship of one event to another. The novel tells the story of a group of people who are not accustomed to clocks and other Western devices for measuring time. Life goes on. It is plotless, a string of events for which only the Western reader tries to find a cause and effect. As in so many other novels from the Third World, *The Crocodile* shows us lives that are influenced by external forces and situations (colonialism, a war that is not understood).* Often these forces are so powerful that they make it impossible for the individual character to act on his own. Eri says of his protagonist, "Hoiri felt entirely passive, exercising no control over his thinking" (p. 104).

Much of the fascination of *The Crocodile* for the Western reader lies in the novel's use of the unexplainable—the use of superstition. I doubt if a Papuan reader bats an eye at this. I am reminded of a conversation I once had with Stanlake Samkange, an African writer, in regard to the manuscript of a novel he had written but had not been able to get published. I told him I thought the Western reader would find the story unbelievable. His reply was that the African reader would have no trouble accepting the so-called "supernatural" aspects of the novel at face value. I have seen this divergence of opinion many times with "supernatural" passages in other Third World novels. They are only supernatural for those of us outside these cultures, trying to look in.

Sorcery is the explanation Eri gives for both of the deaths by crocodiles in his novel—Hoiri's mother and his wife's sudden deaths. Hoiri accepts these as a viable explanation and so do his villagers. The plot—if one wants to call it that—depends upon it, and the story itself is filled with examples of the acceptance of the invisible, the unknown world of the ancestors. Early in the novel, for example, Eri states, "Their eyes ate the food as it was being cooked. And you never knew: spirits of the dead, wandering by the pot of food, might spit into it" (p. 19). When he sleeps in the family cemetery, Hoiri hears his ancestors speaking around him. This is the animistic world so common to peoples of Africa and the South Pacific: the dead are not dead, but living in the world around us.

Signs are constantly received from the spirit world. Birds flying over-head in the night, flying foxes—these foreshadow ominous events in *The Crocodile*. References to the cargo cult are ubiquitous, especially the way these beliefs have been adjusted to fit the arrival of the white man. Of Hoiri's mother and her journey to the afterworld we are told: "...if she survived the journey, she would shed her dark skin and become a European. She would be in a land of plenty and one day she would send gifts to them" (p. 14). But these gifts (the cargo) never arrive. Hoiri's uncle, Aravape, ponders about the big ships in the harbor in Port Moresby, " 'Actually they stay outside the reef for a couple of days while the goods in the hull are renamed. They change your name and mine on all the goods that our dead ancestors send for us' " (p. 46).

*Hoiri's villagers do not comprehend the events of the war. Eri writes, "It seemed a silly idea that the white men and the yellow men should come to Papua to fight one another" (p. 129).

By the end of the story, the reader should be prepared for the final event. Hoiri sees a woman walking down a street in Kerema. He believes she is his wife. But the woman does not recognize him. She is, in fact, annoyed by his reactions:

> The woman began to run. Hoiri followed in pursuit and grabbed her arm. The woman screamed. Hoiri let go her arm and stood panting with despair. He hardly noticed that people were beginning to crowd around him. Was there no way of winning back his wife? But he knew that it was hopeless. The power of the magicians had put her completely beyond his reach. They had transformed her mind and they wielded absolute power over her tongue. She was the same woman in appearance only. If only he hadn't been brought up a Christian, Hoiri thought. Then he might have known the kind of people who could match magic with magic.
>
> He felt cold in his heart and incredibly lonely. His life seemed a confused mess. He was insensitive to the noisy shouting of the people around him. In a flash he saw in front of his eyes all the wasted years of carrying the white man's cargo. He knew that the white man, with all his wisdom and power, could not help him to get his wife back. He did not see the policeman striding up to him and he was only vaguely aware of the hot rusty grip of the handcuffs around his wrists. As he started walking, he felt the square shape of the bank book in his pocket. "Maybe this money will send Sevese [his son] to the white man's school, maybe he will grow up to understand the things that baffle me," he thought numbly, as he was led back to the office he had wished never again to see. (pp. 177–178)

I do not interpret the ending as indicative of any major revelation on Hoiri Sevese's part. He has known all along that Christianity prevents him from following certain traditional ways of getting revenge over the sorcerers. He has known for some time who the sorcerer is, but he has done nothing about it (in part because his father was a deacon in the church). Rather, I interpret the ending as one of almost total confusion. Hoiri has no more understanding of his situation than he had at the beginning of the novel when he was trying to discover the reasons for his mother's death. His experiences with the white man have been as bitter as Batouala's. Once again, exposure to the West has begun a process of destruction. The cycle of life has cracked open and the old world has been fractured.

Other aspects of *The Crocodile* could be mentioned, other traits of Eri's novel that appear in many novels from the Third World—for example, the rather extensive use of folklore and mythology, growing out of the oral tradition. The conflict here is against the Australians instead of the Europeans, but this is still black against white, the emotional versus the analytical. In a number of powerful scenes in the novel in which Eri shows us Hoiri's direct involvements with the white men, Hoiri almost always comes out the worse. Once again, then, we are dealing with a kind of protest novel. But there is much more than that. In *The Counterfeiters* (*Les faux monnyeurs*) André Gide spoke of the "pure" novel, refined of all of its non-essentials. For me, this is what Eri has created (though for different reasons) in *The Crocodile*. Unlike Yambo Ouologuem who studied the novel as a literary form and consciously tried to deceive us into accepting his result, Vincent Eri has shown us that an engaging novel can still be written spontaneously, without the writer's having to concern himself with the rhetoric of three hundred years of fiction.

# 3
# Survival of a Culture
## Hyemeyohsts Storm's *Seven Arrows*

One of Yambo Ouologuem's intentions in writing *Bound to Violence* was to "correct" what he felt was a commonly-held misconception of the African past. A related intent was also in René Maran's thoughts when he wrote *Batouala*, though—as already noted—Maran also wanted to expose the French colonial system in tropical Africa. This objective of correcting what is generally a Western stereotype of another culture is a goal of many Third World writers—coupled with the need for recording traditional life patterns (that is, traditional culture) before they are forgotten or systematically wiped out. The writer in the Third World, then, has a kind of dual role as recorder and interpreter of his society's traditional values. For his own people, he records traditional life as it was—so it will never be forgotten. For his other readers (usually from the West) he acts as defender of his society's right to be different.

For many peoples in the Third World life is changing so rapidly that already the accounts they read of their forebears seem foreign to them. Ibo students in Nigeria have told me that when they read Chinua Achebe's *Things Fall Apart*, many aspects of traditional life come upon them as a surprise—their culture has changed that radically. I suspect that this will be equally true for the Native American reader of Hyemeyohsts Storm's *Seven Arrows*, as it will be even more so for the book's other readers, though for opposite reasons. We think we know all about the black man. We think we know all about the Native

American—at least enough to tell him how to live his life. Some of us can remember, too, seeing Indians dressed in colorful blankets during trips we made out West for summer vacations. But usually when we think beyond such memories—and beyond a few literary examples like Natty Bumppo's friends*—we realize that our image of Native Americans is at best blurred: Hollywood, television, and an occasional cigar store Indian sadly in need of repair. We might expect, too, that the literature by Native Americans would share few similarities with that of the peoples, say, of Africa—or of Eri's Papuans. Again, however, it is not simply culture that has the ability to surprise us but the literary geography of that culture.

There are few books that have a genuine hypnotic effect on the reader. Fewer still are those occasions in our reading lives when we come across a work with magical properties so hypnotic that we immediately sense that we will be haunted by it the rest of our lives. *Seven Arrows* is such a book, a novel—one of a handful of fictive works by American Indians.[1] It is, in fact, one of the most extraordinary books I have ever read. Already it has forced many readers to reconsider some of their basic conceptions of American literature and look at the American artist in a way never regarded before. In the short time since its publication (1972), *Seven Arrows* has, in fact, become a kind of underground classic, with hardbacked sales alone at almost 100,000 copies—a sales record rarely achieved by any novel by a Third World writer.

Topographically, the book is unique: almost square in shape, printed in double columns, illustrated by dozens of photographs of animals and of traditional Indian life, and nearly a dozen color paintings of medicine wheels created especially for the volume. But this is not to suggest a novel with pictures in the sense of a Victorian novel or a children's story told primarily by illustration. Instead, the photographs and color paintings have been carefully integrated into the text of the novel itself. It is impossible to think of the story without them, and our memories of the novel, after reading it, are also images of haunting Indian faces, reprinted from the archives of more than half a dozen museums and historical associations, all reproduced in brown and white, as is the text of the novel itself. The color plates depicting the medicine shields are as important to our appreciation of the story as the events in the narrative or the characters who embellish the story with their analyses of the religious significance of the shields' origins. This perfect union of word and image may be said to constitute the prime achievement of *Seven Arrows:* the growth of our perceptions of the world we live in.

If *Seven Arrows* is different in design from the other Third World novels we have examined thus far, at the same time it shares a number

---

*We remember Natty Bumppo, but usually we cannot remember the names of his Indian companions.

of characteristics. Once again we turn to a book which describes a world outside of time in the usual Western sense: a closed world, with its own rhythms and cycles and self-perpetuating patterns of life—a safe, traditional world similar to that of Batouala's kinsmen before the coming of the Europeans. Like Ouologuem's, Storm's treatment of historical time is almost non-existent—time is cyclic, not linear. *Seven Arrows* spans the time of several generations of confrontation between Native Americans and white men—perhaps as many years as a hundred, though the focus is not upon one family like the Saifs or the Kassoumis but on the Plains Indians in general. An historical thread can be worked out from internal clues in *Seven Arrows*, but for the most part events here are outside of history, and time itself has only one major defining factor: repetition.

The major element Storm's work shares with those by African writers is his reliance upon the oral tradition for structure and form. We have already noticed the incorporation of oral tales in Maran's *Batouala*. Anglophone African writers (Amos Tutuola, Chinua Achebe, Gabriel Okara, and others) have often relied heavily on this technique for developing characterization, foreshadowing, and other novelistic devices, but most of these authors, with the probable exception of Tutuola, have not used the oral tale as ubiquitously as Storm has in his novel. So powerful a role does the interpolated oral tale play in *Seven Arrows* that it is accurate to say that if the outer narrative depicts the slow extermination of the Plains Indians by white invaders, the inner narrative records the survival of the oral tradition and the richness of traditional Indian customs in the face of this genocide. As the destiny of the Indian becomes increasingly that of extermination only, Storm gives growing importance to the oral tale—as if these tales were a final song of praise by a group of people about to be wiped off the face of the earth.

Once again, our concern is with protest literature but not with the death of a culture in the way we have already seen in *Batouala*. If Hyemeyohsts Storm is presenting an accurate picture of a way of life of the people, the Plains Indians, then this is not the demise of a culture but an example of adaptability, for the traditions are very much alive, even by the end of Storm's saga which takes us up to modern times. I am not trying to suggest in any sense an optimistic picture because there is, of course, great loss, but this loss is in land and people while the culture lives on. A counter argument can be made that if the land is gone and the people have been decimated, of what value is the culture? But that is exactly what Storm wants us to perceive: a way of life can exist as long as there is one person to live it, and that way of life can retain its own strength and dignity. The hero dies; his way of life lives on.

Because of the wide expanse of years covered in *Seven Arrows*, the result is a heroless world—somewhat similar to Ouologuem's *Bound to*

*Violence.* The major difference, however, is that we never really become close enough to Ouologuem's Africans to think of them as heroes of their culture or of their people. Raymond Spartacus Kassoumi is, at best, a passive figure, kicked around like a broken calabash. In *Seven Arrows,* however, although Storm repeatedly describes potentially heroic characters—Grey Owl, Hawk, Night Bear—they are not present long enough for us to think of them in that context. Characters are introduced, we follow them for a few sections of the narrative, we come to love them, and then they are dead—mostly shot in the back, dying with little dignity. The "heroes" vanish, killed off by whites, before they have a chance to become heroes. The result is, once again, a situational novel—a novel without a main character in the traditional sense.

*Seven Arrows* begins with three introductory sections, designed to prepare the reader for the story that will follow and expand his perceptions of the basic cultural tools used in the novel. The first of these, "The Pipe," is an invocation, inviting the reader to participate in the voyage that is about to be undertaken. Storm says, "You are about to begin an adventure of the People, the Plains Indian People,"[2] and adds, "The story of these People has at its center and all around it the story of the Medicine Wheel. The Medicine Wheel is the very Way of Life of the People. It is an Understanding of the Universe" (p. 1). The invocation concludes with a reiteration of the novel's themes of perception and adaptability:

Come sit with me, and let us smoke the Pipe of Peace in Understanding. Let us Touch. Let us, each to the other, be a Gift as is the Buffalo. Let us be Meat to Nourish each other, that we all may Grow. Sit here with me, each of you as you are in your own Perceiving of yourself, as Mouse, Wolf, Coyote, Weasel, Fox, or Prairie Bird. Let me See through your Eyes. Let us Teach each other here in this Great Lodge of the People, this Sun Dance, of each of the Ways on this Great Medicine Wheel, our Earth. (p. 1)

In the second section, "The Circle," Storm gives us more of the tools we will need for our understanding of his novel; and he connects perception with "teaching," giving as his example a circle of people around a drum or an eagle feather. Each person views the drum and the feather from a slightly different perspective, from his own apartness. But each person's understanding of the medicine wheels (the peace shields) is further increased by his ability to become part of the whole: "The perception of any object, either tangible or abstract, is ultimately made a thousand times more complicated whenever it is viewed within the circle of *an entire People as a whole*" (p. 4). It is this basic desire to increase the reader's own perceptions that is so painstakingly explained by Storm:

"to Touch and Feel is to Experience," to eliminate loneliness, the "only one thing that all people possess equally" (p. 7). *Seven Arrows* is "a Teaching Story," a novel about growing and seeking, about understanding one's relationship to the world around one.

Storm is careful to explain his intentions. He has not written an anthropological study of his people, nor has he edited a casebook of Indian traditions. Rather, he has written a unique work of imaginative literature. Storm informs us, "Within *Seven Arrows* there are many ancient Stories taught to me by my Fathers and Grandfathers. But there are also new Stories that I have written from within my own Understanding and Experience" (p. 11). We must turn to other books if we want cultural facts; in *Seven Arrows* we can expect something else.*

In the third introductory section, "The Flowering Tree," we can see the tools put in to practice. Storm begins,

> The Medicine Wheel Circle is the Universe. It is change, life, death, birth and learning. This Great Circle is the lodge of our bodies, our minds, and our hearts. It is the cycle of all things that exist. The Circle is our Way of Touching, and of experiencing Harmony with every other thing around us. And for those who seek Understanding, the Circle is their Mirror. This Circle is the Flowering Tree. (p. 14)

Storm then speaks directly about the Indian art of storytelling, illustrating various ways of interpreting the tales that will follow in the novel. After telling a tale of "The Flowering Tree," he concludes, "As we learn we always change, and so does our perceiving. This changed perception then becomes a new Teacher inside each of us" (p. 20). Then he tells us a second story ("The Singing Stone") about a young man on a quest, deriving help from a number of animals. In the analysis that follows, many things have changed. The tale itself concerns a young boy; in

---

*The only adverse criticism I have been able to discover about *Seven Arrows* is a brief review of the book by Rupert Costo in *The Indian Historian*, V (Summer 1972), pp. 41–42. The review, titled " 'Seven Arrows' Desecrates Cheyenne," attacks Storm for distortions and inaccuracies concerning Cheyenne beliefs and religion:

> His description of the Sun Dance is wrong. His drawing of the Sun Dance Lodge is not Cheyenne. The Four Sacred Directions are inaccurately described as North, South, East, and West. They are in fact not the cardinal directions, but the semi-cardinal directions, Northeast, Northwest, Southeast and Southwest. The sacred number given is wrong. The Cheyenne shield colors are wrong. They are red, black, white and yellow—and not the monstrosity of color assemblage shown in the plates. The shield designs are wrong and actually blaspheme the Cheyenne religion.

The reviewer apparently has forgotten that *Seven Arrows* is a novel and not an anthropological study; and he has forgotten that Storm has given us a composite picture of the Plains Indians—not just the Northern Cheyenne, his own tribe—but others including: Arapahoe, Sioux, Comanche, Little Black Eagle, Painted Arrow, Black Feet, Shoshone, Kiowa, People of the Perfect Bow—at least, these are the ones he mentions.

the analysis the sex has been changed to a young girl, but Storm has already warned us about a basic androgyny within the Indian's view of life: "within every man there is the Reflection of a Woman, and within every woman there is the Reflection of a Man. Within every man and woman there is also the Reflection of an Old Man, and Old Woman, a Little Boy, and a Little Girl" (p. 14).

Storm refers to the novel itself as an "endless vision Quest," once again reiterating the necessity of our training ourselves to perceive more clearly—for, as soon as we learn one way of increasing our perceptions, we become aware of others we have not even begun to comprehend. The seven arrows in his title are teaching arrows:

> When you have learned to place these Seven pieces of Mirror together within yourself, you will discover that there are Seven more. Their Reflections will go on and on forever.
>
> Four of these same Seven Arrows are symbolized by the Four Directions. They are the North, South, West and the East. As you remember, these symbolize Wisdom, Trust and Innocence, Introspection and Illumination. These are known as the Four Ways. The Mother Earth is the Fifth Mirror. The Sky, with its Moon, Sun and Stars, is the Sixth Mirror. The Seventh of these Arrows is the Spirit. Among the People, this Spirit is spoken of as the Universal Harmony which holds all things together. All of us, as Perceivers of the Mirrors, are the Eighth Arrow. (p. 20)

Twenty-five unnumbered sections comprise the narrative of Storm's *Seven Arrows,* varying in length from a few paragraphs to fifty-eight pages. Some of these sections depict self-contained episodes, but more frequently a section records several events. The episodic nature of the narrative is in large part the result of the exclusion of a central, developing character. Instead of following a main character as he changes, we follow a culture as it undergoes the bombardment of shock from without: the world around the Indian is changing. His own world will die if he does not adapt to the multiple changes. For a time, it is possible to survive by moving away from the white man's encroachments, but after a while there is no place left to go. By then, change is the only inevitability. Once again the white man is playing the numbers game with someone whose skin is not the same color as his own.

At the beginning of *Seven Arrows,* Storm depicts a culture that is still safe and pure. The white men have yet to invade the territory, though they are just about to. As the story progresses, Storm's characters move from indirect to limited contact with the whites. Guns are heard of, then seen for the first time, and soon Indians are being killed by them. Material objects from the white man's world are non-existent at the beginning of the story; by the end they are ubiquitous. After the influence of the traders, the Indians are exposed to the missionaries, and finally to complete political control. Yet few white characters appear in *Seven Arrows*. As Chinua Achebe shows in *Things Fall Apart*—his novel of traditional Ibo life—the dissension from within is often more difficult to withstand than brute force from without. Well before the end of the story, Indians are killing other Indians. They move from free spirits to wards of the state in just over one hundred years—roughly from 1830 to 1930.

At the opening of *Seven Arrows*, Storm introduces a number of natural elements in the cycle of life: winter is coming to an end, the days of sunshine are increasing; morning arrives and Flying Cloud's Camp is waking up; during the night there has been a birth. The focus is mostly upon the women and the children: Day Woman is making a dress out of doeskin; children are playing by themselves; Dancing Water has returned to the camp with her child. The women are excited by the birth, but they are surprised by the suddenness of Dancing Water's presence in Flying Cloud's camp. Their happiness is short lived. The men of the camp suddenly run off, leaving the women alone and confused.

In the brief section that follows, the narrative abruptly shifts to a meeting of the men of two camps who have come together to call a Sun Dance, a peace conference. Even this early in the narrative, Standing Eagle states that the red man's world is falling apart, "that the People are being exterminated like rabid camp dogs" (p. 36). Falls Down tells of two or three camps that have been attacked by " 'packs of mad wolves. These unnatural white wolves [white men] can be fought and beaten' " (p. 36). There is disagreement among the men as to what should be done—the white men have been heard of but no one has seen them. Already, then, Storm has introduced an element of frustration among the ranks, implying that anything they do may already be too late. For Grey Owl, Storm's main focus of character in the early episodes, it is his first Sun Dance.

Two months later, in the midst of a hot summer, Grey Owl watches his mother embroidering a Sun Dance belt, another symbol of peace like the shields. They are interrupted by the arrival of Painted Elk and his family. Grey Owl sees a "thunder stick" for the first time. Through the use of sign language, indicated in the text of the novel by italics, the men (of different tribes) talk about the forthcoming Sun Dance. Storm explains, " 'Their talk was all with sign language, so that each could understand and take part in it' " (p. 44). In the evening, the young men engage in tests of endurance and skill; then the concentration shifts more specifically to Grey Owl and his rivalry with other men for Morning Song, the girl he loves.

I have mentioned these events—besides the call for a peace conference —because for the most part the early passages of *Seven Arrows* concentrate on the day-to-day activities of communal life, similar to the depiction of like events in Maran's *Batouala*. We see happy children, young men and women in love. Storm shows a number of village activities, such as the entertainments, and he includes a trial of sorts that settles a dispute between two young men (Grey Owl and Stiff Arm). A birth and a marriage occur. Life goes slowly on, in spite of an awareness of a new threat to stability: the white men.

At the beginning of the fourth section—at a period of time that we can only conclude is considerably later, perhaps even several years later—Storm introduces a number of additional characters and a greater amount of instability into their lives. Again there is speculation among the men about the power of the white men. Curious Antelope says, " 'We must find out more about the foreigners. I am told that their wars are fought not for the honor of touching the enemy, but to kill' " (p. 54). Already those men who stand for the traditional ways of the Peace Chiefs are referred to as women, a belief that will be expressed by the younger men many times throughout the novel. Hawk, a younger man than Grey Owl, uses sign language and explains the importance of the four directions as the sources of man's wisdom. Man is superior to animals because he is illuminated by his mind. At the end of Hawk's tale, Grey Owl states ironically, " 'The Peace Chiefs' Ways are dead.' " (p. 57). There is general disagreement about the old ways of life.

Already there is a sense of uprootedness—the Indians (like Batouala's tribesmen) move their camps more frequently than they did in the past, especially as the white man moves closer. During one such move, Grey Owl and Falls Down come upon a camp where no children are playing, where there is only silence. Grey Owl recognizes Painted Elk's peace shield, and shortly thereafter, Painted Elk tells them,

> Our camp was struck by People of the Brotherhood and the Shield. Foreigners rode with them and they were many. All that you see here is what is left of our great camp. A hundred of us are gone, many of them women and children. They were killed for their hair. The whitemen offer valuable goods for the hair cut from their heads. Your brother is still alive, and is taking his turn as guard. Dancing Water is also alive. Your brother Stiff Arm and his family are dead. I saw him fall in front of his lodge, felled by a thunder stick. (p. 60–I)[3]

Storm's implication here—an idea that has been expressed by others—is quite clear: scalping was introduced by the white men, not by the Indians. Grey Owl's reaction is one of incredulity.

But far more significant is Painted Elk's statement that Indians have joined the whites and participated in the massacre: "the whiteman's Way is already travelled by many of the Brotherhood. The Sun Dance has been dying among us for years. Fewer and fewer still carry the shields" (p. 62–I). Painted Elk's pessimistic statements continue—the power of the white men's arms and his numbers has made the Brotherhood look weak. Many of the People have thrown away their shields and adopted the white man's teachings.

> Whitemen in black robes, and others, move among the People and teach about a new Way, the Way of Geessis. This Geessis appears to be a new Power, one which loves death and rewards mightily those who kill. Because of this the camps of the whitemen are rewarded most. (p. 62–I)

The white man's religion has in some ways been a lesser threat than the power of the material possessions to which he has exposed them. Storm's strength is always to describe these possessions from the Indians' point of view—often illustrating an inability to grasp the function of a specific object. "This is a robe that the color will not rub off from, and it is very warm. It is called a 'ba kit' in the language of the white man" (p. 62–I). Four Bears and Painted Elk lead Grey Owl to the center of their camp where a number of young men and women are dancing naked. When Grey Owl asks if they have gone mad, Four Bears replies, "They are crazy on stinging water.... This is more deadly than all the other whitemen's things combined. Some have even killed their brothers and sisters while they were crazy with it" (p. 63–I). Since there has been murder, Grey Owl asks if there has been a renewal, a peace conference. Four Bears replies that the last one he saw was long ago, at Grey Owl's camp. Late at night when they are asleep, the camp is attacked again. Grey Owl, Painted Elk, and Four Bears are among those killed.

Lame Bear tells Day Woman and the other survivors that they will have to move their camp again: " 'The people who murdered your brothers and uncles were not whitemen .... The Brotherhood is dead' " (p. 66). In the argument between Lame Bear and one of the Medicine Chiefs that follows, Storm makes his strongest condemnation of the white man. Lame Bear tells the others, " 'The whitemen are determined to destroy all People whose Ways do not reflect their own. They have set the People one against the other and will kill whichever is left when the wars have ended' " (p. 67). Lame Bear's statement is the most pessimistic in the novel, and although "People" here refers to the Native Americans only, his condemnation is one we might have expected from many other characters in Third World novels. If Batouala has not expressed his feelings in the same words, he has thought about it in the same way. Unfortunately, it is a statement that could be superimposed on the text of almost every novel we will examine. Lame Bear's frustration is mixed with a feeling of utter futility. What can be done about a world that is dominated by objects? As he says, " 'The universe has given them even the Power to have talking leaves' " (p. 67). He knows it is objects that will destroy them in the long run. The Medicine Chief asks him, " 'Is the love of the universe reflected only in material gifts?' " (p. 67). Hawk answers his question with another, " 'If they have these wonderful gifts, then why do they kill?' " (p. 67).

In *Seven Arrows*, the white man's world is represented almost exclusively by objects: stinging water, bak its, talking leaves, thunder sticks. Storm illustrates the Native American's reactions to these objects as one of confusion coupled with fascination at the same time. Although he does not express the reaction in exactly the same words, he reminds one of the *négritude* poets in the 1930's. They too felt that Western man had been stripped of his humanity and had become an extension of objects, the machines around him. In *The Dilemma of a Ghost* (1965), by Ghanaian playwright Ama Ata Aidoo, the main character—an Afro-American girl who has married a Ghanaian student—is thought of by her husband's family as being sterile, made so by machines. Similarly, Storm implies that the Brotherhood broke up in part because Indians began killing other Indians for the possessions they had learned about from the white man. The closed, locked universe that supplied the Indian with all of his needs has been unlocked by the white man's goods. The old medicines have been neutralized by the power of the white man's objects.

At the times of greatest instability in their lives, the Indians rely on the oral tradition for comfort and solace. After the massacre that takes the lives of Grey Owl, Painted Elk, and Four Bears, Great Shield tells the story of "Jumping Mouse"—one of the longest and undoubtedly the most important of the interpolated tales in the novel. When a little mouse learns of something strange and new, he is determined to discover what it is. His peregrinations to find an explanation for a roaring in his ears take him away from his home. However, his curiosity for understanding what is new and different is not satisfied by this journey to what proves to be a river. When Frog tells him to jump up in order to be able to see something he has never seen before (the mountains), little mouse is given a new name—Jumping Mouse.

Thereafter Jumping Mouse is dissatisfied with life as it is. He wants to journey to the mountains to perceive them more clearly, for a mouse is always characterized as short-sighted and limited in his perception of the world. Jumping Mouse, however, is afraid to cross the prairies to the mountains because he fears an eagle will swoop down upon him and devour him. Then he encounters an old buffalo who tells him, " 'I am Sick and I am Dying. . . . And my Medicine has Told me that only the Eye of a Mouse can Heal me. But little Brother, there is no such Thing as a Mouse' " (p. 78–I). Jumping Mouse is initially shocked, but then he decides he only needs one eye. He thinks that a buffalo is a greater creature, so he gives him one of his eyes and the buffalo is cured. Then the buffalo tells Jumping Mouse to run under his belly across the prairies, and in that way he will reach the mountains safely. Once there, Jumping Mouse meets a wolf who has lost his memory, and this time without batting an eye, Jumping Mouse tells him, " 'I know what will Heal you. It is One of my Eyes. And I Want to Give it to you. You are a Greater Being than I. I am only a Mouse. Please Take it' " (p. 82–I). The wolf is cured.

Blind and alone, Jumping Mouse fears that he will now be easy prey for flying creatures. He goes to sleep, knowing he will soon be killed, but when he wakes up, he can see again. A blurry shape tells him to crouch down and jump up as high as he can. The tale continues,

> Jumping Mouse did as he was Instructed. He Crouched as Low as he Could and Jumped! The Wind Caught him and Carried him Higher.
>
> "Do not be Afraid," the Voice called to him. "Hang on to the Wind and Trust!"
>
> Jumping Mouse did. He Closed his Eyes and Hung on to the Wind and it Carried him Higher and Higher. Jumping Mouse Opened his Eyes and they were Clear, and the Higher he Went the Clearer they Became. Jumping Mouse Saw his Old Friend upon a Lily Pad on the Beautiful Medicine Lake. It was the Frog.
>
> "You have a New Name," Called the Frog. "You are Eagle!" (p. 85–I)

Jumping Mouse's story is the story of the Plains Indians, a distillation of many of the most important themes of *Seven Arrows*: giving, perception, change, the seen and the unseen world. Jumping Mouse's curiosity has prepared him for his adaptability. His willingness to give of himself is his humanity. His perceptions are expanded in the same way that Storm wants his reader's awareness to be changed by reading *Seven Arrows*. From the limited world view of a mouse, he has developed a hawk's keen overview of the universe. He has incorporated these opposites into his being and become whole. Quite fittingly, Storm uses Jumping Mouse's story as a leitmotif throughout the remaining episodes of his novel—referring to the story six additional times. Like Jumping Mouse, man too, has to learn to jump up, to seek, to change his perception of life, to combine opposites into his nature. Storm's tale is a brilliant commentary on man's potential to develop his vision.

After Jumping Mouse's tale, the narrative returns to short, episodic scenes—often communal events interrupted by more and more raids by white men and those Indians who have left the Brotherhood. One attack interrupts an evening dance. The focus of attention moves to Hawk and Spotted Calf, and for a time Storm makes a number of references to two historical figures: Sitting Bull (1834?–1890) and Crazy Horse (1840?–1877) whom Storm calls Crazy New Way. Sitting Bull plans to call the Brotherhood of the Shields together. Crazy New Way says that the white man can only be defeated by his own ways: " 'We must kill as he does, and his Gifts will be ours' " (p. 114).

Increasingly, there is talk of the white man's powers. Many of the camps no longer appear to be Indian. Storm states, "There were many new things to see. The miracles of the whiteman's magic were visible everywhere" (p. 104). Shortly thereafter he adds, "Evidence of the disintegration of the Brotherhood of the Shields and the Sun Dance Way was everywhere" (p. 105). Indians continue to kill other Indians. Yellow Robe expresses his horror at the idea of killing: " 'We have been taught by the Men of the Shields all of our lives not to kill, that it is a greater man who simply touches his enemy and shames him. Any animal can kill. It is only man, the great Medicine Animal, who has the Power of Decision' " (p. 114). This belief—that man is higher than the animals —is reiterated several times in the narrative: " 'Our old wars were for touching the enemy and shaming him, not for taking his life. We cut off his braids, not his whole hair and scalp! And every four years we met within the Renewal Lodge and were brothers' " (p. 114). Yet the attacks on even the most isolated camps continue.

Spotted Calf is killed in a raid that decimates the brothers of the Painted Arrow. Hawk survives the attack with Singing Water, and later they come upon Day Women and Prairie Rose who were raped by a pack of white soldiers. Day Women had killed two of the men. Yet somehow in spite of all this violence and chaos the traditions survive. New camps are organized by the survivors of each attack—often comprised of Indians from several tribes. The traditions continue to be passed on from adult to child; the education of the youth is not interrupted. When Bull Looks Around is ready to go on his Vision Quest—his initiation into adulthood—Hawk is there to act as his teacher. At the end of the quest Bull Looks Around is given a new name, Night Bear. The Medicine Wheel survives; the years pass by. Yet as the Indian way of life is altered by the white man's world, more confusions develop. Storm makes it clear that there were times when accidental murder resulted from avenging the wrong people, when Indians lost their ability to distinguish one group from another. Night Bear and Hawk are involved in one such incident—attacking their peaceful brothers. Yellow Robe asks pessimistically, " 'What will become of us?.... Are we all to die?' " (p. 141).

Storm interrupts his story of warfare and extermination to develop a brief idyllic episode between Night Bear and his mother, Sweet Water. During a snowstorm forcing the camp of Yellow Robe to move, the two of them become separated from the others. The blizzard is so intense that Night Bear realizes they will not survive unless he builds a makeshift lodge where they will wait until spring. During that time, an incestuous relationship develops between the two of them—certainly one of the most beautiful accounts of incest that I can recall reading in any literature, certainly one of the sections of exceptional beauty in the novel. In a way, of course, Storm includes the incident as an indirect commentary on the chaos around them, but there is more than that here. For once incest is not tainted by a touch of guilt, Freudian suggestibility, or the Puritan ethic. Sweet Water's only concern is that no children should be born of their union. Their relationship is not frowned upon by the others of the tribe when it is revealed later on, nor is it met with shock or outrage. White Wolf comments,

> "Sweet Water has told me she slept with her son the whole winter. And they found truth in what they did. It was a Gift to them and they have learned from it. They have called us here together for us to hear of their Gift so that we might enjoy the sound of its truth." (p. 152)

In the central section of *Seven Arrows*—the fifteenth and the longest —the episodic structure suddenly becomes phantasmagoric as the madness of the outside world closes in upon Storm's characters, turning the realities of their life topsy-turvy. Ironically, the section begins with another attack on the wrong people. It is the white man's possessions that have once again led to homicide. White Wolf reiterates an idea expressed earlier:

> "It is not the whitemen who are changing our world. It is our own brothers who are doing this. Our own brothers, like some of you young men here in council before me, have given in to these new Ways of the whiteman, and have become victims to it. And what you propose would only add to this terrible thing. We must not go out to seek the enemy in war. We can save our camp only by holding strong to the Way of the Sun Dance, and by remembering the Teachings of the Shields. There is a place for every man within the Great Lodge, because it is a whole Medicine Wheel." (p. 163)

In the winter that follows, there is mass starvation among the Plains Indians—"worse than anyone living could remember" (p. 164). The white man has killed off the buffalo for the sheer sport of hunting; the self-renewing source of food, clothing, and shelter no longer exists. Day Woman, Prairie Rose, and Sweet Water die. When spring arrives, Night Bear and Hawk make their way back to the camp of the Painted Arrow only to be met by mockery and derision. Storm has already shown that the younger Indians have begun to talk of the Brotherhood as "old men's dreams" (p. 159). Now he injects a new inversion into his story.

The younger Indians refer to those who remain faithful to tne way of the shields as feminine. Instead of regarding the elders as their teachers, they refer to them as women. It is the ultimate humiliation.

Storm's use of masculine and feminine roles is not unique in Third World literature. The old way of life strictly defined these roles. In Achebe's *Things Fall Apart*, Okonkwo, the most important character, refers to those younger men who adopt Western ways as women—weak men. We have already noted somewhat related treatment in *Batouala* and in *Bound to Violence*, yet in all of these works it is the person who embraces the new dispensation who is regarded as feminine. Those who remain faithful to the past are looked at as true men, warriors of their people. Storm's novel reverses this pattern; the weak are those who do not accept the white man's way: killing must be met with killing, not with peace. When Hawk and Night Bear propose to organize a renewal, they are accused by the younger men "of having women's meetings" (p. 193). At a later time in the narrative, Not Afraid of Knowledge says, again reflecting the teachings of the white men,

> "Many of the young men have talked about what we do now, and older men too. They say that in the days of the Shields, and of the Brotherhood of the Shields, the men were like women. They were afraid of their own shadows. The whiteman has taught us that this whole Way was a simple minded thing of old women." (p. 220)

As we will later see, this attack on the past as a feminine way of life will also be applied to the white man's own traditions. It is important to notice, then, that masculine and feminine roles are another aspect of traditional life that become blurred in the face of the onslaught of the white man's world.

Several of the tales that Night Bear and Hawk tell to the shrinking band of younger males comment indirectly on what has happened to the traditional way of life. Night Bear, for example, relates the story of a scattered tribe of people—a story of separateness and isolation in which adaptability is seen as the most important factor. Hawk comments, " 'These things of the Medicine and the Spirit must flow like the water or they will die' " (p. 177). Explaining another value of the Medicine Shields, Hawk equates their importance with the white man's talking leaves. The traditions of the past are embodied in the shields as the white man records the past in his books: " 'We have no talking leaves like the whiteman, so we have to memorize these Stories' " (p. 181). Night Bear tells a Story about the origin of eating buffalo meat. The reader becomes aware of the increasing number of such stories included in the narrative. Like René Maran in *Batouala*, Hyemeyohsts Storm recognizes the need for recording the past before it is forgotten.

The oral tales are interrupted for more direct commentary on the white man. Two such men—a trader and a missionary—are expected to visit the camp. When they arrive, Hawk and Night Bear think (for this is the first time they have seen white men): "Both men were monstrously ugly. Their faces appeared nearly identical, with only the coloring of the hair upon their faces different" (p. 189). The missionary appeared to be frightened to death. He tells Hawk, " 'The Big Medicine that hugs the People is bad. . . . Geessis is heap plenty good power. Kills people who are bad' " (p. 192). The Geessis talker then emphasizes the importance of the white man's material possessions. " 'If people Geessis path follow they rewarded rich Gifts. Medicine Father talking leaves Gift people giving. You too follow path Geessis and many plenty prizes giving. Iron horse took sharing with ' " (pp. 192-193). One wonders how many times Christian missionaries have used worldly possessions to gain their converts. Late at night, Hawk and Night Bear watch the warriors who have traded with the white man, "staggering drunk with the stinging water" (p. 193).

The inconsistencies of the white man's religion have rarely been presented more clearly and bitterly than in *Seven Arrows*. One can almost imagine an entire generation of missionaries turning over in their graves. Later in the novel Pretty Weasel places the confusion that Christianity produced within the Indians in its cultural context. One surmises that his interpretation might be valid for people spread throughout the entire non-Christian world:

> The talkers among them spoke of the Medicine Power that was called Geessis. This Geessis was a Power among them, a chief whom they later killed. He was not surprised that they killed him. After they killed him these men decided he was a Power, and they began to like him. He came back as a ghost and even now he walks among them invisible. . . .
>
> This Geessis . . . is the greatest killer of them all. He kills all of their enemies. And he rewards those who follow his path with many things. Believe me, my brother, it is a very confusing thing, this Geessis. . . .
>
> These talkers of the Geessis say that it is bad to do many things. And, believe it or not, killing is one of them. But, as clearly as I can understand it, this only means not to kill those who follow the warpath of Geessis. All others are to be feared and killed. (p. 240–I)

Night Bear later concludes, " 'Geessis is truly the most horrible of things devised' " (p. 274).

In the oral tales that follow, narrated mostly by Hawk, one sees the origin of many Indian customs and attitudes. One cannot help believing that the poverty of Westernization and its bastardization of language is in large part the result of the printed word—the commercial media. The richness of the oral tradition must be sacrificed for modernization.

Even as Night Bear concludes his last tale, the warriors of the camp are raiding a group of white men for their possessions. The oral tradition (the imagination) has been exchanged for objects; that aspect of the intellectual life may soon be lost.

In the rapid series of episodes that follow, the terrorism by the whites and those Indians who have left the Brotherhood increases. When Night Bear and Hawk seek a more peaceful camp, they are ambushed, and Hawk is tied to a tree and tortured to death. Hawk notices the strange appearance of his tormentors:

> It was no surprise to Hawk to see that there were whitemen with them. The entire group of men that finally gathered around him looked like a mixed pack of angry animals. Hawk could tell by their unwashed appearance and their dirty clothes that they had been riding together for quite a while. Their gear was a confused mixture of the things of the whiteman and of many other Peoples. (p. 230)

Hawk's death is not without its dignity, however. As peace maker and mediator who tried to meet the new way of life without killing, Storm equates him with Jumping Mouse in his quest for wisdom and selflessness:

> Then the man who was still standing in front of Hawk took his knife from his belt and thrust it deep into Hawk's belly. Hawk winced with the fire that tore into his body. Through his pain he dimly saw a small frog hop from the creek near where he was tied, and leap soundlessly toward his feet. It seemed to look up at him before the world turned into darkness. (p. 231)

Hawk, too, has jumped up to expand his perceptions.

Night Bear survives the massacre that takes the life of Hawk and others. When he reaches White Clay's camp, he is shocked by what he sees. There are no older people; there are few people in the camp who are older than eighteen—only those who have survived the terrible massacres. Night Bear discovers that no one speaks his own language, though there are three other languages spoken in the camp. Communication has to be by sign language. Pretty Weasel states that henceforth it will be survival of the fittest: "The whiteman kills everyone without compassion, and the Brotherhood now does the same. . . . Only the strongest will survive!" (p. 242-I). Shining Arrow expresses an idea central to our understanding of Storm's novel—the communal consciousness of a people breaks apart as soon as a few people begin to doubt the old ways:

> We are Each a living Spinning Medicine Wheel, and Each of us Possesses this Power to Destroy or to Create. When Ten of the Hundred

do not Care, it Makes our Shield that much less Capable of Stopping Sickness. This Sickness Strikes out at Random, and can Hurt Anyone. (p. 243–I)

White Clay knows that this oneness is a thing of the past: "It is not numbers, it is completeness. I am an old man, and I have seen clearly what happens when a People are not one. Before the whiteman began to destroy the unity of the camps, there was very little sickness" (p. 243–I). Everyone must be a part of the whole.

In the tale that follows, Night Bear shows the results of trying to escape this whole, of avoiding one's communal obligation: two old men lived together who could see the past and the future by closing their eyes. Increasingly, they kept their eyes closed, avoiding their present lives, until one day their eyes stuck closed, and they told the community to take care of them. The people replied that it would be better for them to learn to care for themselves, and this so upset the two men (" 'We are very Self-Sufficient,' they said to Each Other," p. 246–I) that they left the community, thereby rendering their powers of hindsight and foresight useless. For a time all goes well, until a raccoon begins to play tricks on them, taking advantage of their blindness and confusing the two men so thoroughly that they fight with each other. Finally the raccoon tells them to listen to the water and it will give them an answer to their problems. The tale concludes, "But While they Both Listened, Raccoon Sneaked Up Behind them and Pushed them Into the River—and their Eyes were Opened," (p. 251–I). Once again Storm has given us a story about seeing, perception and helping one's fellow men. By avoiding these qualities, a people can never remain whole. But the story of the two blind men is also a story about a lack of adaptability—what the two blind men refuse to do. Instead of adapting to their blindness as the community suggests, they ask to be taken care of, so that the old way will remain unaltered. This conflict is one of the central themes of the novel.

Storm continues to chronicle the horrors of the new dispensation. When Night Bear and his younger friend, Grey Fire Mouse, go trading, they are no longer able to identify the people they encounter. Night Bear speaks of the spiritual death of his people: " 'The most painful of all deaths is the one that is a Spiritual Death. . . . If a man, woman, or child breaks the spirit or will of another and brings loneliness upon them, he not only separates these people from himself, he also causes separation and loneliness among all the People' " (p. 264). Night Bear and Green Fire Mouse realize that the old way of the peace shields is a thing of the past; Left Hand shows them many camps that have come together for a council of war, and he tells them, " 'The Brotherhood is now only a thing of memory' " (p. 272). The white man's illness, presumably smallpox, has killed off untold numbers of Indians; the extermination of the buffalos has continued unchecked.

> "It has made them even more afraid that they will starve.... They fear now that the whiteman will kill all of the buffalo, elk, and deer. There are even stories among the People that others of the Peoples further to the east have been killed by the whitemen like the Buffalo, and that some of them were even eaten by the whitemen." (p. 274)

Even Green Fire Mouse begins to believe that it is time for war, " 'not for a Renewal' " (p. 274).

What follows is one of the most painful discussions in the novel. Left Hand tells Green Fire Mouse that he can fight if he wants to, but

> "I walk the Way of the Shield. I can never talk for war. I must talk always for Peace."
> "Then you are my father," said Night Bear. "But where is your Shield?"
> "I have only the cover of my Shield, my brother," Left Hand answered. "I will make another frame for it. A young Medicine Song Bird, who was maddened with anger by the killing of his entire family, smashed the Shield." (pp. 274–275)

It is the symbol of the broken shield that jars the reader's sensibility. Green Fire Mouse states that there is death in every direction, and Left Hand replies, once again reiterating the idea of change and adaptability, " 'What you say may indeed be true.... But I believe it is equally true that the Power, the Power of Truth, will never allow the total death of the People' " (p. 275). Or—as Storm would have us believe—the total death of a culture.

As the Brotherhood itself breaks up, the Indian's physical world, his environment, also undergoes rapid change. Not only are the buffalos being killed off, but often, Storm tells us, when Night Bear and Green Fire Mouse cross the plains, they see no signs of Indian camps. Yet these two and Hides On the Wind never cease teaching the old way of life. Hides on the Wind tells a tale of "Fallen Star," the story of a young man overcoming a vast number of obstacles and endurance tests, embarking on a quest for stability. The irony is that as the heroism of the Indians becomes impotent in the face of the white man's superior armaments, the tales depict a past peopled with cultural heroes. In this tale, Fallen Star heals his people, cures them of the sickness in their midst in a way that can only be regarded as selfless—a vivid contrast to the heroless world produced by the white man's shots in the back. Throughout, the oral tales are interrupted for questions by the listeners and for lengthy interpolations. Thus, they become once again communal events, glorifying the past, but more importantly, perpetuating the culture, strengthening it, and helping it to survive. When Night Bear visits another camp, he is once again struck by the multiple changes that have made it almost unrecognizable, struck, too, by the frequent coming and going of the white men. Night Bear becomes increasingly pessimistic, knowing that death is only a short time off. Thunder Bow tells of an even greater horror: " 'When I looked inside myself, I saw a whiteman' " (p. 309).

Thunder Bow knows that the future will be controlled by the white men, the men of war. The Native American will lose because the medicine shield can never become a power of war. As he tells Night Bear, when he saw himself as a white man, he also " 'saw how [the whites] had frozen their Medicine Wheel. This frozen thing caused them to see their own Power, twisted within its Reflection. The freezing of the Medicine Wheel Water has caused their blindness and their wars' " (p. 328). The white men cannot change, adapt—they have frozen their way of life and lost their sense of brotherhood. Killing has become a way of life. It comes as little surprise when shortly after this conversation Night Bear is killed by a shot from behind.

The talk of the need for a Renewal becomes less frequent. Green Fire Mouse, increasingly militant, envisions the time when all Indians will combine forces and fight the white men. Then Storm makes an abrupt shift to a much later time and jolts his reader by presenting a number of extreme situations. White Rabbit (Green Fire Mouse's wife) and Red Star dominate the beginning of the next to the last section—the only place in the narrative, with the exception of the opening paragraphs, where women become the center of focus. White Rabbit tells Red Star about the Medicine Shields, because Red Star has no knowledge of them. Red Star tells her, " 'When I was little we lived near the forts of the whitemen. The only teachings I received from my mother were those of the stinging water' " (p. 341). White men's forts? This is the only time they have been mentioned—the only time in the narrative when we are conscious of the white men actually *living* near the Indians. Red Star continues, " 'She made love to many whitemen, but the men who slept with her treated her cruelly' " (p. 341). An alcoholic red woman, living near the white man's forts? The times have indeed changed. Red Star knows none of the teachings. She has grown up outside of the Medicine Wheel way, cut off from the roots of her heritage. White Rabbit tells her about Seven Arrows, the spirit of her people. It is as if Storm is making a final plea for understanding the past. Painstakingly he has White Rabbit instruct Red Star about the Brotherhood.*

The trajectory changes. Green Fire Mouse, Thunder Bow, and a group of other males prepare for an ambush of some white men, but the

*It is significant, also, that this time the instruction is made by a woman—not a man, as in all other instances in the novel.

men they stalk have already taken care of themselves. In the middle of the prairie they come upon three white men who have killed one another. It is Storm's final picture of the whitemen; symbolic of the final fate of the white man's world as seen by the Indians. If the red man can somehow wait it out, the whites will eventually kill themselves off. The white world will in time destroy itself. It is only a matter of time. Time, here, is on the Native American's side. As they strip the bodies of the dead men, one of them discovers a bright shining object:

> *It is alive!* the man signed who held it. *Listen, you can hear its heart beat!* The object was then passed around from hand to hand, everyone listening to it and examining it carefully.
> "It is alive indeed!" Green Fire Mouse said out loud to Thunder Bow. "It is iron that has a heartbeat." (p. 353)

The next morning, however, the strange object no longer possesses a heartbeat. One of the men remarks, "The amazing object died early this morning. Its heart beats no more" (p. 353–I). Time has run out for the white man but it has also stopped for the Indian: both have been catapulted into strange new worlds. Little remains as it was.

One day when Green Fire Mouse, White Rabbit, and a girl called Dancing Moon are on their way to Medicine Water's camp, temporarily stopping for a rest, they notice an old man slowly riding a horse toward them. When he comes closer, Dancing Moon remarks that he looks a thousand years old. She is surprised that the dogs have not barked at his approach. When they ask him where he is going, the old man replies, " 'Why, this Camp of course!' " (p. 356–I). He seems to have an uncanny ability to read their minds. He tells them a tale about a character named Seven Arrows, and his encounter with a young boy who does not want to believe in his existence. The reader soon realizes that the old man is Seven Arrows, telling a story about himself. The boy within the story changes forms a number of times—into a wolverine, a hummingbird, and then back into a boy again. The old man ends his tale suddenly by projecting the people to whom he has been telling his story into the tale itself:

> That Evening, Green Fire Mouse Went for a Swim with White Rabbit and Dancing Moon. The Old Man Sat at the Edge of the River and Watched White Rabbit's Two Children. The Three Young People Swam Until the Moon was Bright and Full Overhead. Then, Tired and Refreshed at the Same Time, they Warmed themselves by the Fire at the Lodge. They Ate Fresh Berries White Rabbit had Gathered and Enjoyed the Meat Dancing Moon had Boiled in Preparation for the Evening. It was an Evening that would be Remembered Forever. (p. 367–I)

Green Fire Mouse, White Rabbit, and Dancing Moon have become a part of the oral tradition, a part of the tale they were listening to, a part of a culture that has survived.

In the remaining section of the novel, a mere two pages in length, Storm surprises his reader once again. White Rabbit asks Green Fire Mouse where he is taking the children. " 'Buffalo hunting,' Green Fire Mouse answered looking up from the book he had been reading" (p. 370). Green Fire Mouse takes his grandchildren outside, "toward the waiting pickup" (p. 370). He lights a cigarette, and one of his grandchildren named Rocky complains about the school he is attending, about the white man's religion. " 'They haven't understood about the seven arrows yet,' " (p. 371) Green Fire Mouse tells him. Rocky tells his grandfather that no one knows about seven arrows any longer.

All of these events come as quite a shock. Storm has again skipped a large block of time. When we last saw Green Fire Mouse and White Rabbit, they were young; now they are grandparents, living on a reservation. Green Fire Mouse answers Rocky's questions, "from under his reservation hat," (p. 371), explaining to him,

> "What's happened to Christianity is that it has become an old woman, a wicked witch. You see, the child of this old woman's marriage was poisoned by the apple, and has been asleep. She is a beautiful young maiden waiting for the spirit of peace that is in each of us to kiss her. Then she will awaken. And the paradox, my son, is this. This symbol of the young maiden is multiple. The young maiden is every woman. And she is the symbol of the way, the new lodge, like in the story of the buffalo wives." (p. 371)

Green Fire Mouse has mixed up his stories so they now include bits and pieces from the red man's past, other borrowed artifacts from the white man's myths (Adam and Eve, the fall of man). He has adapted his own tradition so that is has incorporated some of the white man's myths. But, perhaps more importantly, he has hinted that just as the oral tradition for the Native American has had to become flexible in order to survive, so too the white man's religion will have to learn to incorporate opposites or it will not survive. The allusions to the feminine are also important when we remember the multiple references made throughout the novel by the younger characters: the medicine shields have become weak, feminine.

Rocky tells his grandfather that he must be kidding; no one talks about religion any longer. Green Fire Mouse replies,

> "No, I'm not. . . . It's a teaching. And there are seven arrows in the story too. They are called dwarfs. They give away the gems of

wisdom of the north to all those who understand. And their hair is white, these seven dwarfs.... The name of the story is Snow White...." (p. 371)

Rocky asks if there are other stories, and his grandfather replies, in the final paragraph of the novel,

"Sure.... There is the entire world and everything in it that can teach you much, much more. There are the songs, the bibles, the cities, and the dreams. Everything upon the earth and in the heavens is a mirror for the people. It is a total gift. Jump up! And you will see the Medicine Wheel." (p. 371)

The first few times I read Hyemeyohsts Storm's *Seven Arrows* my reactions to the concluding section were ones of discomfort and pity. Discomfort because of the abrupt change to the twentieth century—to life now lived not on the openness of the plains, but on the confines of a reservation. Green Fire Mouse cannot take his grandchildren buffalo hunting because there are no buffalos left. He takes them fishing instead. His voice has become a sound from under his "reservation hat." The poverty of the white man's mythology ("Snow White and the Seven Dwarfs") has overshadowed the richness of the Native American's traditional stories. I felt pity and compassion for the forgotten world of the shields, of the Brotherhood. I believe these are accurate reactions to the end of *Seven Arrows* but there is another side that has been skillfully argued by Faith Gabelnick in her article, "Identity within the Melting Pot: A Critical Reading of *Seven Arrows*."[4] Ms. Gabelnick points out, correctly I believe, that the events of the last scene are consistent with much of the imagery and rhetoric of the earlier sections of the novel, that Green Fire Mouse is an example of the novel's central theme: the need for change, adaptability, if the Indian is to survive. In this context, it is especially important that he tells his grandson to "Jump Up!" just as the voice instructed the blind Jumping Mouse to do. " 'Jump Up! And you will see the Medicine Wheel' " (p. 371).

On an ethnological level, *Seven Arrows* tells us that the survival of a culture is often dependent upon the extent of its malleability, that the white man's stereotyped image of the Native American is in drastic need of revision. On a literary level, it shows us that our concept of the American novel is going to have to be expanded so that it can include a work as rich as Storm's novel. For too long we have assumed a paternal relationship with the American Indian, telling him what he should do, failing to notice that the meeting of cultures presupposes a giving and a receiving on both sides. The Native American has something to teach us, too, if we will only sit down and listen and learn from him.

# 4
# Toward a Sense of the Community

George Lamming's
*In the Castle of My Skin*

Moving from René Maran, Yambo Ouologuem, Vincent Eri, and Hyemeyohsts Storm to George Lamming, we can begin to see a major change in the content and form of the Third World novel. The works by Maran, Ouologuem, Eri, and Storm record—in varying degrees—the patterns of traditional life and the early stages of exposure to the West. *Batouala* and *Bound to Violence* are the most hopeless of these, chronicling, essentially, the death of a culture. Eri's *The Crocodile* is not much more optimistic; his main character, Hoiri Sevese, has reached a state of total bewilderment by the end of the novel. Only Hyemeyohsts Storm has begun to move in a direction towards self-assertion—in this case through cultural adaption and change. However, the Native Americans in the last episodes of his novel have had to give up much of their traditional culture in order to survive.

In all four of these novels, there is an overriding image of cultural chaos and collapse, often implied by the diffuseness of the narrative itself and the lack of a central character. The situation that has brought about this radical change in each of these cultures is colonialism. There is a ubiquitous feeling of frustration because of an inability to confront the colonial power and overthrow it. The political consciousness of these societies has yet to evolve to any significant degree; the emphasis is still on the unorganized masses, without a leader to guild them toward a revolution.

George Lamming's *In the Castle of My Skin* reflects a change in this pattern. His novel takes us to the Caribbean island of Barbados. Here we see a different form of exploitation: it is an area that was not simply colonized, but also a place to which slaves were transported. The time is different also—at the end of 350 years of subjugation—not the beginning and the middle stages we have generally seen portrayed in the other books. Psychologically, the colony is approaching self-awareness and, eventually, independence. The psychological shift also takes on new meaning in the form of the work itself, certainly an experimental novel—though when it was first published in 1953, *In the Castle of My Skin* was described not as a work of fiction but as an autobiography. The combination of these two forms gives us both personal and private history, culminating in a new political awareness emerging from a racial identity and an incipient Marxist revolt.

Lamming was born in Barbados in 1927. When he completed his secondary schooling, he taught for four years in Trinidad. In 1950, he left Trinidad for England—where he published poetry and worked as a broadcaster for the BBC's colonial service. *In the Castle of My Skin* was published in 1953, with an introduction by Righard Wright which described the book as an "autobiographical summation of a tropical island childhood . . . ."[1] Though other works followed —*The Emigrants* (1954), *Of Age and Innocence* (1958), *The Pleasures of Exile* (1960), *Season of Adventure* (1960), *Water with Berries* (1971), and *Natives of My Person* (1972)—none has achieved the brilliance of Lamming's first work. During the years when he wrote these works, he lived for the most part in England with occasional periods spent in Canada and the United States as writer-in-residence at a number of American universities.

The narrative development of *In the Castle of My Skin* is three-sided—the result of Lamming's merging the autobiography and novel forms. However, the result is not so much an autobiographical novel as Lamming's personal story superimposed on a fictive account of the village in which he grew up. The tripartite nature of the work can be detected in a splitting of the areas of concentration: first, Lamming himself; second, the community; and third, the elderly couple, Pa and Ma. Lamming's own story is told in chapters one, two, six, and parts of chapters three, seven, eleven, and twelve. The story of the village is related in chapters five, nine, thirteen, and parts of chapters three, seven, and twelve. Pa and Ma's story is narrated in chapters four, eight, ten, and part of chapters twelve and thirteen. In the "village" sections and in the sections devoted to Pa and Ma the point of view shifts from first person to third person, the omniscient novelist. All three threads come together in the last chapter, number fourteen. The symbolic time perspective for these three configurations is rooted in the past for Pa and Ma, in the present for the community, and in the future for the narrator himself, though there is some shifting here too. In total number of pages, the concentration of the work divides almost equally into halves; that is, approximately half of the work is the story of Lamming's own life. The rest of the novel is the account of the villagers he lived with including Pa and Ma. Our analysis of *In the Castle of My Skin* will follow these demarcations.

The autobiography/novel begins with the day that George Lamming (though he is never named as such in the book) is nine years old. It rains throughout the day—so intensely that there is a flood in the village, which destroys a number of houses. Lamming states, "Floods had chosen to follow me in the celebration of all my years . . ." (p. 2). Though his mother refers to them as "showers of blessing" (p. 1), the rains ruin his birthday. Thus, at the outset water imagery becomes a leitmotif to symbolize a time of change in the village. In a practical manner, the flood forces Mr. Creighton, the white landlord and owner of the land in the village, to reaffirm his obligation to the villagers: new roads and help for those harmed in the storm—morsels thrown at the villagers to prolong the feudal system.

While the ambiguity of cultural change has been a theme of all the books we have considered, the institutions of continuity—the family and the community—are portrayed quite differently here. We notice this first in Lamming's treatment of the role of women in the society he is describing. Of his mother, he writes: "My father who had only fathered the idea of me had left me the sole liability of my mother who really fathered me" (p. 3). The women in this novel are tough, strong—they have to be to raise their families unaided for the most part by men. This is especially evident in the multiple conversations devoted to "women talk" and in other passages where Lamming stresses the matriarchal order. Such thoughts flow in and out of his mind

> Miss Foster. My mother. Bob's mother.
> It seemed they were three pieces in a pattern which remained constant. The flow of its history was undistrubed by any difference in the pieces, nor was its evenness affected by any likeness. There was a difference and there was no difference. Miss Foster had six children, three by a butcher, two by a baker and one whose father had never been mentioned. Bob's mother had two, and my mother one. (p. 18)

Attitudes toward the female-dominated family are a key topic of conversation among the central character's peers. When alone together, the boys speak of the harshness of fathers, the gentleness of mothers.

One boy is happy his father does not live with him: "My father couldn't hit me 'cause he don't support me. An' that's why I alright. My mother won't let him hit me 'cause he don't support me" (p. 42). Another boy speculates, "Mothers stupid, that's why most of us without fathers" (p. 43). Yet, one boy thinks that the fatherless household is a good thing: "If there ain't no father in the house, you get the feeling you is the man in the place" (p. 43). Such a relationship develops with Lamming and his own mother, culminating in the poignant scene the night before his departure for Trinidad, when she does not want to give him up.

Among Lamming's pals—Bob, Boy Blue, and Trumper—there is an intense feeling of camaraderie which is a clear outgrowth of their need to escape the world of their mothers and thereby create their own male identity. A number of sub-stories in the narrative exemplifying this need center upon male/female relationships which do not end in marriage but in illegitimate children. The story of Jon, Susie, and Jen illustrates the carefree masculine world in which the male sows his wild oats and then moves on to the next woman he can find.

Although the result for Jon is frustrating, it is not tragic as is Boy Blue's account of Bots, Bambi, and Bambina. Bambi lived in quiet harmony with two women—Bots and Bambina. He fathered children by both of them and each woman was content with the arrangement. " 'Bots an' Bambina wus the best of friends, an' the children who wus half brother an' half sister live like real brother and sister without any talk 'bout half or quarter' " (p. 145). Then a female anthropologist—a little like Fritz Shrobenius in Ouologuem's novel—began meddling in their relationship. She told Bambi he was living in sin and that he ought to marry one of the women. The result of the eventual wedding was a catastrophe, not so much for the two women as it was for Bambi, who began to harbor Western puritanical hang-ups about his life of sin. Bambi turned to alcohol, eventually drinking himself to death. Trumper concludes from Boy Blue's story: " ' . . . it don't matter who marry who, as soon as they is that marryin' business, everythin' break up, break right up' " (p. 154). These stories and similar prolonged discussions between Lamming and his pals serve as their initiation into manhood, fulfilling the role played by the rites of passage in African and Native American societies, as we have seen in *Batouala* and *Seven Arrows*.

The outer world for Lamming in his autobiography is described by his relationships with his mother and his boyhood friends, by his activities at school, and by the life of the village itself. This overlapping setting gives us a sense of totality of immersion into the collective consciousness of a community—even in the passages which focus almost exclusively on Lamming himself. Although his own life later becomes centered in the future—since his education is designed to help him succeed at some distant time—as a child, his affinity with the village is focused upon the day-to-day aspects of communal life. That is why the early sections so painstakingly stress the elements of continuation of life as it is, without flux. Lamming and his pals have not yet begun to direct their lives toward the future as they later will. They are still of the community. Hence, Trumper says, " 'Everything's all right, 'tis the same yesterday an' today an' tomorrow an' forever as they says in the Bible' " (p. 129). The boyhood world is experienced in the present continuous. Boy Blue states, " '...I get the feelin' that I always this size, an' all I try to remember, I can't remember myself bigger or smaller than I is now' " (p. 129). Trumper develops this idea of cyclical time even further, stressing the communal motif: " 'Everybody in the village sort of belong. Is like a tree. It can't kind of take up the roots by itself; we all live sort of together, except for those who don't really belong' " (p. 157).

At the same time, the inner world created through the autobiographical sections of *In the Castle of My Skin* moves us far away from the other Third World novels we have examined, resulting in one of the most introspective pieces of writing we are likely to find from this area of the world. Most of the sections devoted to Lamming himself are illustrations of his own developing consciousness. Lamming is always analyzing, rationalizing, whether that be at the beginning, when the physical flooding of the village extends to his mind and the "phantoms" that he says "populated" his brain; or at the end of the narrative, where he states that "words and voices [fell] like a full shower" (p. 341) on his heightened consciousness. In a way, it is proper to think of Lamming's work as foreshadowing the later inward turning of the Third World novel—personal history depicted through introspection, stream of consciousness, the interior monologue.

Lamming's mind is constantly bombarded by ideas and impressions over which he has no control. Often they interrupt sections of the narrative in which he is not talking about himself. Words and expressions are repeated over and over as they impinge on his consciousness: "The image of the enemy. My people" (p. 24). "Three, Thirteen, Thirty" (p. 27). "The landlord. The overseer. The flood. Miss Foster. Bob's mother, my mother. Not thirteen, but three" (p. 29). The waves have a similar effect on his mind, when Lamming is lying on the beach, talking to Trumper and Boy Blue.

It is in the eleventh chapter that Lamming's story becomes the most introspective, the most personal in the sense of using autobiographical material. Lamming is much older, eighteen or nineteen, looking back upon his estrangement from his boyhood friends. High school has cut him off from both these friends and the rest of the villagers. Suddenly he is regarded as someone different—because of the possibilities of his education connecting his life to some goal in the future. He is aware of the changes in his life; he describes a mystical experience with a pebble he once hid on the beach. As he buried the pebble, so he will soon bury his own past and present. He describes his sensations, after he had hidden the pebble:

> this feeling, no longer new, had grown on me like a sickness. I couldn't bear the thought of seeing things for the last time. It was like imagining the end of my life. Now it had happened again. The pebble wasn't there. (p. 236)

Lamming knows that no one has taken the pebble, that the sea has not washed it away. Rather, he has experienced the force of the invisible world that Batouala felt in the forests of Africa. As he reflects on the pebble, he muses,

> it seemed to me that there were certain things one couldn't lose. Things which had grown on you could be risked since they had an uncanny way of returning. And above all I had a vague feeling that there was no reason one should see things for the last time. I selected the spot and placed the pebble under the leaf on the even slope. A day had passed. There was no change in the weather, and the waves were as quiet as ever on this side of the sea. They rode up gently, tired themselves out and receded in another form towards the sea. But the pebble had gone. The feeling sharpened. It had really started the evening before when I received the letters, and now the pebble had made it permanent. (p. 238)

One of the letters he refers to informed him that he had been granted a teaching position in Trinidad. Life will henceforth be lived in flux, as he realizes it has been for some time now: Trumper has been in America for three years, Boy Blue and Bob have left school and have "drifted into another world" (p. 240). High school cut him off from his mother, who became obsessed with a fear that he would fail. "Gradually the village receded from my consciousness although it wasn't possible for me to forget it" (p. 243). Lamming knows that the changes in himself are complemented by a number of changes in the village, mostly the result of World War II:

> Then the pebble returned present in its image on the sloping sand under the grape leaf, and I thought of them all in turn. Trumper, Boy Blue, Bob. The High School, the village, the first assistant. They had all arisen with the pebble, making the feeling of separation a permanent sickness. The thought of seeing things for the last time. And my mother? She seemed in a way too big for this occasion. I waded out of the water and walked to the rocks where my clothes were bundled. For the last time I looked at the spot where I had

placed the pebble, and then quickly turned my thoughts to Trumper's letter. It was difficult to decide which was less perplexing. I repeated the sentence with which he ended the letter. "You don't understand, You don't understand what life is, but I'll tell you when I come and I am coming soon." (pp. 252-253)

Lamming has learned that the past can never be recaptured.

The sections devoted to Pa and Ma serve as a connecting bridge between Lamming and his changing perception of the place of the village in his life. The earliest reference to them appears in the first chapter. Lamming thinks,

> Pa and Ma . . .what did happen to Pa and Ma. They weren't related to us by blood, but they were Pa and Ma nevertheless. Everyone called them Pa and Ma. They were the oldest couple in the village, so old no one could tell their age, and few knew what names they had besides those we had given them, Ma and Pa. (p. 7)

They are a bridge of kindness to the past, to what was—the titular king and queen of Lamming's castle. They fulfill much the same function that the elders do in African societies: they are respected, cared for, consulted. They live at the center of communal life, not on its edge as old people do in our world. Lamming devotes four crucial sections of his narrative to them—often told from their point of view, as if he were privy to their innermost thoughts.

The first of these sections (the fourth chapter) begins as a play: Old Man, Old Woman, and what they say to each other. It is a year since the flood described in the opening sequence. Ma says she is worried about what will happen when Mr. Creighton, the landlord, dies. He has no sons. Who will be their new landlord? Pa's thoughts are about Mr. Slime, former teacher at the village school, who has formed a Friendly Society and a Penny Bank. Both fear the future; it will only bring change. Lamming shifts the narrative to the third person point of view, ending his playlet, to tell us about Pa's strange dream. While Pa knows that death cannot be far away, Ma seeks refuge in her religion.

In the eighth chapter, Ma comes through more clearly as a representative of the past than Pa does. She has had a conversation with the landlord who has also expressed his fears about the changes taking place in the village, including riots and other demonstrations of unrest. Ma—faithful to life as it was—sides with the landlord more than Pa, who thinks the changes are good as long as they do not involve violence. When they reappear in the novel, it is several years later (the twelfth chapter): "The years had changed nothing. The riots were not repeated. The landlord had remained" (p. 231). Most of their appearance this time is devoted to a dream Pa has about Africa, a dream that is crucial to

our understanding of the novel. Lamming places us inside of Pa's mind,
in a dream in which the old man reflects on the black man's past in
Africa and on a common West Indian belief that when a man dies
his soul returns to Africa.*

Pa's dream telescopes the black man's romantic origins in Africa, the
horrors of the beginning of slavery followed by the middle passage,
the shift to the new culture in the West Indies:

> Strange tribe my tribe and the tribe of your father my brother's son.
>     And strange was the time that change my neighbor and me, the
> tribes with gods and the one tribe without. The silver of exchange
> sail cross the sea and my people scatter like clouds in the sky when
> the waters come. There was similar buying and selling 'mongst tribe
> and tribe, but this was the biggest of the bargains for tribes. Each
> sell his own. (p. 233)

Pa also lucidly develops an idea we have already seen in Ouologuem's
*Bound to Violence*: Africans must share the guilt of slavery because they
sold each other. We will also see this idea—that the past must be exorcised
—in Jean Toomer's *Cane*. Pa's dream continues,

> A man walked out in the market and one buyer watch his tooth and
> another his toe and the parts that was private for the coming of
> a creature in the intimate night. The silver sail from hand to hand
> and the purchase was shipped like a box of good fruit. The sale
> was the best of Africa's produce, and me and my neighbor made
> the same same bargain. I make my peace with the middle Passage
> to settle on that side of the sea the white man call a world that was
> west of another world. The tribes with gods and the one tribe without
> we all went the way of the white man's money. (p. 233)

The dream continues, as Pa thinks of his ancestors being transported
to the West Indies. Then, like many dreams, this one ends in confusion.
Pa thinks that returning to Africa will not solve the black man's problems,
yet life in the New World has not been a solution either, because black
people will always be exploited by someone—even their own people:
"Slime and Creighton, landlord and politician . . ." (p. 234). Pa is the
first to realize that Mr. Slime has become faithful to his name—one
of the exploiters.

The flood of thoughts here should remind us of the end of *Batouala*,
when the old chief is talking to his ancestors, for Pa, also, is close to
the spirit world. The thoughts in his subconscious are thoughts that
others are afraid to express. That is why the chapter does not end

---

*See, for example, the following two peoms: Jacques Roumain's "The Slow Road to
Guinea" (Guinée") or Carl Brouard's "Nostalgia" ("Nostalgie").

with Pa's death, as one expects, but with Ma's. Pa—that connecting bridge now to the future as well as the past—must live on for a while. This we see in his next appearances in the story, the days before Lamming is ready to leave his village for Trinidad. In the first of these appearances (Chapter Twelve), Lamming visits the old man to say his farewells. Pa remarks how the face of the village has changed. The second time (Chapter Thirteen), Lamming is not present, but again assumes omniscience to relate Pa's fate, what he had seen in his earlier dream: the demise of the white landlord and the rise of the black politician who exploits his fellow men. The headmaster from the school tells Pa that his property has been sold, that he will have to move to the Alms House, the ultimate humiliation: "the final stage of human degradation, the grave of those who though dead had been allowed to go on living..." (p. 282). Pa has been toppled from his former respected position as symbolic head of the village. His strange dreams have turned into reality; the community has turned topsy-turvy.

At the beginning, however, the  community seems to have a kind of inherent stability. Lamming describes the village (Creighton's village) as composed of nearly 3000 people—set off from the landlord who lives on a hill, surrounded by a wall. "From any point of the land one could see on a clear day the large brick house hoisted on the hill" (p. 19). At night, it looks like a castle.

> It was a castle around which the land like a shabby back garden stretched. When the lights went out, and the wood was dark, the villagers took note. The landlord's light had been put out. The landlord had gone to bed. It was time they did the same. A custom had been established, and later a value which through continual application and a hardened habit of feeling became an absolute standard of feeling. I don't feel the landlord would like this. If the overseer see, the landlord is bound to know. It operated in every activity. The obedient lived in the hope that the Great might not be offended, the uncertain in the fear it might have been. (p. 23)

The villagers exist in a kind of feudal relationship with the landlord. They are not yet organized in any political way. They pay their respects to the landlord and he takes care of them. Each is a part of the other: "the landlord couldn't do without the village any more than they could" (p. 104). It is part of the presentness of everything—life seen without any changes.

As the story progresses, Lamming begins to develop the gradual shift that takes place between the villagers and the landlord. In fact, he skillfully uses the change in this relationship as a symbol of the village's ascent to modern political consciousness. At first it is a protective relationship; the landlord is father of the village—the one patrarchial relationship suggested in the book. Then things change as the power base begins to crack. Slime sets up the penny bank, begins to talk about land ownership, and manipulates the workers during a strike. Later, there is a riot in the town and though its effects on Ceighton's village are nominal, Slime has played the dubious role as mediator between the Great (including Creighton) and the lowly—Lamming's villagers. The landlord's house, referred to later in the narrative, is described as a fortification designed to keep the peasants out. When Lamming and his pals sneak into the landlord's garden, Lamming states, "The house looked so much bigger than I had thought. It was like some of the castles we had seen in pictures" (p. 188). After the war begins and the trees are cut down, the landlord's house stands out alone. The power base has shifted drastically. Creighton has sold the land to Slime and his cohorts, who soon begin to exploit the villagers as Creighton did.

Lamming's early pictures of village life, however, concentrate almost exclusively on its collective nature. The reader thinks this is not a novel about an individual but about a community—a way of life for a group of people. In scene after scene the author establishes this collective image of the village's pulse: the public bath house; the streets at night, clotted with lovers and drunks; men gathering together at the shoemaker's shop; Savory, the foodseller, in the morning and the villagers clustered around him for their daily purchases; a street brawl between two women, of which Lamming states, "It was like a public ball to which everyone had been invited and where there were no restrictions at all" (p. 113); open-air revival meetings. All of these give us the quotidian throb of village life. These are the aspects of the story which develop its situational plot—a village, a group of people undergoing the final stages of colonialism, just before the revolution that will lead to independence. It is as if the village impinged so strongly on Lamming's consciousness that the autobiography he planned to write became almost totally effaced. (Lamming is in fact missing in episode after episode—except as the recording consciousness.)

Structurally, the communal sections of Lamming's novel are those that reveal his strongest traits as a shaping novelist. Again and again there are passages (in both the community sections and in the passages devoted to Pa and Ma) that illustrate Lamming's intense awareness of the great changes that were taking place in his village—even if the villagers themselves have not yet made these realizations. Lamming has two roles to play: as a character in the book, he does not realize the magnitude of the changes that have begun to take place until almost the end of the story; as the novelist, telling his story in retrospect, he sees all and understands the significance of these events. Assuming total omniscience in order to describe these events, Lamming has to step aside from his own story that slowly becomes of lesser importance. How fitting that these communal sections, then, also illustrate the villagers' shifting awareness from acceptance to questioning of the status quo.

The first major section of the novel that develops the communal aspect is in Chapter Three—a day at school—Empire Day. Though the point of view shifts back and forth from adult to child, from teacher to pupil, both illustrate the psychological impact that the colonial idea of the "obedient child" has had on Barbados—or "Little England" as she is called. Lamming describes the educational process as "an enormous ship whose cargo had been packed in boxes and set on the deck" (p. 31). Of the colony itself, he says, "Barbados or Little England was the oldest and the purest of England's children," (p. 32), another way of saying that the people have effectively been kept in their place. The school masters are mostly concerned with pleasing the English school inspector instead of educating the students in the true history of their past.*

The English school inspector represents more than just the false aspects of colonial education based on indoctrination (the result of which is civil servants and teachers who continue to perpetuate the cycle without questioning its merits). Cheap education leads to cheap labor, always buffered with a degree of hard work and practicality—the Puritan ethic. The inspector tells the boys, just before giving them each a penny, " 'You must all when you go to spend your penny think before you throw it away. Queen Victoria was a wise queen, and she would have you spend it wisely' " (p. 38). He naturally assumes that they will throw their pennies away. After the coins have been distributed, the boys sit quietly, examining them, questioning how the King's imprint got on the penny.

> This face on the penny was very fascinating. Could you have a penny without a face? They looked at it closely and critically, and made notes of their observations. How did the face get there? The question puzzled them. Some said it was a drawing of the king made with a pin while the copper was soft. They had seen lead melt. The hard, colourless slab was put in the pot and when you looked again it was a shining crystal liquid that gradually grew solid again. (p. 51)

Just as the pennies have been cast in a mold to make them all identical, so these students in Barbados are being molded to continue the cycle of colonialism. Education is a subtle means of economic exploitation; the mother country milks the colony, occasionally throwing a penny at her subjects to keep them from rising up in anger and frustration: " . . .the English . . .the only people in the world to deal with pennies were very sensible" (p. 51). The boys continue their musings on the nature of penny production:

*The past that Pa's dream recalls.

Someone said it was the same penny all the time. One penny, that is the first penny ever made, was the real penny, and all the others were made by a kind of stamp. You simply had to get the first penny and the necessary materials and thousands followed. That meant, someone asked, that you couldn't spend the first penny. (pp. 51–52)

The pennies will always be made in England; Barbados will always be a dependent child. The passage concludes with a discussion of "the shadow king" (p. 53), who casts a pall over the entire colonial system. It is a most subtle attack on colonialism.

The students' inability to understand the subtleties of economic exploitation is tied to their confusion about freedom and bondage. Queen Victoria is referred to as "a good queen because she freed them" (p. 55), but this makes no sense to them because they have no context to place it in. An old woman has told one of the boys that they were once slaves. The boy repeated to "the teacher what the old woman had said. She was a slave. And the teacher said she was getting dotish . . .it had nothing to do with people in Barbados. No one there was ever a slave, the teacher said" (p. 56). The teachers refuse to admit to the past history of their people, rejecting their racial origins and embracing the role of the obedient child introduced by the British: " . . .slavery was thousands of years [ago]. It was too far back for anyone to worry about teaching it as history" (p. 56). Slavery was so far back that it never happened.

Modern slavery—the economic exploitation of the colonies—is one of the major themes of Lamming's *In the Castle of My Skin*. The people are duped into believing that what they have is the best of all possible worlds. As Mr. Foster tells a number of men when they are sitting in the shoemaker's shop, " 'I don't think there's any part of this God's world barring England sheself where the education is to such a high pitch' " (p. 110). The myth of the superiority of their education is rooted in a past that does not exist. As the shoemaker says, if you tell the average worker about his racial heritage, that " 'they have somethin' to do with Africa they'd piss straight in your face' " (p. 110). The African past has been hidden; the present white world offers everything one needs.

That is why when the power shift takes place in the village, so few people realize what has happened. Slime uses the money from the Penny Bank (the people's money) to buy the land from the landlord—after he has misled the villagers into believing that he is working for them. During the strike, he subdues the men, because he is really working for Creighton. When a riot breaks out, he intervenes so the landlord is not harmed. By the time his power is firmly entrenched in the village, he has surrounded himself with a number of other questionable characters (such as the head teacher, once his greatest enemy) who have aided him in making the transition a success. Only old Pa seems to have foreseen what has happened, but he is powerless to do anything about it. Hence it comes as a jolt to the other villagers when they are told (in Chapter Thirteen) that they must move out of their houses and make way for the new owners. Little remains but impotence and frustration. "But the villagers didn't understand. Their ways had been formed, and their life like their certain death knew its roots" (p. 269).

A quotation from Ayi Kwei Armah's *The Beautyful Ones Are Not Yet Born* is revealing here, since Armah's picture of Ghana is similar to Lamming's picture of Barbados:

> the same men, when they had power in their hands at last, began to find the veils useful. They made many more. Life has not changed. Only some people have been growing, becoming different, that is all. After a youth spent fighting the white man, why should not the president discover as he grows older that his real desire has been to be like the white governor himself, to live above all blackness in the big old slave castle? And the men around him, why not? What stops them sending their loved children to kindergartens in Europe? And if the little men around the big men can send their children to new international schools, why not? That is all anyone here ever struggles for: to be nearer the white man. All the shouting against the white man was not hate. It was love. Twisted, but love all the same.[2]

Slime and his henchmen are the new white men in Lamming's novel. They can be displaced only by a frontal attack, by the combined force of the community as a whole.

The last chapter of Lamming's work describes such a confrontation, though only in a symbolic way, by bringing together the three main threads: Lamming, the community, and the story of Pa and Ma. At the beginning of the chapter, Lamming presents us with several entries from his journal. They contrast vividly with the earlier Lamming we have seen. His interests have shifted to his future teaching position, and, to a lesser extent, women. One of the entries describes an incident with a prostitute; another an overheard conversation between Slime and the Head Teacher talking in a bar, plotting to take over the village.* The last entry shifts to Lamming's preparations for his departure. He muses about the isolation of men, the difficulty of knowing others, concluding, "They won't know the you that's hidden somewhere in the castle of your skin" (p. 291). He feels that it is time for him to get away from his people so he can be safe. He thinks about the relationships he has had with several of his so-called friends, which now seem so odd. "I am always feeling terrified of being known; not because they

---

*Some of these entries describe incidents that take place before the narrated time of the previous chapter.

really know you, but simply because their claim to this knowledge is a concealed attempt to destroy you .... As soon as they know you they will kill you ..." (p. 291). Although Lamming does not realize it, he is running away—from family and community. His education has cut him off from his people; he has been molded like the face on the penny.

The journal entries are followed by a lengthy conversation between Lamming and his mother the night before his departure. It is a painful meeting for both of them, masterfully told. Both realize that their relationship will never be the same again. It is a symbolic rebirth for Lamming, who can no longer be the child his mother wants him to be. Independence assumes adulthood. Their dialogue is a fitting climax to the autobiographical aspects of Lamming's narrative: the child become a man. Lamming states, "When I looked at her and the pebble came back the feeling was like being a tooth which had been taken from its snapped roots, leaving the gum a space to occupy the probing tongue" (p. 312).

Then the narrative shifts again. Trumper has returned from America, after living abroad for three years. He and Lamming go out to a local bar for a farewell drink and conversation, and Lamming realizes that his friend has changed, though he cannot tell exactly in what way. After criticizing Slime's land purchases, Trumper says, " ' ...this world is a world o' camps, an' you got to find out which camp you're in' " (p. 323). Lamming does not understand what his friend is saying. Trumper has a tape recorder with him and a recording of Paul Robeson singing "Let My People Go," but Lamming does not know who Robeson is.

> "Paul Robeson," he said. "One o' the greatest o' my people."
> "What people?" I asked. I was a bit puzzled.
> "My People," said Trumper ....
> "Who are your people?" I asked him. It seemed a kind of huge joke.
> "The Negro race," said Trumper. The smile had left his face, and his manner had turned grave again. I finished my drink and looked at him. He knew that I was puzzled. This bewilderment about Trumper's people was real. At first I thought he meant the village. This allegiance was something bigger. I wanted to understand it. He drained the glass and set it on the table.
> "I didn't know it till I reach the States," he said. (p. 331)

Trumper has discovered who he is, who his people are. His years spent in the United States have given him a new identification with his people. He contrasts the blacks in Barbados with those in the United States:

> " 'Course the blacks here are my people too, but they don't know it yet. You don't know it yourself. None o' you here on this islan'

know what it mean to fin' race. An' the white people you have to deal with won't ever let you know." (p. 332)

Trumper tells Lamming that blacks in the United States have found their identity through suffering, while in Barbados they are still content to play the roles the British have thrust upon them. Lamming confusedly asks him, " 'Am I one of your people, Trumper?' " (p. 333). Trumper replies that he is, but he does not yet understand. They leave the bar with Lamming trying to sort out what Trumper has told him. "Trumper made his own experience, the discovery of a race, a people, seem like a revelation. It was nothing I had known, and it didn't seem I could know it till I had lived it.... To be a different kind of creature. This was beyond my experience" (pp. 334-335).

Lamming thinks, it isn't simply a black/white issue: "Certain blacks employed a similar subterfuge to exclude other blacks who weren't equal to their demands" (p. 335). The furniture of his mind begins to fall into place: Slime, the land, his villagers—the exploiters and the exploited. Lamming wonders what Trumper will do to help the villagers since he knows that he himself can do very little. He asks Trumper if he ever feels lonely, isolated. Does he remember a day on the beach years ago, " 'A feeling you were alone in a world all by yourself, and although there were hundreds of people moving round you, it made no difference' " (p. 338). This is the feeling responsible for Lamming's leaving his people. Trumper replies, " 'A man who know his people won't ever feel like that...' " (p. 338). A man who knows his people won't ever be trapped in the castle of his skin.

Trumper has come home, to his people, to his community. He has returned from a voyage that has taken the shape of a circle, safely restoring him to the heart of his people. Lamming's own voyage is about to begin—a quest of similar discovery. As he walks slowly home after saying farewell to his friend, he encounters old Pa—alone, out on the street. Pa says he is taking a last look at the village. In the morning he too will make a final trip—to the Alms House. Then Pa mentions the flood, ten years ago, the deluge that started the village on a new pathway,

> "You wus small then," he said, "too small to care much 'bout the calamity that happen. But it wus the beginnin' o' so much in this place. 'Twus strike an' then 'twus riot an' what with one rumour an' a next, now 'tis the land. We see Penny Bank an' Society an' now 'tis the end." (p. 340)

He kisses Lamming on the brow, telling him that they will never meet again. The novel concludes, returning us to Lamming's own thoughts:

The village/my mother/a boy among the boys/a man who knew his people won't feel alone/to be a different kind of creature. Words and voices falling like a full shower and the old man returning with the pebble under the grape leaf on the sand: You won't see me again, my son.

The earth where I walked was a marvel of blackness and I knew in a sense more deep than simple departure I had said farewell, farewell to the land. (p. 341)

The power of Lamming's novel owes much to the uniqueness of its composition—personal history and private history, the individual and the collective identity. Lamming's genius is his ability to weave the two skillfully into a tapestry of rare beauty. Out of materials similar to those used in other Third World novels, he has created a unique entity, a powerful statement on the plight of the individual cut off from his people's collective consciousness, of the individual seeking refuge in a community unsure of its own heritage. I can think of no other Anglophone novelist from the West Indies—with the exception of V. S. Naipaul, whose works are confined to a slightly different domain—who has written with such force and magnitude. Much of the power is due to Lamming's subtlety. This is not the usual protest novel, though there are rumblings here—in almost every scene—of what broke forth into the West Indian black power movements in the late 1960's and the early 1970's. Hence, Lamming can be seen as a prophet, a man ahead of his time.

When we place him next to Maran, Ouologuem, and Eri, the differences are more obvious than the similarities. The Barbados of *In the Castle of My Skin* is not at all like the colonial worlds depicted in the works by those other writers. Things fell apart here much earlier. The African traditions hardly exist any longer—there is not the richness of the oral tradition captured by Maran or Storm, for example. Much of that was lost during the middle passage. The people have become docile, almost apathetic. They are ready for a new leader to guide them toward the future; they are ready for a counter force like Trumper to stand up to the corruption of Slime and his like. The time, of course, is crucial. Though it may run parallel to the same years of *The Crocodile*, that is the only point of contact; colonialism is shown as much more firmly entrenched in Lamming's work than in any of the others we have examined so far. The other works, for the most part, depicted the early stages of exposure to the West. Lamming gives us the penultimate stage, after years and years of steady indoctrination into the mythos of "Little England." It is for this reason that one finds so few white characters in Lamming's novel. They are no longer necessary; the colonial machinery runs smoothly by itself. The English school inspector appears once; Creighton appears briefly two or three times. There are even speculations that he may no longer live in his castle on the hill. But the symbolic power of the edifice is enough to hold the people in check: economic exploitation feeds upon itself. The few outer changes in the village are telling since they indicate the total power of the mother country. She can do whatever she wants and there will be no reaction from the people in the colony. When the train is no longer necessary, the tracks are pulled up and sold for scrap. The trees that used to surround Creighton's castle are cut down—the land is decimated by proxy. These are the economics of colonialism.

Historically, it appears that Barbados was better off than some of the other English colonies,* and that is one reason the movement toward self-identity was so slow. Lamming indicates this quite early in his narrative, since it is, after all, a narrative written out of his own realization of his people's identity. In the second chapter he refers to the "overseers" as those men who collect rent from the villagers and take it to the landlord. "Each represented for the other an image of the enemy" (p. 20). The image of the enemy flows in and out of his mind as the passage continues: "The image of the enemy, and the enemy was My People. My people are low-down nigger people. My people don't like to see their people get on" (p. 20). This is the period during the years of acceptance, before the later questionings that will lead to racial identity: "The obedient lived in the hope that the Great might not be offended..." (p. 23), playing the role of the well-minded child. Only time, Lamming knows, will make the child grow up.

A major difference between Lamming's and the other Third World novels is not only in content but in form. His technical skills are comparable to the Western novelists'. We have already noted the relatively minor importance the oral tradition plays in his work, though Lamming often structures individual chapters like Maran does in *Batouala*: they begin with references to the sun in the morning and conclude with references to the moon at night, the cycles of day and night. The opening paragraph of *In the Castle of My Skin* describes the morning of Lamming's ninth birthday; the concluding paragraphs of the last chapter take place in the darkness of his last night in Creighton's village ten years later. More important than the daily cycle of life, however, is Lamming's use of water imagery throughout the entire narrative: the flood at the beginning, disrupting the village; Pa's comment at the end of the novel about the importance of that flood. Lamming wants us to think of this as more than a Biblical reference. The water imagery—especially the constant references to waves—calls our attention not only to the passing of time but to the passing of out-dated ways of life. There are multiple references to the flooding of water and waves not only in such obvious places as the scenes that take place on the beach ("The sea heaved and our laughter was lost in the wash of the waves," p. 135); but also at

*Independence was achieved in 1960.

other unexpected places, such as at the school ("The water flowed, carrying the boys' laughter down the canal and beyond the school yard," p. 50). So frequent are these images that Lamming could have titled his novel *The Waves* if Virginia Woolf's novel had not preceded his.

The ways in which Lamming is different from other Third World novelists are equally important. We have already noted the extensive use of introspection in this novel, a trait we rarely find in early novels by writers from Africa and the West Indies. My students have often found the lack of introspection in Third World novels a major hurdle they have to overcome before they can accept these works on an equal footing with Western writing. Characters in Third World novels are often presented totally from the outside, as we noted in the discussions of *Bound to Violence* and *Seven Arrows* and to a lesser extent in *Batouala* and *The Crocodile*. Characters in Third World fiction often do not "develop." They are the same at the end as they were at the beginning: Hoiri Sevese, Raymond Spartacus Kassoumi, Batouala. But this is not true in Lamming's *In the Castle of My Skin*. We are inside of the narrator's mind for much of the novel, aware of his innermost thoughts via the use of stream of consciousness and the interior monologue. Because of the constant shifting from the first to third person point of view, we are often given the stream of consciousness of other characters: Pa and Ma and the head teacher, for example. There are flashbacks and flashforwards. The narration of time is constantly interrupted and not presented in strict chronological order as is the general case in novels by African and West Indian writers. Furthermore, there are places in the narrative where Lamming stops the time and interpolates dramatic scenes similar to those in James Joyce's *Ulysses*. In every sense we are dealing with a radically experimental novel that makes skillful use of a variety of techniques common to twentieth century fiction.

Ultimately, however, it is the content (the use of the symbol of the community) that relates Lamming's novel to other Third World novels. In a way, this is only an implied recognition of the emergent new revolutionary consciousness, since Lamming, as a character in his work, has become separate—isolated from his people. He is not capable of understanding everything that Trumper tells him, though his travels (and his writing) will shortly give him this comprehension. For Trumper, however, the sense of the community's potential (the rise of the masses) has already been discovered. He has developed the wider consciousness of Pan Africanism—the struggle of oppressed peoples—during his years with black people in the United States. We are led to believe that he has come home to organize his people politically. Lamming (as narrator) has already made it clear that the time is propitious; the people in his village are ready for a leader to guide them in their struggle against the new élite; the feudal system of the past is about to evolve into a

Marxist struggle. A combination of these two forces—the communal organization under the careful guidance of individual leadership—is important. Lamming's thesis is that a recognition of the power of the community marks the first stage of identifying one's own self—an identity found in the life-giving culture of one's people.

# 5
# Return to the Past
## Jean Toomer's *Cane*

With George Lamming's *In the Castle of My Skin* we witnessed the discovery of a new form of communal consciousness (the beginnings of black power), emerging from an increased emphasis on the individual self. The transition from Lamming to Afro-American Jean Toomer is an easy one, for Toomer also recognizes the potential power of this same new community as an extension of the individual's search for his cultural roots. In his only novel, *Cane* (1923), the individual's relationship to the communal consciousness is always an incipient force, lurking below the surface. Toomer, however, would argue that the potential of the group cannot be harnessed until black people have come to grips with a deeper frustration—the inheritance of the past, in this case slavery. *Cane* shows us that the scars of slavery for the black man in the United States are not very different from the scars of colonialism for the black man in Africa or the West Indies.

Jean Toomer's biography is an unusual one. He was born in 1894, in Washington, D.C., of racially mixed parentage—of seven blood mixtures, as he related it: French, Dutch, Welsh, Negro, German, Jewish, and Indian.[1] He attended public schools in Washington, later spending some years at the University of Wisconsin and City College of New York—never, however, completing a degree. In 1920, he taught briefly in the South, in a public school in Georgia, returning there in 1921 for a trip with Waldo Frank. In 1923, Boni and Liveright published

*Cane,* his major piece of writing. Though it was generally received favorably by the critics, and went through a second small printing in 1927, Toomer's novel was not readily available or known until the late 1960's.

In the mid- to late twenties, Toomer dabbled in psychology, underwent Jungian psychoanalysis, and spent a time at the Gurdjieff Institute in Fontainebleau.[2] A privately published collection of definitions and sayings, *Essentials,* appeared in 1931, by which time Toomer was having little success with editors and publishers. They misdirected him—recommending among other things that he not write about black people—and Toomer himself did not seem to be able to decide about whom he should write. He was married twice to white women (his first wife died in childbirth), and then, about 1934, like the main character in James Weldon Johnson's *The Autobiography of an Ex-Colored Man* (1912), Toomer decided to let the world take him for whatever it would:

> I finally made up my mind that I would neither disclaim the black race nor claim the white race; but that I would change my name, raise a moustache, and let the world take me for what it would; that it was not necessary for me to go about with a label of inferiority pasted across my forehead.[3]

In short, Toomer passed for white, moving later to Bucks County, Pennsylvania, with his family, where he continued to write for the rest of his life, though his publications were by and large limited to religious tracts for the Quaker Society of Friends.

When Toomer died in 1967, there were no obituaries; it was months before the literary world realized it had lost one of the most talented writers of the Harlem Renaissance of the 1920's. In his introduction to the 1969 paperbacked edition of the novel, Arna Bontemps states:

> *Cane's* influence was by no means limited to the joyous band that included Langston Hughes, Countee Cullen, Eric Walrond, Zora Neal Hurston, Wallace Thurman, Rudolph Fisher and their contemporaries of the 'Twenties. Subseqent writing by Negroes in the Untied States, as well as in the West Indies and Africa, has continued to reflect its mood and often its method and, one feels, it has also influenced the writing about Negroes by others.[4]

*Cane's* influence has rarely been in question—rather, critics have been puzzled by the nature of the work itself, and by Toomer's decision to renounce his blackness after writing a work that so emphatically asserts the necessity for proclaiming one's heritage.

It is its form that has particularly confused *Cane's* readers—beginning with a dispute as to whether the book is a novel or not. Robert Bone includes discussion of *Cane* in his book, *The Negro Novel in America* (1958), and this appears to have upset Darwin T. Turner, who states in his book, *In a Minor Chord*: "It is not a novel, not even the experimental novel for which Bone pleaded to justify including it in his study of novels by Negroes."[5] Turner refers to Toomer's *Cane* as "a collection of his works. . . ."[6] This confusion is the result of *Cane*'s unusual combination of poetry, prose, and drama. Many readers have regarded the work as little more than a series of short stories or vignettes, intermixed with lyrical poems, and concluding with a play called "Kabnis." They have been perplexed by the work's supposed lack of traditional unities: character, setting, action, time. Once again with a Third World novel, we encounter the problem of categorization, of trying to force a work into conventional literary pigeonholes.

Clearly this will not work with *Cane*. It is a unique piece of writing in the panorama of American literature and in the panorama of Third World writing—though it shares a number of similarities with works we have already examined. I suggest—as others have suggested[7]—that *Cane* is a lyrical novel, and, hence, structured by images. In fact, the lyrical novel is not that rare. Toomer's friend, Waldo Frank, published one the same year that Toomer did. It was called *Holiday*, also published by Boni and Liveright, and it grew out of the trip Frank took with Toomer in the South in 1921. *Holiday*, though not nearly as diffuse as *Cane*, also shares a racial theme. (The story ends with a lynching.) But while Frank's *Holiday* disintegrates into clichés, Toomer's *Cane*, structured as it is by a series of lyrical counterpoints or tensions, achieves a rare beauty and power which make it, for me, the most important novel ever written by an Afro-American writer. There is no way to illustrate this power better than by examining—at least briefly—its tripartite structure, a similarity *Cane* shares with Lamming's *In the Castle of My Skin*.

Part I of *Cane*\* is composed of six prose sections and ten poems. The time is shortly after World War I, the setting is the South, and the concentration is, for the most part, upon a number of women: Karintha, Becky, Carma, Fern, Esther, and Louisa. Except for the last of these, the women's names are used as titles for the prose sections. Almost all of them have led rather frustrated lives, usually dominating the men who lust after them. Karintha, for example, drives men mad, leaves no man fulfilled, though men lose their control around her. Becky, a white woman, is misunderstood by men and women and ostracized by the community because of her two mulatto children. Carma's husband is so jealous of other men and their attraction to her that he kills a man and ends up on a chain gang. The implication is quite clear: Carma has emasculated her husband. Fern, too, is unwilling to give of herself in any satisfying way. Esther, a mulatto, is frigid. Louise, in "Blood-

---

\*The three sections are not numbered but separated by circular markings which I will discuss later.

Burning Moon," is involved with two men: one black, one white. Her black lover kills her white lover and, in turn, is lynched by the white men of the community.

In all of these portraits, the focus is upon the women—the way they frustrate the men around them. All of the male/female relationships also leave something to be desired, two of them ending tragically for the men involved. Although these women are usually stronger than the men in their lives, they achieve little satisfaction from their domineering roles. Karintha leaves her child to die in the woods; Becky dies, her spirit haunting the forest; Esther lives in a dream world; Louisa does not realize that she is in large part responsible for the death of her two lovers. Sexual frustrations lead to illegitimacy, frigidity, and murder—and to no lasting peace for any of the characters involved.

Almost all of these stories take place in the dead of night, in darkness or at dusk—a characteristic *Cane* shares with Sherwood Anderson's *Winesburg, Ohio* (1919), which had a certain influence on Toomer's novel. Karintha's story begins with a fragment of poetry which is repeated several times throughout the story: "Her skin is like dusk on the eastern horizon/ . . . When the sun goes down."[8] Carma's story takes place in the darkness of the crescent moon; the narrator of "Fern" refers to the dusk that hides her; Esther's dream world disintegrates after dark; Louisa's two men are killed under the blood-burning moon. The implication is that all of these events happen only in the security of the dark, that black people are free to act and be themselves only after the sun goes down. The darkness liberates them, but it also destroys them.

In addition, darkness is used repeatedly throughout the poems in Part I of *Cane*—often a darkness related to the end of a unit of time, such as the cycle of planting and harvesting. "Reapers," the first poem, introduces this image of the termination of things—the end of the growing cycle. "November Cotton Flower" speaks of "winter's cold" and "dead birds" (p. 7). In "Face," and imagist poem, a woman's face is highlighted against the "evening sun" (p. 14). "Cotton Song" again describes a time of harvest; and "Song of the Sun"—the most important of the poems—states that "the sun is settin on/A song-lit race of slaves" (p. 21), thereby introducing the theme of slavery and the black man's past. The setting sun is referred to, again, in "Georgia Dusk," in "Nullo," which describes the western horizon, and in "Evening Song" which speaks of the full moon and a desire to sleep. Only the last two poems in Part I, "Conversion" and "Portrait in Georgia," contain no specific references to darkness, though "Conversion" describes a shift from the African past to the new world of Christianity.

These images of darkness and dusk establish a major tension in Toomer's novel, creating a nightmarish world of frustration and violence. They are important primarily because they depict a people living on the fringes of reality, repressing the horrors of the past and the conditions of the present. The future, Toomer implies, will be a continuation of these frustrations unless the black man comes to grips with the realities of his past, rooted as it is so horrendously in slavery and its tragic aftermath.

The aftermath of slavery is presented even more chaotically in Part II of Toomer's novel, in which we see the results of the great migration. Here the emphasis shifts from the South to the North, to Washington, D.C., and Chicago, during and after World War I. As a counterpoint to Part I, the focus is mostly upon black men, instead of black women, and the crippled lives they lead in industrialized Northern cities. The second part of *Cane* is composed of seven prose sections interspersed with five poems. While most of the stories in Part I take place outside in the natural world of cane fields and pine forests, most of the stories of the second take place inside of buildings which confine man's basic yearnings. The implication throughout *Cane* is clear: Toomer generally feels that the black man is better off in the South than in the North.

A mood piece, "Seventh Street," opens Part II, describing the "whitewashed" world of Washington. It begins and concludes with a four-line poem:

> Money burns the pocket, pocket hurts,
> Bootleggers in silken shirts,
> Ballooned, zooming Cadillacs,
> Whizzing, whizzing down the street-car tracks. (p. 71)

"Rhobert," the second prose segment in this part, describes Rhobert as wearing a dead house on his head, a burden so heavy that he is slowly sinking down. The narrator of "Avey" complains about Avey's untouchable nature. She gives him no peace; their relationship only frustrates him. "Theatre" treats a similar theme: John is frustrated because Dorris does not respond to his desires; he feels that his "body is separate from the thoughts that pack his mind" (p. 92). "Calling Jesus" briefly describes a woman cut off from her roots in the South, hiding in her religion.

The remaining two prose sections of Part II, longer than the earlier ones, develop more directly the tension of unfulfilled sexual desires. In the first of these, called "Box Seat," Dan Moore can hardly contain his feelings of anger and impotence. The city emasculates him; he has no job; he lusts after a young teacher numed Muriel, whose puritanical attitudes toward sex will not permit her to let herself go. She loves Dan but is afraid to express her feelings. Houses box Dan in, walls confine him: "The house contracts about him. It is a sharp-edged, massed, metallic house. Bolted" (p. 107). In the theatre at night, Dan thinks, "I am going to reach up and grab the girders of this building and pull them down" (p. 126). Dan Moore is powerless to act because he is exiled from his natural element: the soil of the South.

"Bona and Paul" shows us another sexually sterile relationship, this time between a white girl and a mulatto youth. The setting is Chicago, where both of them go to school. Paul tries to hide his black identity, not realizing that that is what makes him so attractive to Bona. She asks him, " 'Since when have men like you grown cold?' " (p. 150). Because of his indecisiveness, Bona eventually leaves him, and though Paul has begun to desire her, it is too late.

Many of the prose passages in Part II are set after dark, as are several of the poems, though the urban theme with its multiple infringements on man's freedom is also crucial to these poems. In the first poem, "Beehive," swarms of bees pass "in and out [of] the moon" (p. 89). The narrator refers to himself as a drone,

> Lying on my back,
> Lipping honey,
> Getting drunk with silver honey,
> Wish that I might fly out past the moon
> And curl forever in some far-off farmyard flower. (p. 89)

He fulfills his sexual role with the queen, but drone that he is, he has no sting, he gathers no honey. "Harvest Song," another poem set at sundown, speaks of the exile and alienation the narrator feels as he hungers for the cane fields of the South.

The setting shifts back to the South in "Kabnis," the third part of *Cane*. Some critics have referred to "Kabnis" as a novella, others have called it a play. My own feeling is that it reads as if it had been intended to be a movie scenario. Whatever it is, there are stage directions, occasional lines of poetry, and movement in and out of the main character's mind. Characteristically, much of Kabnis' story is set in the darkness of night.

At the beginning of the section, Ralph Kabnis, a teacher at a Georgia girls' school, is alone in his cabin, frightened by the noises outside. He longs for his home, Washington, D.C., from where he feels estranged. Other significant characters introduced in later passages in "Kabnis" include Fred Halsey, a shop-keeper and proprietor of the village forge; Hanby, Kabnis' Booker-T-Washington-like principal; Lewis, a fellow teacher and Northerner; three women, and an old man. Kabnis expresses his opinions on a variety of topics: black religion, slavery, color. The scenario ends the morning after Kabnis, Halsey, and Lewis have spent a night in the basement (known as the "hole") of Halsey's shop with two women, Stella and Cora. During that night, Kabnis renounces his color and his religion. Hidden away in the hole Halsey keeps an old man Lewis refers to as Father John.

What is of utmost significance in the third part of *Cane* is that the imagery of darkness continues until the last scene when it suddenly alters, providing the symbolic climax of the novel. The morning after the debauchery, Halsey's young sister, Carrie Kate, brings a plate of food to the old man, Father John. The images begin to change to lightness and rebirth. Kabnis pays little attention to Father John, though Carrie Kate tries to get him to talk. Father John mumbles, "Th sin whats fixed . . . upon th white folks . . . f tellin Jesus—lies" (p. 237). Kabnis climbs the stairs to the forge, leaving them alone, as the story concludes:

> Carrie's gaze follows him till he is gone. Then she goes to the old man and slips to her knees before him. Her lips murmur, "Jesus, come."
> Light streaks through the iron-barred cellar window. Within its soft circle, the figures of Carrie and Father John.
> Outside, the sun arises from its cradle in the tree-tops of the forest. Shadows of pines are dreams the sun shakes from its eyes. The sun arises. Gold-glowing child, it steps into the sky and sends a birth-song slanting down gray dust streets and sleepy windows of the southern town. (p. 239)

This is the first time that light has been used in any significant way in the novel. Always before we have seen the sun going down; now it is rising for the first time. Toomer implies that the symbolic unity of Carrie Kate's innocence and Father John's past will lead to a rebirth of the black race. Carrie Kate realizes this, for she is not embarrassed by the old man as her brother is. Father John, representative of the black man's past in the United States—that is, slavery—must not be hidden away but brought out into the light of truth and understanding. Carrie Kate knows that black people should not be ashamed of their past, but acknowledge it and construct their present lives out of this comprehension. Only then will they be free of the frustrations that Toomer has illustrated in all of the relationships (male/female, black/white) in his novel.

The imagery modulation of *Cane* is far more complex than I have been able to illustrate in this analysis. Images of darkness saturate the novel, related as they are to most of the other dramatic tensions within the work: the land itself, and the cycles of planting and harvesting; the contrasts between North and South, city and country; the references to past and present (especially as they are related to slavery and the African theme); industrialization and exploitation of the black worker; the conflicts of black and white, male and female; the place of religion in the black man's life. All of these contrasts are woven in and out of Toomer's novel, giving it a rare emotional and intellectual complexity—for, if nothing else, *Cane* is an intellectual challenge. These themes are also related, as we will shortly see, to the problem of the narrator or narrative consciousness within the novel.

Perhaps the most significant of the images is that of the land itself, the soil in which, according to Toomer, the black man's heritage is rooted. Toomer did, after all, use cane as his title image: tall, proud like the black man, strongly rooted in the land. Dozens of references to sugar cane punctuate the work, though the image is not totally positive. After all, it is northern industrialism and exploitation that keep black people in the South on the farm, forever tilling the soil. Cane takes on a number of disparate meanings. In "Blood-Burning Moon," Bob Stone relates boiling sugar cane to sex, as if the odor of the cane were responsible for his attraction to Louisa: "... it was because she was nigger that he went to her. Sweet... The scent of boiling cane came to him" (p. 61). Tom Burwell kills Bob on a pathway through the cane fields. In "Box Seat" Dan is aware of a "portly Negress" sitting close to him in the theatre:

A soil-soaked fragrance comes from her. Through the cement floor her strong roots sink down. They spread under the asphalt streets. Dreaming, the streets roll over on their bellies, and suck their glossy health from them. Her strong roots sink down and spread under the river and disappear in blood-lines that waver south. Her roots shoot down. Dan's hands follow them. Roots throb. Dan's heart beats violently. He places his palms upon the earth to cool them. Earth throbs. Dan's heart beats violently. (p. 119)

In "Kabnis," Ralph thinks of the land, "The earth my mother" (p. 161), but he refuses to pay homage to the earth's magnetic pull. Lewis looks at Kabnis and thinks, "Kabnis, a promise of a soil-soaked beauty; up-rooted, thinning out. Suspended a few feet above the soil whose touch would resurrect him" (p. 191). Earlier, in "Fern," Toomer noted the potential of the land by stating, "When one is on the soil of one's ancestors, most anything can come to one..." (p. 31).

The conflicts between North and South are closely related to the land and its economic base—an idea that W. E. B. DuBois used similarly in his novel, *The Quest of the Silver Fleece*. We have already noted the shift from South to North to South again in the three major divisions of the novel, along with Toomer's implications that black people are less inhibited in the South than they are in the North. (Toomer's black women in the North, for example, are not as free as those in the South since they suffer repressions that make them frigid.) The narrator of "Avey" who lives in Washington thinks back to the South, referring to it as the "soil of my homeland" (p. 85). In "Bona and Paul," Paul looks out of his dormitory window and thinks of his home in the South, a "pine-matted hillock in Georgia. He sees the slanting roofs of gray unpainted cabins tinted lavender. A Negress chants a lullaby beneath the mate-eyes of a Southern planter" (pp. 137–138). Like the portly Negress in "Box Seat," Paul knows he is out of his element in the North. In both the poems and prose sections that combine to make up Part II, then, Toomer depicts the black man as an exile in the North, uprooted from the land that would give him nourishment.

The South, of course, suffers its own multiple problems, not the least of which is economic exploitation from the northern industrial giants. Again and again Toomer contrasts the softness and the beauty of the land with the destruction wrought by the industrial age, foreshadowing a later Afro-American novel that gives much the same picture: William Attaway's *Blood on the Forge* (1941). A major image of Part I is the sawmill, ripping apart the pine trees. In "Karintha," Toomer mentions the smoke from the sawmill several times, a sharp contrast to the bed of pine-needles "smooth and sweet" (p. 4) on which Karintha drops her child. The image of the sawmill is repeated in "Carma" and linked to the railroad that comes in and transports the cut wood to the North. It is similar to the use of the railroad in Lamming's *In the Castle of My Skin*—economic exploitation by proxy, rape of the land until it is barren.

In "Becky" the railroad is mentioned several times; Becky builds her cabin on "the narrow strip of land between the railroad and the road" (p. 9). "Song of the Son" mentions the "sawdust glow of night,/Into the velvet pine-smoke air to-night . . ." (p. 21), and "Georgia Duck" describes the

> Smoke from the pyramidal sawdust pile
>     Curls up, blue ghosts of trees, tarrying low
>     Where only chips and stumps are left to show
> The solid proof of former domicile. (p. 22)

All the trees will soon be gone from here, just as they were cut down in Lamming's village. The industrial theme reaches a crescendo in "Blood-Burning Moon," in which there are multiple references to the "factory town" of the story's setting—this time, however, pre-war cotton factories. Toomer repeats the following lines of poetry three times:

> Red nigger moon. Sinner!
> Blood-burning moon. Sinner!
> Come out that fact'ry door. (p. 53)

His meaning is clear. For the black man in the South, slavery did not end with the Civil War. The economic exploitation that continued results in its own emotional scars. Modern slavery, no matter what you call it.

Slavery—as I have already suggested—is one of the main themes of *Cane*: acknowledging it, coming to grips with the past. The word is first used in "Song of the Son," in which Toomer refers to his characters as "A song-lit race of slaves" (p. 21). His own role is to carol "softly souls of slavery" (p. 21), to sing of all black men in America, of all victims of slavery. In "Esther," slavery is given a more historical perspective, which should remind us of Pa's dream in *In the Castle of My Skin*. While in a religious trance, Barlo mumbles,

> "I saw a vision. I saw a man arise, an he was big an black an powerful . . . but his head was caught up in th clouds. An while he was agazin at th heavens, heart filled up with th Lord, some little white-ant biddies came an tied his feet to chains. They led him t th coast, they led him t th sea, they led him across th ocean an they didnt set him free. The old coast didnt miss him, an th new coast wasnt free, he left the old-coast brothers, t give birth t you an me." (pp. 38–39)

Proud, strong Africans were stripped of their identities by slavery. In "Box Seat," Dan Moore uses "slave" and "slavery" several times to refer to the people around him in the North. We have already noted that Father John in "Kabnis" was born a slave before the Civil War, for which reason Halsey and others keep him hidden away in the hole. But other characters in "Kabnis" are also referred to as slaves. Lewis looks at Kabnis and the word "slave" enters his mind. Kabnis also carries the slavery idea into the current day, asking Father John, "Do y think youre out of slavery? Huh? Youre where they used t throw th worked-out, no-count slaves. On a damp clammy floor of a dark scum-hole" (p. 233). Slavery has no historical demarcation.

The slavery motif is related to Africa a number of times throughout the novel, as we have already seen in Barlo's soliloquy in "Esther." In "Carma" when Carma is walking through the forest, her mind suddenly conjures up an African image, and she thinks she has returned to her homeland: "She is in the forest, dancing. Torches flare . . . juju men, greegree, witch-doctors . . . torches go out . . . The Dixie Pike has grown from a goat path in Africa" (pp. 17–18). This belief that the African heritage is manifested in the woods is reiterated in a stanza in "Georgia Dusk":

> Meanwhile, the men, with vestiges of pomp,
> Race memories of king and caravan,
> High-priests, an ostrich, and a juju-man,
> Go singing through the footpaths of the swamp. (p. 22)

But it is in "Conversion" that Toomer speaks most bitterly of what the Africa heritage has become:

> African Guardian of Souls,
> Drunk with rum,
> Feasting on a strange cassava,

Yielding to new words and a weak palabra
Of a white-faced sardonic god—
Grins, cries
Amen,
Shouts hosanna. (p. 49)

There is something about the grin of the new God of Christianity that speaks most tragically about the failures of organized religion for blacks in the New World, thus introducing another important theme of Toomer's *Cane*—natural versus organized religion. Ultimately, that African God, drunk with rum, is preferable to Christianity.

We have only to remember Toomer's own later life, when he wrote for the *Friends Intelligencer,* to realize that there is more than one inconsistency between Toomer's ideas as expressed in *Cane* and those practiced in his later life, for organized religion in *Cane* is generally depicted as a form of escapism for the black man. In "Cotton Song," it is true, religion is a welcome release from the back-breaking work of the cotton fields: Judgment Day is the day the shackles will fall and man will be free. Here religion has a positive function—as it does in many traditional Negro spirituals; it permits one to endure the toils of the present. In several later places, however, religion is mocked as a kind of fraud, a white man's con game to take advantage of innocent black people. Barlo plays this kind of role, a little like Rinehart in Ralph Ellison's *Invisible Man* (1952). In "Calling Jesus" Toomer describes an old woman who relies on her religion: "Her soul is like a little thrust-tailed dog that follows her, whimpering" (p. 102).

In "Kabnis" the pot shots at organized religion are ubiquitous. Kabnis rants and raves about black folks' religion: "This preacher-ridden race. Pray and shout. Theyre in the preacher's hands. Thats what it is. And the preacher's hands are in the white man's pockets" (p. 174). Kabnis says that he gave up going to church because he couldn't stand the shouting. Father John's indictment of religion is total: whites used the Bible to justify slavery ("Th sin whats fixed ... upon th white folks ... f tellin Jesus—lies," p. 237); or, as Nancy Carter Goodley has written, "The white people made the Bible lie by not telling their slaves that Christ was black."[9]

Toomer's concern with religion grows from his interest in race relations, and the tenuousness of black/white relationships is at the heart of *Cane* as it is in so many Third World novels. Becky is ostracized by the community for mothering two mulatto children. Esther and Paul's problems develop in large part because they are mulattos—so light skinned they can pass. Kabnis, Toomer's alter-ego, belongs to the same category: he cannot decide how important his color should be. It is this repeated interest in the potential of passing, in the issue of the mulatto who is of neither race, that takes us directly to the question of narrative voice and point of view in Toomer's *Cane,* the place of the narrator and that narrator's dilemma about his color. For me this is the singular most fascinating aspect of Toomer's novel, its emotional center.

In his introduction to the paperbacked edition of *Cane,* Arna Bontemps hints at the importance of the narrative voice in the work: "A young poet-observer moves through the book."[10] Bontemps did not have the space in his introduction to illustrate how this is achieved or to indicate the multiple places where this poet-observer is present. In many first person narratives the "I" is not necessarily identical with the author, but there are indications that such an identification should be made in *Cane.* I suggest that this narrator-observer, this fictive persona, is a disguise that Toomer has employed to hide his own presence in the novel. Expressed another way, it is possible for us to speak of a "main character" in *Cane*—Jean Toomer himself, skillfully playing the role of the narrative consciousness. Toomer's function in *Cane,* then, is much the same as George Lamming's in *In the Castle of My Skin. Cane* is every bit as much an autobiography as is Lamming's work—except that Toomer has gone to even more extreme pains to hide his presence in the novel than Lamming did in his. We always know where Lamming is in his work; of Toomer we can not always be certain. Both works, however, employ the effacement of the main character in order to emphasize the greater importance of the community, the collective consciousness of a race.

Jean Toomer is present as the first person narrator in twelve of the twenty-eight sections of Parts I and II of *Cane:* in "Reapers," "Becky," "Carma," "Song of the Son," "Fern," and "Evening Song" in Part I; in "Avey," "Beehive," "Her Lips Are Copper Wire," "Calling Jesus," "Prayer," and "Harvest Song" in Part II. In some of these sequences Toomer is a character, a participant in the activities described; at other times he is an observer, like Joseph Conrad's Marlow. In most of these sequences Toomer uses the first person singular—often so infrequently, however, that the reader may not notice its presence. In two other major sections ("Bona and Paul" and "Kabnis") I think we can say that Toomer has disguised himself as the mulatto who cannot decide whether he should be black or white. Given this reading, *Cane* must be regarded as the story of Jean Toomer's inability to accept his racial origins—not just his blackness, but his whiteness too.

Toomer's first appearance in *Cane* is in the first poem, "Reapers," in which he is an observer. The poem, about harvesting, relates the end of the growing cycle to violence and death: "I see the blade,/Blood-stained, continue cutting weeds and shade" (p. 6). Ostensibly the blood referred to is that of a field rat, but the laborers themselves are victims

of similar sudden deaths. "Reapers" serves to set the scene, to introduce
Toomer, the poet-observer of the novel. It also introduces a number
of tensions we have already noted, but Toomer's presence here is not
nearly as important as it is in "Becky," the first prose section in which
he appears as a participant.

"Becky" is one of the most important sections of the entire work—the
only story of a white woman. Her tale opens with four brief lines of
retrospective narrative:

> Becky was the white woman who had two
> Negro sons. She's dead; they've gone away.
> The pines whisper to Jesus. The Bible flaps
> its leaves with an aimless rustle on her mound. (p. 8)

Who gave her these sons? The white folks say it was a "Damn buck
nigger" (p. 8). The black folks reply, "Low-down nigger with no self-
respect" (p. 8). A dual point of view, then, is introduced early in the
story—the only time in the novel that Toomer expands his viewpoint
to express both black and white sentiments in a commonly-felt response:
their reactions to Becky's mulatto child. Although Becky is ostracized,
forced to live outside of the town, nevertheless the community extends
a kind of protective, almost maternal attitude toward her. "White folks
and black folks built her cabin" (p. 8), Toomer says, on a piece of land
near the railroad, and various people from the town supply her with
food. Then Becky has a second mulatto child and somewhat later the
villagers believe that she has died. They refuse to permit her two sons
to work in the town, so Becky's boys seek refuge elsewhere. When smoke
again curls up from Becky's chimney, the villagers believe she may not
have died—or, perhaps, that her ghost is living in her cabin. But they
are never certain.

These are the facts that Toomer develops in the first four pages of
his story—a kind of thumb-nail sketch, poetically drawn as if we were
in Edwin Arlington Robinson's Tilbury Town. Then the emphasis shifts
in the remaining two pages, where Toomer introduces himself as the
first-person narrator, employing at the same time the first person plural
to typify the black part of the community, now separate from the white.
Toomer, as member of a church congregation returning from Pulverton,
passes Becky's cabin near the railroad:

> the ground trembled as a ghost train rumbled by. The chimney fell
> into the cabin. Its thud was like a hollow report, ages having passed
> since it went off. Barlo and I were pulled out of our seats. Dragged
> to the door that had swung open. Through the dust we saw the bricks
> in a mound upon the floor. Becky, if she was there, lay under them.
> I thought I heard a groan. Barlo, mumbling something, threw his
> Bible on the pile. (p. 12)

When they return to the village, they tell others about their experience. The story concludes with the same four lines with which it began, this time used as summary.

"Becky" is one of the most significant stories in *Cane,* not simply because it introduces Toomer as a first person narrator participant, but because it places him within the communal center—a community expanded so that it represents more than just the black or the white villagers. Toomer is a part of the community—much more centrally involved than he will be in most of the later sections of the novel, where he becomes increasingly distanced from his fellow blacks.* In the character of Becky herself we see a kind of microcosmic treatment of black/white relationships in the South as a whole: willingness to render limited aid and recognition, buffered at the same time by social ostracism. Becky is an embarrassment to both groups, yet she must be taken care of. Her estrangement from the community will be the same as Toomer's own as the narrative continues.

In "Carma," Toomer's voice is again that of an observer witness, the teller of Carma's tale. At the beginning of the story, Toomer states, "I leave the men around the stove to follow her with my eyes down the red dust road" (p. 16). He re-enters the story at the end, by asking, "Should she not take others, this Carma, strong as a man, whose tale as I have told it is the crudest melodrama?" (p. 20). Toomer is linked to the other men in the story, fascinated by the strong-armed woman, but his primary role is that of story-teller, witness.

In "Song of the Son" Toomer's position is symbolic of his place in the entire novel: the recording consciousness of a race before its past is forgotten, a position similar to that of the griot in traditional African life. In a rich, hymn-like chant, the poem begins with Toomer's voice, singing of the "parting soul in song" (p. 21). As his song passes over the valley, Toomer says,

> Now just before an epoch's sun declines
> Thy son, in time, I have returned to thee,
> Thy son, I have in time returned to thee. (p. 21)

Toomer speaks of his obligation, the poet's duty to his people: before a period of their history is forgotten, before the sun sets on the aftermath of slavery, he will record this past on paper. Though the sun is setting "on/A song-lit race of slaves, it has not set," (p. 21), it is not yet too late to record this past "to catch thy plantive soul, leaving soon gone,/ Leaving, to catch thy plantive soul soon gone" (p. 21). As he addresses his people ("Negro slaves"), comparing them to "dark purple ripened

*In "Becky" Toomer still has his religion, still participates in organized religious functions. He is quite different from what he will become in "Kabnis."

plums," he tells them that one seed from the past has survived and that seed will become

> An everlasting song, a singing tree,
> Caroling softly souls of slavery,
> What they were, and what they are to me,
> Caroling softly souls of slavery. (p. 21)

"Song of the Son" (of Toomer as a son of slavery, of the sun setting on slavery) is Toomer's most direct statement in the novel of the need for understanding the past before it is forgotten. We have already seen in Lamming's *In the Castle of My Skin* how slavery and the African heritage can be forgotten, how the teachers at Lamming's school teach European history only, thereby renouncing their own traditional customs. Toomer does not want this to happen to his people. "Song of the Son" is his vow that it will not happen, and *Cane* is the fulfillment of that vow: it shows black people as they would perhaps not always want to be depicted, but Toomer believes that even out of slavery something good may come. Man has only these examples in his past to learn from.

Toomer's next appearance in *Cane* is in "Fern," this time as a participant rather than a witness as he was in "Carma." Fern's story is told from his point of view, stressing his lack of fulfillment in their relationship. A number of autobiographical facts are revealed:

> I first saw her on her porch. I was passing with a fellow whose crusty numbness (I was from the North and suspected of being prejudiced and stuck-up) was melting as he found me warm. I asked him who she was. "That's Fern," was all that I could get from him. (pp. 27–28)

Toomer speaks of his strange attraction to her, the same attraction that so many other men felt: "I felt bound to her. I too had my dreams: something I would do for her" (p. 28). He becomes obsessed with helping Fern, improving her lot. One night when he gets up his courage, he asks her to take a walk with him. As they stroll down the pike, a strange feeling comes over him, introducing—for Toomer now—the belief that he is out of place in the South, a clue that he will later renounce his own people: "I felt strange, as I always do in Georgia, particularly at dusk. I felt that things unseen to men were tangibly immediate. It would not have surprised me had I had [a] vision" (p. 31). As he holds Fern in his arms, he thinks he is holding God. Then Fern faints and Toomer later gets ugly looks from the townspeople who believe he has taken advantage of her. As he looks back at this incident in his life, he realizes he is perplexed because nothing had happened between the two of them, except for the strange attraction and the quasi-religious experience. The fact is that nothing happened (though Fern was apparently willing) because Toomer could not make up his mind to act. And this indecisiveness, we will see, is a trait demonstrated frequently in *Cane*. Toomer's last appearance in Part I of the novel is in "Evening Song"—one of the few love poems in the book—wishfully describing Cloine sleeping next to him, her lips pressed against his heart.

In Part II of *Cane*, Toomer first appears as a participant in the prose section titled "Avey." The story appears to be the most autobiographical section in the entire novel, again relating an unconsummated sexual desire on the part of the narrator. Toomer begins, "For a long while she was nothing more to me than one of those skirted beings whom boys at a certain age disdain to play with. Just how I came to love her, timidly, and with secret blushes, I do not know" (p. 76). Toomer jealously watches Avey's visits to a college fellow's room late at night. Once when they were still in school, he had been alone with her on the upper deck of a steamer on the Potomac River: "I could feel by the touch of it that it wasnt a man-to-woman love" (p. 80). Another time when he is alone with her, Toomer describes her as indifferent to his presence, yet his passion for Avey does not die. When he goes away to college in Wisconsin, he begins to think of her as "no better than a whore" (p. 84). Their last encounter five years later is the least satisfactory of them all. Avey falls asleep as he talks proudly about his future hopes and ideals.

We have already noted Toomer's role of the "drunk" drone in "Beehive." He appears next in "Her Lips Are Copper Wire," another quasi-love poem, describing what must be a dream instead of reality: romantic fantasies. In the short prose piece, "Calling Jesus," Toomer is the observer/recorder of the sad, puppy-dog woman. In "Prayer," Toomer begins,

> My body is opaque to the soul.
> Driven of the spirit, long have I sought to temper it unto the spirit's
>     longing,
> But my mind, too, is opaque to the soul. (p. 131)

Here Toomer relates himself to the other Northern males in Part II who also feel a separation of mind and body—an idea continued in "Harvest Song," the last use of the first person singular in the novel:

> I am a reaper. (Eoho!) All my oats are cradled. But I am too fatigued to bind them. And I hunger. I crack a grain. It has no taste to it. My throat is dry . . .
> O my brothers, I beat my palms, still soft, against the stubble of my harvesting. (You beat your soft palms, too.) My pain is sweet. Sweeter than the oats or wheat or corn. It will not bring me knowledge of my hunger. (p. 133)

The remaining two sections of the novel are "Bona and Paul" and "Kabnis." In the first, Toomer's role is a prefiguration of his position in "Kabnis." In both of these sections, however, his identity is disguised as the mulatto unable to act decisively. The night Paul takes Bona to the Crimson Gardens, Bona says she loves him. Paul finds this disturbing because Bona loves him for what he does not want to recognize: his blackness. He is unable to return her love because he is incapable of accepting his black blood. When the two of them go to a segregated night club, even the Negro doorman does not realize that Paul is passing. "What is he, a Spaniard, an Indian, an Italian, a Mexican, a Hindu, or a Japanese?" (p. 145). Paul feels the icy stares of the other people at the club, fearing, of course, that they will realize he is a Negro. It is when they begin to dance that Bona asks him. " 'Since when have men like you grown cold?' " (p. 150). In her frustration, Bona says she wants to leave the club, and the two of them walk to the door. The black doorman realizes that Paul is a Negro, passing, and he smiles because he guesses that the two of them are leaving to go somewhere and make love.* They leave the club, but Paul, still embarrassed about his color, returns to the doorman to inform him that he is wrong—thus renouncing both his blackness and his passion. When he returns to the place where he left Bona, she is gone. In the character of Paul we see the central dilemma of Toomer's own life: indecisiveness coupled with an inability to come to grips with his racial heritage. At the end of the story, there is a hint that Paul has decided to accept his black heritage, that he has begun to understand who he is.

Ralph Kabnis (cannabis?), unfortunately, totally rejects his heritage, just as Toomer did later in his own life. I have referred to Kabnis as Jean Toomer thinly disguised because of the similarities he shares with his creator: a Northerner teaching in the South, a mulatto light enough to pass. Toomer also refers to him as a would-be poet, and the description he gives of him is similar to pictures of Toomer published in recent anthologies that have included his work: "Kabnis' thin hair is streaked on the pillow. His hand strokes the slim silk of his mustache. His thumb, pressed under his chin, seems to be trying to give squareness and projection to it. Brown eyes stare from a lemon face" (p. 158). Like Toomer, Kabnis has come South to find his identity, yet he longs for the North: "Christ, how cut off from everything he is. And hours, hours north, why not say a lifetime north? Washington sleeps. Its still, peaceful streets, how desirable they are" (p. 163). There is, of course, an inconsistency here which Toomer explains as "impotent nostalgia" (p. 163).

Many of Kabnis' fears are the result of his feelings of exile. Halsey speaks of him as the "Coldest Yankee I've ever seen" (p. 170). When Kabnis hears the shouting coming from a black church, he says, "We dont have that sort of thing up North" (p. 175). After a stone crashes

*He may also be smiling because he realizes that Paul has been successful in passing.

through Halsey's store window, Kabnis—though he has already spoken of himself as a "gentleman" the whites would not dare touch—fears he will be lynched. The stone was meant for Lewis, of whom Toomer states, "He is what a stronger Kabnis might have been, and in an odd faint way resembles him" (p. 189). Accurately stated, Lewis is what Toomer wishes he were. Together, Kabnis and Lewis represent the split in Toomer's own personality—what he wants to be (Lewis) and what he will soon become (Kabnis). When Kabnis first meets Lewis, Toomer says of the latter, "As he steps towards the others, he seems to be issuing sharply from a vivid dream," (pp. 189–190) marked contrast to the dream world that Ralph Kabnis lives in. Lewis has quit his job and intends to return to his home in the North when the month is up. I have already noted the passage in which Toomer develops his contrast of the two men, describing Kabnis as "suspended a few feet above the soil whose touch would resurrect him" (p. 191). Lewis, though a Northerner, does not suffer a sense of estrangement from his home. He is confident, aware of his identity—qualities that bother other blacks and lead them to force him to leave the southern town.

When Lewis sees Carrie Kate for the first time, there is a kind of spontaneous reaction between the two of them, an immediate affinity:

> Their meeting is a swift sun-burst. Lewis impulsively moves towards her. His mind flashes images of her life in the southern town. He sees the nascent woman, her flesh already stiffening to cartilage, drying to bone. Her spirit-bloom, even now touched sullen, bitter. Her rich beauty fading . . . He wants to—He stretches forth his hands to hers. He takes them. They feel like warm cheeks against his palms. The sun-burst from her eyes floods up and haloes him. (p. 205)

Lewis' reactions to the old man in Halsey's cellar are the same; when he first sees him, he is unable to take his eyes off him. He refers to the old man as "A mute John the Baptist of a new religion—or a tongue-tied shadow of an old" (p. 211). Both descriptions are accurate. Lewis calls him "Father John," thinking as he does so,

> Slave boy whom some Christian mistress taught to read the Bible. Black man who saw Jesus in the ricefields, and began preaching to his people. Moses- and Christ-words used for songs. Dead blind father of a muted folk who feel their way upward to a life that crushes or absorbs them. (p. 212)

When the prostitutes, Cora and Stella, arrive for a night of debauchery, Lewis pays no attention to them, concerned as he is with the old man: "Lewis, seated now so that his eyes rest upon the old man, merges with his source and lets the pain and beauty of the South meet him there" (p. 214).

Kabnis' reactions to Father John are cold and impersonal. For him, the old man looks like "any done-up preacher" (p. 217). For him, Father John does not represent the past. As he tells Lewis, "Jam some false teeth in his mouth and crank him, an youd have God Almighty spit in torrents all around th floor. Oh, hell, an he reminds me of that black cockroach over yonder. An besides, he aint my past. My ancestors were Southern blue-bloods—" (p. 217). It is a most revealing remark. Bluebloods had such light skin that their veins shone through, making it possible for them to pass. Kabnis has made his choice of identity as white instead of black. "Aint much difference between blue [that is, Caucasion] an black" (p. 218), he adds. Lewis replies that the difference is that between master and slave, but getting little response from Kabnis or the others, he leaves the cellar and plunges out into the night.

In the morning, when the final scene takes place, Kabnis continues haranguing the old man, reacting to his mutterings by telling him to shut up. In the midst of Father John's mumblings about sin, Kabnis refers to the black race as "that bastard race thats roamin round th country" (p. 237). Then he climbs up to Halsey's shop, too soon to witness the miracle between Carrie Kate and Father John (the sunrise, symbolizing a rebirth for the black race).

Toomer's portrait of Kabnis is an accurate picture of himself. One suspects that the publication of *Cane* must have acted as a kind of exorcism, bringing Toomer's own identity problems to a climax. Just months after Boni and Liveright published the novel, in the summer of 1923, Toomer protested against the publisher's suggestion that the book be publicized as the work of a Negro writer. Darwin T. Turner has written that Toomer replied to their request by saying, " 'If my relationship with you is to be what I'd like it to be, I must insist that you never use such a word, such a thought again.' "[11] Turner adds, "Afterwards Toomer never again wrote about people who can be identified as Afro-American."[12] The results were tragic for his writing. Scholars who have sifted through the 30,000 manuscript pieces Toomer left Fisk University Library have concluded that very little of the material is of publishable merit. Again, Darwin T. Turner's conclusion here is particularly apt: "What matters is that Jean Toomer's artistic stature diminished after he repudiated his African ancestry and rejected Afro-American subjects. "[13]

None of this, however, diminishes the brilliance of *Cane*. Its position in the center of the Harlem Renaissance is described by Nathan Huggins in his excellent history of that movement:

The real power of Jean Toomer's conception and its superiority to the romanticisms of McKay and Cullen was that *Cane*, though symbolic and mystical, dealt with the past as a palpable reality. It faced the fact of the South and slavery. The final, and perhaps supreme, irony of the primitives was that they were, in their quest of Africa, in their fancy of Timbuctoo and Alexandria, forsaking their actual past. They were in effect denying that which was immediate, personal, and discernible for something which was vague, distant, half-myth. Toomer asked to embrace the slave father, while Countee Cullen fancied "spicy grove and cinnamon tree." For all of its search for ancestral roots, the quest for Africa denied the soil in which the particular plant had sprouted. It is a supreme irony because it is so characteristically American. Black Americans, like white Americans, dissatisfied with and unfulfiilled by the selves that they had, sought escape in exotica.[14]

*Cane* is the most original piece of writing an Afro-American writer has fashioned; it is one of the most innovative works of twentieth century American fiction—a landmark in American literature, anticipating the soon-to-follow experimental works of John Dos Passos and William Faulkner. The experimental novel in America begins not with those writers but with Jean Toomer's *Cane*. Besides the mixture of the three genres (poetry, prose, and drama), many of the techniques used by Dos Passos and Faulkner are present in *Cane*: stream of consciousness developed primarily by the use of the interior monologue; the use of multiple points of view; disruption of the temporal element; alteration of the traditional unities of plot, character, setting.* There is even some attempt to make use of pictorial designs in the circular lines that introduce each section of the novel:**

These have been variously interpreted as male and female symbols and as signs representing the sun and the moon. When they are superimposed on top of one another, they do not form a complete circle as some readers have suggested, but, rather, a circle not quite whole, which reflects

---

*There is more unity of character than I have illustrated in this analysis. If Toomer is the main character, Barlo is at least of supporting interest, since he appears in three sections of the novel: "Becky," "Esther," and "Blood-Burning Moon."

**In reproducing the plates of the original 1923 edition for the 1967 hardbacked reprint and the 1969 paperback—and for the 1975 new edition of the work—the first of these designs was left out. Presumaby, the publishers have felt the designs are of no importance.

Toomer's central theme: the instability of black lives, the unfulfilled nature of their existence because of an inability to understand the past.

As an example of Third World fiction, *Cane* is as difficult to pigeonhole as it is to categorize in American fiction. Certainly Toomer's disguised image of himself as the main character and the concentration on the community places him with other Third World novelists who have relied on situational conflicts. The common experience here is of slavery and its aftermath, of understanding that slavery is not circumscribed by historical dates. The symbolic ending with the burst of sun between Carrie Kate and Father John can only be considered emblematic of the potential for an entire race of people, not simply for these two minor characters, since the work (and its image pattern) must ultimately be regarded as a whole—the way of life of an entire race of people.

Toomer's personal vacillation between black and white damaged his own psyche beyond repair. I think Darwin T. Turner is correct when he says that in the end Toomer did not identify himself as a Caucasian any more than he did as an Afro-American, that he was "self-exiled from all races."[15] That is why the biography of Jean Toomer serves to illuminate our interpretations of his masterpiece, for *Cane* was not only his swan song but his attempt to wrestle with the central problem of his life—his racial heritage. If Toomer was in the long run unable to accept his mixed heritage, *Cane* has made it possible for others to realize theirs. We have only to remember W. E. B. DuBois's prophetic statement made in 1903, in *The Souls of Black Folk*: "The problem of the twentieth century is the problem of the color-line . . . ."[16]

# 6
# Revolt and Rebirth, Cultural Renewal

Raja Rao's *Kanthapura*
Kamala Markandaya's *Two Virgins*

The geography of the Third World is so extensive, embracing the peoples of so many disparate countries and continents, that any attempt to single out one novel as representative of all the others would be impossible. Yet literary criticism thrives on categorization and comparison. It is difficult to talk about any individual novel without mentioning others, a problem we encounter when we write about a work even from our own culture. The problems of interpretation can only be multiplied when we examine novels from half a dozen different areas of the world. It becomes almost impossible to speak of one of them in singular fashion. Novel X shares a number of similarities with Novel Y, and these affinities, of course, only stand to be increased if the cultures that produced them share a number of basic similarities.

It is not, however, only a similarity of cultural practices but the common experiences these cultures have undergone that connects the fiction from different areas of the Third World. The shock of exposure to the West and its multiple aspects of exploitation coupled with the threat of cultural extermination is the common background to all of the works we have examined in this study—whether they be African, West Indian, Papuan, Afro-American, or Native American. It is the centuries-old upheaval generated by the West that relates Indo-Anglian fiction to the novels written by authors from the other areas we have already examined. Indian writers who use English as their language of expression have also reflected upon the various stages of colonialism as it controlled Indian life. Colonialism is in the fiction of still another group of writers, but this time a number of other apparent similarities disappear.

As we begin our examination of three Indo-Anglian novels,* we can see that when the novels from the different Third World countries are placed together, their subject matter falls into several categories; by topic they cluster around certain themes. Some novels record the initial exposure of these peoples to the West, such as we saw in *Batouala,* when the West appeared to be so strong that the other culture would be completely destroyed. We also saw this shock of the initial exposure in *Seven Arrows* and in *Bound to Violence,* though both of these works, since they cover so many years, extend beyond this period. For a time it looked as if total extermination of a race or at least the cultural tenets of that race of people would be the outcome in a number of these instances, but at a later stage, after colonialism has been a reality for an apparently never-ending period of time, a different kind of shift begins to take place. Certain checks and balances, rooted in the cultures themselves, begin to take hold, perhaps even without an awareness in these peoples of what is happening. Events begin to occur. Call it cultural reorganization if you want: a struggle for life or death played out between the colonial powers and their "possessions" in the colonies.

Perhaps the earliest of these shifts within the cultures themselves is the surfacing of the communal consciousness, the collective nature of traditional life. People begin to band together to meet the common force, and the literary result, as we have seen, is the situational plot: content influences from. The subject matter of the novel is not the individual's confrontation with his own problems but the conflict between two collective groups, two cultures, worked out in any number of permutations: Batouala's villagers against the French; the Plains Indians against the white invaders, the Afro-American confronting the white American. The situation is the same in all of these cases: one group of people trying to liberate itself from the stronghold of the other.

The individual, powerless by himself, gets lost in the shuffle; he cannot singlehandedly fight the oppressors. His fate, after all, is the same as everyone else's. They are all being exploited in one way or another by the colonial invaders. Colonialism forced these peoples to band to-

---

*R. K. Narayan's *Grateful to Life and Death* will be discussed at the beginning of the next chapter.

gether, forced them to renew the cultural roots which have lain dormant
for some time, in the form of group solidarity, the communal collectivity.
No doubt there were cultural heroes in the mythologies of all of these
peoples. Colonialism simply brought a halt to that aspect of their lives—it
became the great emasculator.

In almost all of these books, the group has been represented by the
village or the tribe. In *Batouala* it is both of these. In Eri's *The Crocodile*
and Lamming's *In the Castle of My Skin* it is the village, though Lamming
also develops the idea of a global consciousness, uniting all Third World
peoples. In *Bound to Violence* it is extended to include several neighboring
tribes as it is in *Seven Arrows*. Even in *Cane,* it seems to me, that at
least in Parts I and III one finds a semblance of village life. In almost
all of these works it is difficult to delineate one person as the main
character, since the situation affects all of them. The individual consciousness has not fully emerged—though we know it is about to do so, as
is indicated by the position taken by George Lamming at the end of
*In the Castle of My Skin* and Toomer's cryptic stance in *Cane.*

All of these novels (with the exception of *Cane* because of its special
characteristics) are set before the group consciousness has been able
to strengthen itself and undertake the rigorous struggle necessary for
independence. (*Bound to Violence*, as we have seen, ends supposedly after
independence from France, but Ouologuem's message is quite clear:
the struggle is far from over.) The results these novels depict are dis-
similar, however. In *Batouala* there is hardly anything but total chaos
and frustration. In *The Crocodile,* Eri shows the beginning awareness
of what exploitation really means, but the end is again frustration and
confusion. *In the Castle of My Skin* takes us closer to the revolution that
will be necessary if independence is ever going to be achieved, but it
is still at an inchoate stage. The other novels (*Bound to Violence, Cane,*
and *Seven Arrows*) in one way or another illustrate that political independence must be matched with cultural independence, for the cultures
themselves are no longer what they were.

For the most part, Indo-Anglian fiction represents a somewhat later
period in the Third World/Western conflict: the group consciousness
is shown as a powerful force to be reckoned with; the politics of the
situation indicates that the struggle for independence is about to be
achieved, that the individual consciousness is ready to emerge. It is the
concern with the spirit, with man's spiritual foundations, that gives the
group this power—the age-old teachings of the Hindu scriptures supply
the impetus necessary to undertake the struggle for self-rule. The culture
itself never appears to be walking the pathway of cultural suicide but
rather a road toward basic regeneration. Phoenix-like, it is about to
be reborn out of the ashes of the past. The Indian novels, then, take
us one step further in the evolutionary relationship between the Third

World and the West and, in doing so, bring us closer to the novel as we think of it in the West.

Raja Rao and Kamala Markandaya are two of the most important novelists to have emerged as part of the diverse Indo-Anglian literary scene in the last thirty-five years. Both have achieved solid literary reputations during this time, though Ms. Markandaya started writing later than her compatriot. In the case of the former, her eighth novel, *Two Virgins*, published in 1973, most strikingly illustrates the growing tradition of cultural renewal in Indo-Anglian fiction.* It is also, I believe, her finest achievement in a literary career both stunning and prolific. With Raja Rao, it is the opposite: his major achievement is still his first novel. *Kanthapura*, published in 1938, though it was written some years before that. It was followed by two other exceptional pieces of fiction,*The Serpent and the Rope* (1960) and *The Cat and Shakespeare* (1965). Placing *Kanthapura* and *Two Virgins* side by side, we see that though they represent the opposite ends of the literary careers of two talented writers, several important connections will come to our attention when we begin examining them in closer detail.

The most obvious relationship between *Kanthapura* and *Two Virgins* is the attitude they express toward women. The person who tells the story in *Kanthapura* is not Raja Rao, the omniscient novelist, but a woman named Achakka. *Two Virgins* is essentially the story of a young girl's changing consciousness. Of the two, *Kanthapura* is undoubtedly the more unusual. Raja Rao has abandoned his position as story teller, giving it over to his fictive female persona. I can think of few other instances in Third World fiction where a male novelist has done this.

Women, in fact, are not usually very important as characters in Third World novels. There are very few novelists from the Third World who are women, in large part because the educational systems in many of these cultures have favored men. Of the 594 writers listed in Donald E. Herdeck's *African Authors*, only thirty-one are women—and only four of them have written novels.[1] From the West Indies, only one female novelist has left her mark: Paule Marshall. There are no female novelists from the South Pacific and no Native American female novelists. It is not until the Harlem Renaissance that the first female Afro-American novelists begin to appear (Nella Larsen, Jessie Fauset, and Zora Neale Hurston) though their work is generally considered of lesser importance than that of their male contemporaries. More recently, however, there have been a number of extremely talented female black American writers who have begun publishing novels—indeed their appearance has been

*Her earlier novels are *Nectar in a Sieve* (1954), *Some Inner Fury* (1956), *A Silence of Desire* (1960), *Possession* (1963), *A Handful of Rice* (1966), *The Coffer Dams* (1969), and *The Nowhere Man* (1972).

one of the most interesting aspects of the recent collison between Black Studies and Women's Lib.[2]

With the exception of Afro-American fiction, I would have to say that in most Third World novels female characters play lesser roles than their male counterparts—no doubt in large part because Western (romantic) love is missing as a theme. If women are present in any of these books, they tend to be of incidental importance, functional objects in an otherwise masculine-oriented world.* For the most part, this is true of *Batouala* though, as we have seen, Maran does illustrate the sexual power that women have over men. In Ouologuem's *Bound to Violence*, women are treated as totally disposable objects; they have no power at all. Eri's *The Crocodile* also illustrates the male-dominated world where the women's role is essentially limited to bearing children. Storm's female characters in *Seven Arrows* are often carefully drawn, but they, too, are not seen as capable of bringing about any significant change in the culture itself. Lamming's *In the Castle of My Skin* is somewhat different; his women are strong (they have to be to raise their illegitimate children), though there is never any question about the superior status men hold in the society. Toomer's men and women are equally victims of American racism, though his women often dominate their men.

In all of the novels discussed so far, then, female characters are never presented as holding the key to social or political change. Even in Lamming's novel, in which they are responsible for much of the stability in the village, it is clear that by themselves they will not bring about any significant alteration in the culture. The men will do that when the right time arrives. This attitude toward women begins to change, however, when we turn to the works by Indo-Anglian novelists. In proportion to the total number, there are more female writers of Indo-Anglian fiction that there are from the other geographical areas we have already examined.[3] In *Kanthapura*, women are the vanguard for an entire revolutionary change. In *Two Virgins*, although the revolution has long since come and gone, it is the women who are responsible for retaining any stability in family and village life.

The female sensitivity gives us one marked distinction between the Indian writers and the others, but there is another equally important one. The Indo-Anglian novel tends to be much more introspective than the other writing we have considered, moving us clearly toward what is commonly referred to as the inward turning of the novel. *Kanthapura* is told in the first person, the only first person narrative we have examined besides Lamming's *In the Castle of My Skin* and parts of Toomer's *Cane*. *Two Virgins*, though not related in the first person, must be classified

*For a discussion of the theme of romantic love in Third World writing, seem my article, "Heroic Ethnocentrism: The Idea of Universality in Literatue," *The American Scholar*, XXXXII (Summer 1973), pp. 463-475.

as an introspective novel, for it stresses an individual's evolving consciousness. These two books also move us one step closer to R. K. Narayan's *Grateful to Life and Death* and Bessie Head's *A Question of Power*, which depict even more closely the solitary consciousness.

*Kanthapura* is the story of a village with that name. There is no central character (other than the village, what happens to it, what it becomes). At the beginning—sometime in the late 1920's—the village exists more or less in a state of peaceful harmony. The age-old traditions of Hindu life have not been noticeably altered, except indirectly by British colonial rule. As the story develops, a young Brahmin male named Moorthy terminates his studies in the city and returns to Kanthapura, preaching Gandhi's politics of non-violence, abolition of the caste system, and the revival of home industries so that the Indian will be economically free of the British monopolies on cotton and salt. Moorthy's influence in the village eventually leads to a number of protests and riots, culminating in a final bloodbath that destroys the entire village. The people of Kanthapura have either been killed or have moved on to another village for refuge.

Village life is certainly more closely at the heart of *Kanthapura* than of any of the other works we have examined, in spite of the fact that Raja Rao describes the movement of the village from solidarity to complete and utter annihilation. Much of the early part of the book is spent developing a sense of the village itself, establishing its ambience. In the first paragraphs, Achakka informs us of its geographical location:

> Our village—I don't think you have ever heard about it—Kanthapura is its name, and it is in the province of Kara.
>
> High on the Ghats is it, high up the steep mountains that face the cool Arabian seas, up the Malabar coast is it, up Mangalore and Puttur and many a centre of cardamom and coffee, rice and sugar cane. Roads, narrow, dusty, rut-covered roads, wind through the forest of teak and of jack, of sandal and of sal, and hanging over bellowing gorges and leaping over elephant-haunted valleys, they turn now to the left and now to the right and bring you through the Alambè and Champa and Mena and Kola passes into the great granaries of trade. There, on the blue waters, they say, our carted cardamoms and coffee get into the ships the Red-men bring, and, so they say, they go across the seven oceans into the countries where our rulers live.[4]

The communal point of view is established immediately and placed in its colonial context—the red-man ("Standard Hindu colloquialism for the British," the author states in his notes to the novel, p. 185), the colonial power manipulating the villagers from thousands of miles away.

In the paragraphs that follow, Kenchamma, the village goddess, is first introduced ("She has never failed us, I assure you, our Kenchamma,"

p. 2); the physical lay-out of the village is described (the Brahmin, the Pariah, and the artisan quarters and the surrounding coffee estates controlled by the British); important places (the temple, the river, and so on) and people are mentioned. The communal aspect of the village is further developed in hundreds of references to the collective pronouns *our* and *we*, beginning with the opening words of the novel "our village." The narrator generally effaces herself, avoiding the first person singular, so that the reader often has the impression that several people are telling the story instead of one person alone. Village life is recorded in all of its manifold aspects—reminiscent of what we have seen in other Third World novels—stressing, again, the day-to-day activities that are at the heart of the villagers' lives.

The communal motif is not solely a matter of description or the use of the plural pronoun but a theme reflected innumerable times throughout the story in the statements of others. Well into the novel, when Moorthy explains to the villagers the importance of unity in the face of the colonial power, he states,

> "Now...we are out for action. A cock does not make a morning, nor a single man a revolution, but we'll build a thousand-pillared temple, a temple more firm than any that hath yet been builded, and each one of you be ye pillars in it, and when the temple is built, stone by stone, and man by man, and the bell hung to the roof and the eagle-tower shaped and planted, we shall invoke the Mother to reside with us in dream and in life. India then will live in a temple of our making." (p. 118)

The oneness that Moorthy is extolling here is the same goal that several characters in *Seven Arrows* envisioned as necessary to meet the invading white man. So powerful does the pressure of the communal consciousness become in Kanthapura that only seven families fail to join in the protest. Raja Rao' implication by the end of the story is quite clear: symbolically, Kanthapura is all of India. If all of India were as united as these villagers, if the caste system could break down as quickly as it did here, independence would come tomorrow, for, after all, it is the forces brought in from outside that eventually lead to destruction. Kanthapura today, India tomorrow.

Raja Rao's structural device of relinquishing his omniscient position to the fictive character within the story, coupled with that narrator's use of plural pronouns, is responsible for much of the effectiveness of the basic story and the rooting that it has in the communal consciousness. Not surprisingly, the reader learns very little about Achakka, the narrator. She refers to herself as a "daughterless widow" (p. 5) early in the novel, while she is still a part of Kanthapura; and she is referred to by another as "the aunt who tells such nice stories" (p. 179) at the conclusion of the narrative, when she is living in Kashipura. We know that she owns a little land ("I have seven acres of wet land and twelve acres of dry land..." p. 9) and that she is a Brahmin, but these are the only facts directly revealed about her in the entire narrative.

The most significant of these characteristics undoubtedly are her Brahmin position and the fact that she is female. Achakka's Brahmin status initially presents some problems for her as a narrator, since her past education has told her to uphold the caste system. When she describes the outcaste quarter early in the narrative, she comments, "Of course you wouldn't expect me to go to the Pariah quarter..." (p. 5). Since Achakka is much like the other villagers, she must learn to accept the changes that are taking place in Kanthapura, for Raja Rao's novel recounts an even more complete social change than Storm's *Seven Arrows*. Flexibility, however, typifies Achakka's character; quite early in the story she adopts Gandhi's teachings. In the riots that culminate at the end, Achakka is out there, proudly marching with the others—Brahmins and Pariahs, potters and weavers, coolies, even Mohammedans. Altogether, she becomes an admirable character—perhaps all the more surprising because she is no longer young.

The female point of view, however, is much more important than her Brahmin status, giving us, as I have already indicated, something atypical of most Third World fiction. Much of the novel's power is Raja Rao's determination to keep the viewpoint totally feminine. For this reason, it is expecially important that the village protector is a goddess, Kenchamma, not a god. Her power resides in her past actions, and the origin of the village is attributed to her initial accomplishments:

> Kenchamma is our goddess. Great and bounteous is she. She killed a demon ages, ages ago, a demon that had come to demand our young sons as food and our young women as wives. Kenchamma came from the Heavens—it was the sage Tripura who had made penances to bring her down—and she waged such a battle and she fought so many a night that the blood soaked and soaked into the earth, and that is why the Kenchamma Hill is all red. If not, tell me, sister, why should it be red only from the Tippur stream upwards, for a foot down on the other side of the stream you have mud, black and brown, but never red. Tell me, how could this happen, if it were not for Kenchamma and her battle? Thank heaven, not only did she slay the demon, but she even settled down among us, and this much I shall say, never has she failed us in our grief. (p. 2)

Symbolically, Kenchamma's power, incarnated in the women of Kanthapura such as Achakka (engaging in a similar battle), brings about the great social change that radicalizes the village, for Gandhi and Moorthy are only the catalysts, the inspiration for what eventually happens. They become increasingly insignificant as the narrative continues, Moorthy even disappearing from the village itself. The women are the force, they bring about the real revolution, since their husbands have had to hide in the jungles around the village.* Without the force of the women, there would not, in fact, have been a revolution in Kanthapura.

Achakka's entire story—her narration of the events that take place in Kanthapura—is told in retrospect to other women listeners. There are constant references to these listeners who are identified as "sisters," but what is of more importance is that *Kanthapura* is thereby rooted in oral storytelling. The novel itself is one long oral tale, told by a mature woman who has survived the ordeal she is describing to her listeners. There are other tales also, usually digressions within the main narrative itself, tales related by Achakka that other people have told her. Often they begin with conventional oral tags, "Once upon a time," (p. 103) "And this is how it all began" (p. 61). Other oral characteristics of the narrative include the multiple use of songs and prayers and the more limited use of proverbs, mythology, and epic lists and catalogs. So strong is the oral tradition that if it were eliminated there would be no *Kanthapura*.

Stylistically, all of these aspects contribute a rather fast-paced quality to the prose itself, at times reminiscent of a kind of oral stream of consciousness or automatic writing because of the declarative sentences that go on and on, connected by conjunction after conjunction. Here, for example, is a small portion of a passage from the confusion of the final riots:

> ...and then suddenly from the darkened Brahmin street and the Pariah street and the Weavers' street and the lantana growths came back the cry, "*Mahatma Gandhi ki jai!*" and the police were so infuriated that they rushed this side and that, and from this courtyard and that garden, from behind this door and that byre, and from the tops of champak trees and pipal trees and tamarind trees, from beneath horse carts and bullock carts, men in white jumped out, men at last from the city, boys, young men, householders, peasants, Mohammedans with dhotis to the knees, and city boys with floating skirts and Gandhi caps, and they swarmed around us like veritable mother elephants round their young. (p. 165)

The connectives are piled one on top of the other; there is a sense of a heightened pace—of time rushing by so quickly that it can never be recaptured. Most of the novel is told as a summary of past events, with endless digressions, as is often typical of longer oral narratives, and only limited use of dialogue. The combination of these aspects creates

---

*There is an interesting parallel here with an African novel by Sembene Ousmane called *God's Bits of Wood* (*Les bouts de bois de Dieu*, 1960). It is also the women who bring about the revolution in that novel during times of extraordinarily abrupt social change: a workers' strike against the French who own the railroad.

a style that is altogether breathless, vividly recapturing the abruptness of the social change within the culture itself. Time is not only marching on, but it is bringing about major social changes.

Radical change is, of course, at the heart of *Kanthapura*, from the first to the last page. Initially, these changes are frowned upon—even by those who later become the activists responsible for much of the final outcome. When Moorthy returns to Kanthapura and begins to associate with the artisans, Achakka comments, again mirroring the Brahmin part of the village:

> he even goes to the Potters' quarter and the Weavers' quarter and the Sudra quarter, and I closed my ears when I heard he went to the Pariah quarter. We said to ourselves, he is one of these Gandhimen, who say there is neither caste nor clan nor family, and yet they pray like us and they live like us. Only they say, too, one should not marry early, one should allow widows to take husbands and a brahmin might marry a pariah and a pariah a brahmin. Well, well, let them say it, how does it affect us? We shall be dead before the world is polluted. We shall have closed our eyes. (p. 9)

Moorthy soon begins to gain a following among the Brahmin women, though his own mother turns against his new beliefs. When Badé Khan, a Mohammedan policeman sent in from the outside, arrives in Kanthapura, the villagers understand what is going on: the government is becoming frightened by what is happening in their village.

Towards the end of the novel, when nothing can stop the women from marching against the soldiers sent in by the British, the change has been so complete that the women (in spite of the fact that many of them have been killed) make the voluntary choice to continue their protests. They are driven by an uncontrollable force—not Moorthy, not Gandhi—a new revolutionary consciousness, only dreamed about by Trumper in Lamming's novel.

> ...some strange fever rushed up from the feet, it rushed up and with it our hair stood on end and our ears grew hot and something powerful shook us from head to foot, like Shamoo when the goddess had taken hold of him; and on that beating, bursting day, with the palms and the champaks and the lantana and the silent well about us, such a terror took hold of us, that we put the water jugs on our hips, and we rushed back home, trembling and gasping with the anger of the gods.... Moorthy forgive us! Mahatma forgive us! Kenchamma forgive us! We shall go. Oh, we shall go to the end of the pilgrimage like the two hundred and fifty thousand women of Bombay. We will go like them, we will go ...!(pp.161–162)

The women envision a nationwide women's revolt, liberating all of India. Kanthapura itself has become insignificant—it is simply the village where the riots began. That is why these same women decide to burn down what is left of the village, rather than return to it. For them, life can never again be as it was in Kanthapura. The revolution is now self-perpetuating.

In retrospect, this change from passivity to activity is explained by Achakka as a kind of uncontrollable religious possession, growing out of the foundation of the villagers' beliefs.

> Kenchamma forgive us, but there is something that has entered our hearts, an abundance like the Himavathy on Gauri's night, when lights come floating down the Rampur corner, lights come floating down from Rampur and Maddur and Tippur, lights lit on the betel leaves, and with flower and kumkum and song we let them go, and they will go down the Ghats to the morning of the sea, the lights on the betel leaves, and the Mahatma will gather it all, he will gather it by the sea, and he will bless us. (p. 180)

Something which they had little control over had entered their hearts; their religion has been tested and strengthened by a "renaissance of Indian spiritual life,"[5] according to Indian critic, M. A. Naik. Yet what has happened is only the beginning, for as Achakka says, the Mahatma will gather them all together to fight the common enemy.

The common force against them—British colonial rule—is not so different in this novel from what we have already seen in others, except for the fact that the duration of colonial rule has been longer and more widespread than it has been in some of the societies described in the other novels we have examined. As in many of these other instances, the external force in Kanthapura tends to be indirect. No white men live in the village; there is only one white man at the Skeffington Coffee Estate. Yet indirect control—especially of the basic economic system within the country—is again presented as a force so powerful that it holds every Indian in perpetual servitude. Most frequently, the attacks against the British in *Kanthapura* occur as demonstrations of Gandhi's teachings: " '...millions and millions of yards of foreign cloth came to this country, and everything foreign makes us poor and pollutes us. To wear cloth spun and woven with your own God-given hands is sacred, says the Mahatma.... Our country is being bled to death by foreigners' " (p. 16). We have only to remember that *Kanthapura* was published in 1938—nine years before independence—to realize the revolutionary nature of these remarks. It is surprising that the novel was not banned in India or that its author was not imprisoned.

In a way, what we find in *Kanthapura* is the historical novel Yambo Ouologuem was unable to write in *Bound to Violence,* for Raja Rao's tale is built around several significant events in Gandhi's political career that eventually culminated in India's independence. Time is not presented through cyclical events in the novel, though there are some references to the natural seasons; we are not shown a closed system in which only the timeless present has any reality for the people. Rather, there is a sense of past and future—a sense of history marching on. Achakka herself is aware of this feeling as becomes apparent in her retrospective narrative of what has taken place. The other women also realize that they are a part of history on the march. No doubt much of this sense of historical time is a reflection of events in Gandhi's political life, plus the merging of his image with the oral tradition. Historically, for the Indians, Gandhi became a kind of myth in his own day, and this sense—almost of sainthood—permeates much of *Kanthapura*, as it does other Indo-Anglian novels.*

Gandhi appears only once in *Kanthapura*—the single meeting he has with Moorthy. The effect on the latter is almost mystical; he gives up his studies, his worldly possessions. Gandhi's "don't touch the government campaign" is described in some detail, and the revolutionary expressions referring to his movement are repeatedly mentioned in the text: "*Gandhi Mahatma ki jai!*" ("Victory, Victory to Mahatma Gandhi"). These multiple references to specific events in India in the late 1920's and the early 1930's give us the sense of reading a novel growing out of a distinct historical context where time is the most important contributing factor, for without it things would still be as they were in the past.

At the end of the story, when Range Gowda—one of the Pariah leaders who has gone back to Kanthapura to look at the site that was once the village—tells Achakka " 'There's neither man nor mosquito in Kanthapura . . .' " (p. 182), it might be easy to conclude that what has taken place in Kanthapura is essentially negative. After all, the village no longer exists. Moorthy has run off and joined forces with the Communists, Gandhi has made a truce with the viceroy, and it is suspected that "the peasants will pay back the revenues, the young men will not boycott the toddy shops, and everything they say, will be as before" (p. 180). It is then however that Achakka makes one of the most emphatic statements in the narrative, relating it to her comment about what has happened to their hearts: " 'No, sister, no, nothing can ever be the same again' " (p. 180).

In the concluding summary, Achakka expresses her beliefs that what has happened in Kanthapura is to be interpreted as essentially positive: "They say the Mahatma will go to the Red-man's country and he will get us Swaraj" (p. 181), that is, independence. The time is propitious, the culture has been renewed, things will never again be as they were. The pessimism that has for so long been a controlling factor in Third

---

*See also R. K. Narayan's *Waiting for the Mahatma* (1955), Khwaja Ahamed Abbas's *Inquilab* (1955), Mulk Raj Anand's *The Sword and the Sickle* (1942), and K. Nagaranjan's *Chronicles of Kedaram* (1961). For a discussion of Gandhi's importance in these works see Meenakshi Mukherjee's *The Twice Born Fiction* (1971).

World fiction has begun to shift toward optimism. Cultural renewal can only begin within the culture itself, from within its basic foundations: the village and the family.

Village and family life are central to Kamala Markandaya's *Two Virgins*, but to these she adds a third element: the individual. The time of the story is roughly forty years later, India today, and the setting is once again a small village, though it is never given a name. The incipient revolution of Raja Rao's novel has come and gone. Markandaya makes occasional allusions to the independence struggle, such as the various references to Rangu, now a village hero, who was tortured to death by the British. Evidence of Gandhi's teachings permeates the story, clearly indicating that India today is not what it was during the colonial period: "Appa said all India was one now, and they must learn to live as one. It was a British stratagem, he said, to divide the people up and set them one against another in order to rule them, and they must never make that mistake again."[6] In Appa's house, Markandaya tells us, there are "pottery busts of Gandhi and Nehru and Mrs. Gandhi" (p. 93). But what is probably most indicative of the great changes that have taken place is the fact that there are very few references to the caste system, though a kind of economic class system appears to be emerging out of the older distinctions.

The story of *Two Virgins* is a simple one. It has been told many times before, but rarely as effectively as it is in Markandaya's novel. Two sisters grow up in a village, on a small farm. Lalitha, the older one, is exposed to Western schooling; Saroja, her younger sister, attends a more traditional school. When Lalitha runs away to the city in pursuit of a movie career, the evils of urban life lead to her downfall. Pregnant and abandoned, she returns briefly to the village, but no longer finds any happiness there. Lalitha's parents try to find the man who has seduced her, a movie director; but the pilgrimage that all four of them make to the city (the two sisters and their parents, Appa and Amma) ends in further tragedy. At the end of the story, Lalitha refuses to return to the village with her parents and her younger and wiser sister, Saroja.

The reader sees the events from Saroja's point of view, though the narration is in the third person. Markandaya's intention here is twofold: a feminine viewpoint coupled with an evolving consciousness. The achievement is remarkable, unlike anything else we have seen in Third World fiction: Saroja perceives, she changes, she grows. She is not the same person at the end that she was at the beginning. No longer are we dealing with two-dimensional characterization as we were in *Batouala*, *The Crocodile*, *Bound to Violence*, and *Seven Arrows*. The only other character who can be compared to Saroja is George Lamming in *In the Castle of My Skin*, but the comparison is one limited to age. Lamming has not altered noticeably by the end of his story—the change in him takes place sometime between the end of the novel's actual story and the beginning of the writing of it. This is not the case with Saroja. She is what we can assume a younger version of Achakka would have been like or what she might have been like if Raja Rao had shifted the emphasis from the village to the narrator, for in *Kanthapura* the change is in the village as well as in all the villagers. In *Two Virgins*, the village remains the same, a place of stability. It is Saroja who is altered.

This is not to suggest that Ms. Markandaya believes everything in the village is as it should be. She does not, but the village is stable and comforting—it is a home that offers a kind of safety unknown in the city. She populates the village with a vivid assortment of rural character types: Chingleput, the sweet-seller; Manikkam, the milkman; his wife, a wet nurse; Lachu, the village idiot who molests little girls; the carpenter, the blacksmith, the moneylender—each carefully distinguished from the others. There are the usual references to common events in the cycle of life: birth, marriage, death. The village has a place for all of these people, for all of these happenings, yet Markandaya makes it clear that not everyone can survive in such an atmosphere. In one of his quarrels, Appa asks his wife about their two sons, now living in the town, "Is that what you had in your minuscule mind for my boys, that they should stagnate in this village where there is no outlet whatsoever for their energies and talents?" (p. 122). Saroja knows that the city has done something to her brothers: "The boys' faces were hard, in a way no one's in the village was, even faces that were twice their age" (p. 54). Saroja comes to recognize that a subtle balance exists between village and city life; both have their advantages. She thinks about the tale of the town mouse and the country mouse, concluding, "The moral, as far as she could remember, was that there were snags in both life styles" (p. 193).

The city, however, is more than a contrast to village life. It also represents the West, those aspects of Westernization that have remained in the country even though the British have left: urbanization and industrialization. "The town was full of machines," (p. 4) Markandaya tells us early in the novel—machines that Chingleput knows can produce his sweets much more quickly. Saroja realizes that machines can drive an artisan out of work—they can eliminate Chingleput's business. She prays that the machines will never invade her village: "She always said a prayer though, just in case, asked God not to allow machines into their village which would destroy Chingleput and his skills. She kept her prayers secret, however, because of Appa and the boys who were progressives. They often said machines were the answers to the country's problems" (p. 80). Aunt Alamelu, Amma's widowed sister, has a more basic attitude toward them: "If God had wanted men to be machines he would have embedded wires in their limbs" (p. 84).

When Saroja rides into the city with her family to confront her sister's seducer, she thinks, "Rattling and honking the bus raced toward the city, its birthplace. It had been assembled there, part by shining part. Saroja knew because one of the boys had worked for a time in the factory where it was done" (p. 187). Machines are born in the city; machines make one sterile. Those who live in the city run the risk of becoming machines themselves. When Lalitha tells her sister about her abortion, her voice sounds like a machine, "clear and metallic" (p. 230). The abortion itself was accomplished by another machine:

> They sucked him out, said Lalitha, bit by bit. He came out in pieces. I could feel him going, though they said I wouldn't feel anything. He wouldn't have filled a tumbler, except for the fluid. It took ten minutes. She paused, she was hideously dry. If I hadn't wanted him it might have been different, she said, an unwanted child is better off unborn. But I did want him, I wanted him most when he was going, those last ten minutes of his life. (p. 232)

After this, Saroja has only fear and loathing for the city. The hotel room where they are staying feels like "a prison cell with bars" (p. 239).

The west also infiltrates the village. It may, in fact, be said to contribute directly to Lalitha's downfall. She attends a school patterned after Western educational methods, run by Miss Mendoza, "a Christian, although an Indian" (p. 14). Miss Mendoza is proud of the artistic opportunities she offers her pupils: "moral science, and how to dance around a bamboo pole which Miss Mendoza said was a maypole" (p. 14). These Western dances directly contribute to Lalitha's short-lived movie career: an Indian director, Mr. Gupta, comes to the village and makes a documentary, including shots of Lalitha's dancing. The maypole becomes a kind of leitmotif, mentioned several times later in the story. After Lalitha becomes pregnant and her position in the family changes noticeably, Markandaya states, "No one took any notice of her. They talked round her and about her as if she weren't there but she was, a figurehead, a maypole round which they ran with their tangled ribbons. The ribbons were tatty and mournful, not a bright strand among them, the pattern was altogether woeful" (p. 174). Aunt Alamelu links the maypole even more directly to Lalitha's downfall, "Maypoles . . . dancing around them and such Christian practices, is it a fitting pastime for our young Hindu maidens?" (p. 176).

Part of the problem is with Appa—"he liked Indians to be Westernized, which advanced them into the big world instead of remaining static in a backwater" (p. 57). It is he who decides that Lalitha should attend

Miss Mendoza's school. The differences between his daughters' schools are nowhere more fully described than in the following statement: "In Saroja's school the girls wanted to be rounded and curvy, like goddesses in pictures, but in Lalitha's they were crazy for slimness, the fashion was to be skinny everywhere except for breasts" (p. 61). Lalitha's seducer, the movie-maker Mr. Gupta (educated in the West) is introduced to her through Miss Mendoza. The chain of reactions may seem a little strained, but it is mentioned again and again: Miss Mendoza and Mr. Gupta are the villains. Later in the novel, Appa's feelings about the West begin to pale: "One imbibes what is bad in the West as well as what is good . . ." (p. 113). He has learned that many of the pre-independence problems have not been solved by Westernization.

Contemporary Indian society in *Two Virgins* is, in fact, depicted as a kind of hodgepodge of traditional Indian and modern Western cultures, slowly adding to the breakdown of the class system. Saroja's brothers refer to Western society as "a spreading thing, one cannot escape it" (p. 67). Appa thinks of society in general as criminal, but, initially, at least, he believes that most of the problems are flaws within the old traditions themselves.When Lalitha becomes pregnant, Saroja wonders what will happen to the baby and realizes "it had no future in what Appa and the boys called society as it was organized" (p. 179). Later Appa's hatred toward the West increases, for by then he has related his daughter's abortion to the violence of Westernization. Even Amma, the least critical of Indian life, begins to realize that Indian society has changed so quickly in the last few years that her daughter is no better off than anyone else's. She thinks of other unmarried girls from the village who have become pregnant:

> Not girls from families like ours, said Amma. These are low-class girls of low intelligence. She was wrong. Lalitha was none of these things but Lalitha was pregnant. From time to time there had been other girls like her too. Exceptions that prove the rule, claimed Amma. She stuck to her belief even after Lalitha, but she was less vocal. A family like theirs had produced a girl just like the others. (p. 202)

Modern India is shown as a country undergoing rapid social change from within and from without. The middle class no longer knows the security of the past ways of life; the teachings of Gandhi have been more far-reaching than anyone would have suspected. Whatever stability there is must come from the inner strengths of individual characters.

The shift toward the individual consciousness in *Two Virgins* , although prefiguring our discussion of the inner consciousness of R. K. Narayan's *Grateful to Life and Death* and Bessie Head's *A Question of Power*, is more accurately a move in the direction of the more traditional novel of character. When we finish *Two Virgins* and think about it months after we have read it, we remember specific characters within the story: Lalitha, Appa, especially Saroja. This is a major difference from the other novels we have examined. When we think back to *Seven Arrows,* the characters all seem to blur into one; we remember events instead—situations—and that, I believe, is true of most of the Third World novels we have considered: *Cane, Bound to Violence, The Crocodile, Kanthapura,* and, to a lesser extent, *In the Castle of My Skin. Batouala* is in a class by itself: we remember the great chief, but we are privileged to see his innermost thoughts only occasionally. *Two Virgins* is different from these other works, truly a novel of character and the interaction of its characters. Markandaya's achievement is her ability to write a novel that bridges the gaps between the Third World and the West: introspective characters strongly rooted in traditional village life, the Indian joint family.

Lalitha is her star portrait, though not her most important one. She dominates the story, though the tale eventually becomes her younger sister's. Beautiful, talented, vain—she is always shown as a little out of her element: a seductress with no one in the village worthy of her guiles. Whether she is flicking her eyelashes at Lachu the village idiot, dancing naked in the rain, or asking the doctor to inoculate her on her thigh instead of her arm (so the scar will not be visible), she is always presented as out of her element in the village, as someone not quite real: an oversized kewpie doll—all surface with no inner life. After she has travelled to the city to view the showing of Mr. Gupta's documentary, nothing can keep her at home. "This one-horse town, this backward place, this outpost of civilization, moaned Lalitha" (p. 84). Even her speech—now filled with slang—gives her away. She no longer belongs. "The way we live is *primitive,* said Lalitha" (p. 87). The city simply sharpens the qualities she has possessed all along. Markandaya states, "She developed arts, grew adept at side-stepping, at obliquities" (pp. 161–162). Perhaps no single event is more revealing than an incident Saroja remembers about her sister years ago:

> In Lalitha's school at the end of term Miss Mendoza handed out little books with blank colored pages in which you put a tick for each good deed you had done during the holidays. When school started again the girl with the most ticks was given a prize. One year Lalitha had won a prize, but it wasn't for good deeds, it was for the ticks she had scrawled in the book. She had forgotten about good deeds until the last day, then she simply sat down and penciled them in, they represented nothing. She never bothered about good deeds after that. The ease of substitution, she told Saroja, has been a revelation. (pp. 166–167)

Lalitha has always been a cheater with life.

One cannot help feeling sorry for her at the end. She realizes that she wants her baby, but by then it is too late. There is nothing more painful in the novel than Lalitha's description of her abortion or her answer when Saroja asks her if she is all right: "I'm just fine, it's him that's a bloody pulp" (p. 230). At the end of the story, shortly before she leaves her family for good, rather than return to the village, she tells Saroja, "The thing to remember, my sweet, is never to cry over spilt milk" (p. 233) and she adds, "Over men or babies... I'm telling you now because I shan't be able to tell you later" (p. 233). The city has made her hard like her brothers, but she knows it is the only way of life she can now understand.

Appa is a different matter; he would not hurt a flea. Unlike Lalitha who always tries to take advantage of a situation, he is all giving. A freedom fighter during the independence movement, Appa served time in prison, where he was beaten up by the policemen. When he was released after independence, he was given an acre of land, though he was an educated man, used to other work. Although not especially good at farming, he plays an invaluable part in the village—helping others in need. "Appa was the unofficial moneylender, known as a soft touch for miles around. He didn't charge any interest, was delighted merely to get his own money back" (p. 41). Markandaya states, "His innocence lent him strength" (p. 76). For him, nothing can be as bad as it was when the British ruled the country. Amma tells Saroja, "Your father would make a wedding out of a funeral..." (p. 208). It is as much Appa's permissiveness that leads to Lalitha's downfall as anything else. He has always spoiled her, permitted her to do whatever she wants.

Appa is also the major source of comedy in *Two Virgins*, and in this sense he bears an affinity to many of R. K. Narayan's buffoon characters. A gentle humor runs throughout much Indo-Anglian fiction, unlike anything else in Third World literature. When Manikkam comes to Appa to borrow money for the umpteenth time—his wife has just lost another child—Appa gives him, instead, a prophylactic:

> You should have lived in the era before we got our own government, he cried, then you'd really have had something to complain about! I'm not complaining, said Manikkam humbly, if it weren't for the children—You are, you are, you hideous old bag of bones, roared Appa. He was purple. He bent down and began rummaging in the trunk he kept under his charpoy. Here, he said in a nasty way, then he noticed Saroja, who was curious to see what was changing hands, and he ordered her out. (p. 142)

Needless to say, Appa and Amma are progressives—they practice family planning. The references to birth control are important. At the height of his despair, when Appa is talking to Amma about what should be done with their pregnant daughter, Markandaya writes, "His eyes were misting. He felt in his pocket and drew out a crumpled sheath, this time he made no attempt to conceal it from his daughter. I educated the milkman, he said, but I couldn't do as much for my own child . . . she was innocent, and we let her go out as she was" (p. 178). When one thinks of the great effort the Indian government has made in recent years to publicize birth control, one realizes how contemporary many of the ideas in *Two Virgins* are.

The references throughout the novel to sexual intercourse, birth control, and abortion are filtered through Saroja's consciousness, for *Two Virgins* is much more the story of her slow growth of rational awareness of the sexual part of our lives than of Lalitha's abrupt initiation. Still a child at the beginning of the novel, Saroja has learned how to control her emotions by the end. She will never become another Lalitha. Near the opening of the story, Markandaya writes, "Saroja paid attention when she was told to, and even more when she was told not to because she had discovered you learned more that way, and mostly they were the more interesting things" (p. 21). Even before Lalitha becomes pregnant, Saroja has seen enough of the complications that Manikkam's wife has had with her children to realize that any babies she has will be planned, like Amma's. When her father gives the prophylactic to Manikkam, the reader sees Saroja's reactions:

> Saroja retreated with this new clue under her belt, sat under the tamarind tree to consider. She draped the gossamer over her father's jigger. She stuffed it up her mother's aperture. The improbability was so extreme it drove her to substitute Manikkam. Then Mr. Gupta and Lalitha. It was coming easier now, it fitted, it brought her to the verge of discovery. Her flesh shivered with a foretaste of knowledge. She heard her mother calling. It penetrated her absorption, the sensations subsided. The images, on which discovery was based, grew blurred, vanished. (p. 143)

When the story begins, Saroja has no physical desires. She plays with dolls—an image that shifts from her playthings at the beginning, to Lalitha at the end. Lachu, the village idiot, holds no fascination for her as he does for Lalitha. Saroja feels no sexual sensations until her trip to the city when Mr. Gupta's assistant, Devraj, accidently touches her hand. Then she feels afraid and at night she begins to have erotic dreams. After a second encounter with Devraj, her emotions become uncontrollable:

> the fire refused to die. She wondered if this was what Lalitha had felt like, if it was the cause of her opening herself to *him*, allowing him to put the seed of the baby inside her. It was the only explanation for a girl to be so careless. It was also a frightening thought, made

her speculate on whether she, too, was cast in the wanton mold Aunt Alamelu had described; but the thought would not root. What rooted itself was the suspicion that it wasn't necessary to be cast in Lalitha's mold or any mold, the urge was implanted deep and indestructibly in every human being. (p. 218)

She has become an adult. It is only after Saroja has understood the agony of her sister's abortion that there is a reversal in her emotions. The final time she sees Devraj in the city, she becomes hysterical, yelling at him, "Take your hands off me.... What do you take me for... a virgin in your whorehouse?" (p. 245). Her parents have to drag her bodily from the room. She will not let what happened to Lalitha happen to her.

Saroja's maturity is much more than a sexual awakening. We watch her perceptions expanding throughout the entire narrative. When La- litha returns to the village, the younger girl knows that something is wrong: "Saroja considered her sister, thought she looked older, it was a matter of years rather than the months she had been away" (p. 156). When Lalitha states to her at the height of her despair, "I wish I were you," (p. 209), Saroja no longer feels the jealousy she has felt for her older sister all of her life. It has vanished; she has learned too much about suffering. She has seen Manikkam's wife lose her babies, she has seen the death of a schoolmate, she has learned of Lalitha's abortion. Lalitha's note to her in the city ("Stay if you want to, no one can stop you" p. 241) brings only one reaction: "She couldn't think of anything worse than to stay on in the city" (p. 241). She has learned to hate it.

She didn't belong to it, she wanted to go away and never come back.

She wanted to go home. At home there were fields to rest your eyes on, colors that changed with the seasons. The tender green of new crops, the tawny shades of harvest, the tints of freshly turned earth, you could have told the week and the month of the year by these alone. You knew each grove, each acre, each homestead on it, who owned them, and the owners of the names. You knew every pathway. No one could ever be lost, not by trying. The wells, the fields, each had its name: the well beside the water meadow, the well by the banyan, the field next to the mill. You always knew where you were. You knew who you were. (p. 243)

On the return trip, Saroja feels that she is slowly coming alive again, the further they get from the city. She is surprised that their house is still the same: "Saroja wandered around, touching, feeling, she felt she had been away for years, simultaneously she felt she had not been away at all" (p. 248). She has returned home whole, no longer afraid of life or of her sexuality. The novel concludes, as it began, with Saroja talking to Chingleput the sweet maker:

> He clasped her. His organ was hard, was nuzzling her body. Don't be afraid, I'm a man, I can't help it, said Chingleput.
> Saroja wasn't afraid. She knew too much, she had gone through too much to be afraid of anything. But she knew she wasn't for him, she would never be. So she drew away from him. She got up and mounted her bike. She could hardly see for the tears that were cascading down her face, she couldn't have told for whom they were falling, for her, or Chingleput, or for what was ended. After a while she didn't try. She thought instead of when she was older, felt the wind in her face and the tears drying as she skimmed down the path that led past the fields to the house. (p. 250)

Much of the concern with feminine sexuality in *Two Virgins* is a plea by Kamala Markandaya for women's rights. This is not the blatant forthrightness of Women's Lib in the United States but a subtle commentary on women in modern India running through the entire novel. It embraces all of the adult females in the narrative: Aunt Alamelu, for whom there is no longer any place in the joint family (that is, the status of a childless widow); Manikkam's wife, whose problems in large part grown from the ignorance of birth control and vaccination (one child dies from smallpox, another is the victim of a miscarriage); even Amma, a kind of quasi-earth mother, representative of all village women who cannot have a chat with a peddler without becoming the victims of gossip. Markandaya writes about Aunt Alamelu, but the statement applies to all women in the village, "Appa and Anand could stride off to the coffee shop, Manikkam had his bhang hideout, Bundi's liquor store was always crammed with men. Women had no boltholes. There was no escape for them, they had to stand where they were and take it" (p. 123). All of the women in *Two Virgins* are strong characters, stronger than the men around them. They survive, they endure.

*Two Virgins* is a story of mythic proportions, an archetypal story of the loss of innocence. It embodies a journey, a going forth, and a return. Like Raja Rao's *Kanthapura*, Kamala Markandaya has written a novel of rebirth through cultural renewal. In *Kanthapura*, the village is destroyed, yet the culture survives, remains intact—survives a testing and brings forth a new breed of people, stronger for the struggle, secure in their beliefs that they now have the tools to overcome the ugly colonial machine. The revolution, they know, can only end in independence. *Two Virgins* takes us a step further, beyond that village destroyed in *Kanthapura*. The first revolution is over, the struggle for independence has passed. Now a more difficult revolution is about to begin, rooted in the simplicity and dignity of traditional life.

# 7
# The Singular Consciousness

R. K. Narayan's *Grateful to Life and Death*
Bessie Head's *A Question of Power*

Traditional life in all of the novels we have examined thus far has been strongly rooted in the communal consciousness; the individual identity has just begun to break away from the group. There have been no instances of personal estrangement or alienation from the wider collective unit, though all of these novels have been concerned with the meeting of two cultures. Even those characters who have questioned the validity of traditional life within the culture (Lamming in his autobiographical novel, some of Storm's Indians, Lalitha) have never considered joining forces directly with the insurgents from the new culture.* They have remained victims, a part of the old culture even if they have not totally approved of what it has become. The isolated figure does not exist in these novels; the word itself is never used by any of these writers.

---

*I can think of one immediate exception to this in another work. In Chinua Achebe's *Things Fall Apart*, Okonkwo's son, Nwoye, leaves his father's household and joins the Christian missionaries. This act is as much a rebellion against his father's sternness as it is a rejection of traditional Ibo life.

Even more importantly, these characters never think of themselves in this context. Traditional life assumes togetherness, belonging.

With the two Indo-Anglian novels examined in the last chapter, these matters began to take on a slightly different form. The communal force reigns supreme in *Kanthapura* down through the chaos of the last scene and symbolically even beyond that through the rebirth of basic religious beliefs. In *Two Virgins,* the sister who strays away from the community undergoes a metamorphosis, resulting in personal disaster; the sister who rejects the outer world discovers safety and warmth back in the fold of the village. In the two remaining novels we will examine, the individual's position in relation to the community becomes much more estranged. In the first of these, R. K. Narayan's *Grateful to Life and Death* (1945), the temporary alienation from the group consciousness is eventually resolved by a form of self-education which restores the individual's position in the community. In Bessie Head's *A Question of Power* (1973) the individual estrangement—seemingly total and irreversible—gravitates at the end toward a partial return to the roots that restore the individual sanity and that individual's place in the community.

R. K. Narayan has long been one of the most respected Anglophone novelists of India, repeatedly mentioned as a candidate for the Nobel Prize for literature. He began his writing career in the early thirties, publishing his first novel (*Swami and Friends*) in 1935. It is in his second novel, however, (*The Bachelor of Arts,* 1937) that the pattern of Narayan's work begins to emerge. The narrative recounts a young Indian's (named Chandran) growing awareness of his role in his society. The structure of the narrative is loose, beginning with the last few months of Chandran's undergraduate studies and ending two or three years after his graduation. The initial setting is Narayan's usual fictive world, a city called Malgudi, generally considered the literary synthesis of Mysore, where Narayan has lived most of his life, and Madras, where he was born. After an unrequited love affair, Chandran leaves his home in Malgudi, and undergoes a spiritual crisis, but eventually returns to the fold, supposedly having found a place for himself within the old value system.

There is much in *The Bachelor of Arts* to remind us of Narayan's eight subsequent novels: the effete young man, indecisive, unsure of his role in his society; the crisis of life, often one of spirituality; the symbolic conclusion, indicating a new maturity coupled with a return to the traditional value system. Again and again, these stages are presented as part of an evolving singular consciousness, beginning in isolation and confusion and ending in wholeness, peace within the traditional religious (Hindu) faith. For the most part, *Grateful to Life and Death* (original title: *The English Teacher*) belongs within this same pattern. I have chosen it for inclusion in this study instead of the other Narayan novels, however, not only because I believe it is his finest work but also because it introduces a new theme: the mystery of physical death. Narayan's development of this theme might be looked at as an extension of what we have already seen in *Kanthapura*. In that work, Raja Rao illustrated that a collective revolutionary consciousness could only develop by a rejection of Western political dominance. In *Grateful to Life and Death*, Narayan shows us that the individual's personal spiritual fulfillment (an understanding of the mystical aspects of death), can only be achieved by a renunciation of Western cultural dominance.

The point of view of Narayan's *Grateful to Life and Death* is the first person, the main character's, Krishna's—not only the singular conscious-ness but the questioning consciousness, something we are aware of from the opening paragraph. Krishna (named after the narrator of the *Bhavagad-Gita*) is discontented with his life as it is; he questions what can be done about it. We are thrust directly into his thoughts, though they are usually presented in a conventional manner. The story that Krishna tells us is simple enough, in fact almost plotless: his growing unhappiness with his teaching career, the pain of his wife's death, his later attempts to establish contact with her through spiritualism. Of these events, death is centermost, since it is related to most of the other events in the story and to the novel's other themes.

Although Krishna's discontent with his position (his life crisis) begins before his wife's death, the two eventually become related. In the opening pages of the novel, Narayan depicts him as an aesthetically sensitive man: besides writing poetry, Krishna plants a jasmine tree at the boys' school where he teaches. He also has a sense of humor and a tendency to be a bit of a worrier. In a way, Krishna is a younger version of Markandaya's Appa—part buffoon, still part child himself, refusing to become an adult. He is dissatisfied with things as they are, though he is highly regarded by his colleagues and students. When placed next to the other characters from Third World novels we have examined, Krishna's life is clearly more secure, yet he feels little but discontent with his situation. He is, in short, concerned about his role in life. Is he doing what he should be doing? By the definitions of the Western academic world he inhabits, he is a success. Yet he realizes that something is wrong; he is not happy. He criticizes himself but not the system he has become a part of.

Self-criticism is the issue Krishna confronts—a problem none of the other characters we have examined has faced. The term appears in the opening sentence of the novel: "I was on the whole very pleased with my day—not many conflicts and worries, above all not too much self-criticism."[1] His satisfaction, we soon learn, is only for this specific day. The paragraph continues, developing the self-probing aspect of his personality:

I had done almost all the things I wanted to do, and as a result I felt heroic and satisfied. The urge had been upon me for some days past to take myself in hand. What was wrong with me? I couldn't say, some sort of vague disaffection, a self-rebellion I might call it. The feeling again and again came upon me that as I was nearing thirty I should cease to live like a cow (perhaps, a cow, with justice, might feel hurt at the comparison), eating, working in a manner of speaking, walking, talking, etc.—all done to perfection, I was sure, but always leaving behind a sense of something missing. (p. 1)

This is the first time we have seen a character in any of these novels ask himself "What was wrong with me?" Always before, if there has been any questioning, it has been of the inconsistencies and frustrations of the white man's world.

Krishna comments on his superior status in the community as a teacher at the Albert Mission College where he earns a hundred rupees each month. But he suggests, "...perhaps because I was a poet..., I was constantly nagged by the feeling that I was doing the wrong work. This was responsible for a perpetual self-criticism..." (p. 1). Shortly thereafter, he complains about his inability to control his thoughts. His mind wanders. He broods. How can anything be wrong, since he has everything he needs?

There are hints to the answers to these questions almost immediately, though Krishna is a long time in understanding exactly what they mean. Most of them are couched in the multiple references to Western education, of which Krishna is both product and perpetrator. The Albert Mission College rigidly upholds British educational methods. On the day that Krishna says has gone so well, Mr. Brown, the English principal, gave "a lecture on the importance of the English language, and the need for preserving its purity" (p. 2). Brown tells the Indian teachers he is especially disturbed that the English Honors students do not " 'know till this day that "honours" [has] to be spelt with a "u" ' " (p. 2). When the other teachers uphold Brown's nitpicking, Krishna states, " 'Let us be fair. Ask Mr. Brown if he can say in any of the two hundred Indian languages: "The cat chases the rat." He has spent thirty years in India' " (p. 3). Krishna has yet to realize that it is this educational system he has been locked into (for ten years, as a student and then as a teacher) that is the source of much of his anxiety. Western education has, in fact, become a slow death for Krishna, preventing him from discovering the kind of mystical rebirth he is seeking. Later in the day, while he is teaching a class, his self-questioning becomes more revealing. He thinks,

I was merely a man who had mugged earlier than they the introduction and the notes in the Verity edition of *Lear,* and guided them through the mazes of Elizabethan English. I did not do it out of love for them or for Shakespeare but only out of love for myself. If they paid me the same one hundred rupees for stringing beads together or tearing up paper bits every day for a few hours, I would perhaps be doing it with equal fervour. (p. 9)

Krishna's fellow teachers are all trapped within the English educational system. Narayan shows them as literal-minded and humorless, perfect little automatons perpetuating the same theories taught to them years ago. All of them take their work too seriously. The multiple references to *King Lear* are also of more than passing significance. Like Lear, Krishna is about to experience a total emotional collapse followed by spiritual transformation.

Western education extends far beyond the classroom walls in *Grateful to Life and Death*. Because Krishna is an English teacher, Narayan is able to make fun of a number of Western literary sacred cows. Of his wife, Krishna tells us, "She had been trying to get through *Ivanhoe* for years now, and Lamb's *Tales from Shakespeare*. But she never went beyond the fiftieth page" (p. 44). It is too early (1945) for criticism stronger than this, but we have only to remember that one of the first things most ex-British colonies did with their educational systems after independence was revise the curriculum, changing the reading requirements, especially in areas such as literature. That meant eliminating the English classics and replacing them with the works of indigenous writers.

To the themes of self-evaluation and the limitations of an imported educational system, Narayan adds the dominant theme of death, merging them together in the scenes devoted to Krishna's wife's last days. What precedes them is an extremely low-keyed account of marital bliss between Krishna and Susila, his wife—one of the most poignant I can recall. Once his wife and daughter have joined him, everything goes along well—Krishna even appears to have stopped his self-questioning—until the search for a new house culminates in Susila's illness, contacted supposedly from a squalid toilet in the empty house they intend to purchase. Narayan employs a number of subtle criticisms of Western medicine, again commenting on those Indians who have accepted Western practices and rejected Indian ones. Krishna is disturbed at the doctor's initial abruptness and the coldness he experiences at the medical clinic, but the doctor, he later tells us—once he makes a house call—"radiated health and cheer" (p. 83). The comment is meant to be taken ironically. A friend warns him, " 'Never trust these English [trained] doctors' " (p. 90). When Susila's mother calls in a native doctor, an exorcist, Krishna states, "I felt ashamed and wished I could spirit away this mystic" (p. 93). Then, as everything appears to be getting better, Susila dies. Her death (from typhoid, first wrongly diagnosed as malaria) comes as quite a jolt to the reader. There have been few clues that the happiness between Krishna and Susila would end so abruptly in tragedy.

The truth is that Krishna is no better prepared for his wife's death than the reader is. Narayan intends for it to be a shock to both. When Krishna tries to answer his three-year-old daughter's questions about what has happened to her mother, he realizes that he has no answers. As he tells us, "I'm an imbecile, incapable of doing anything or answering any questions" (p. 106). His education and his years of teaching have given him no preparation for explaining death to his daughter or comprehending it himself. He has reached the bottom of his life, the depth of his confusion: "There are no more surprises and shocks in life . . . . For me the greatest reality is this and nothing else . . . . Nothing else will worry or interest me in life hereafter" (p. 107).

Susila's death—coupled now with his earlier self-questioning about his job and his place in life—results in a period of intense grief for Krishna. "The days had acquired a peculiar blankness and emptiness" (p. 108). The only relief he finds is caring for his child, Leela, who becomes his "chief occupation in life" (p. 116). Little else brings satisfaction. Krishna states, "A terrible fatigue and inertia had come over me . . ." (p. 118). He continues teaching, but it brings him no rewards. He bungles along.

Abruptly, Narayan opens up his story, expands his commentary on death by introducing a number of carefully balanced counterpoints that will eventually change his picture of the irreversibility of death to one of rebirth. But it is a radically different kind of rebirth that we see here, one which takes us away from the norms of Western education and into the mysterious worlds of communication with the dead and astrology. This departure is first evident when a young boy brings Krishna a letter from his father:

> "This is a message for Krishna from his wife Susila who recently passed over . . . . She has been seeking all these months some means of expressing herself to her husband, but the opportunity has occurred only today, when she found the present gentleman a very suitable medium of expression. Through him she is happy to communicate. She wants her husband to know that she is quite happy in another region, and wants him also to eradicate the grief in his mind. We are nearer each other than you understand. And I'm always watching him and the child . . . ." (p. 119)

The second counterpoint is Krishna's own confrontation with death when he poses the question of his own suicide. The third emanates from another Indian teacher—the headmaster of the school Leela begins attending—and the sub-story of his approaching death, predicted by an astrologer.

All of these variations on the death theme come together in the last few chapters of the novel and relate back to the earlier issues of self-questioning and the place of Western education in a non-Western society.

All of them contribute to Krishna's own spiritual development and self-education, returning him to his cultural roots. In the ensuing encounters with the gentleman who acts as the medium in order that he may establish contact with his wife, Krishna acquires the patience necessary for his own eventual psychic development. At first, however he is so excited that the communications are unsatisfactory, bringing more frustration than content. Krisna is in too much of a hurry. When the communications are not immediately revealing, he begins to doubt the validity of the entire sequence of events. Then, on one occasion, Susila explains to him the need for looking at death in a new way:

> "Between thought and fulfillment there is no interval. Thought is fulfillment, motion and everything. That is the main difference between our physical state and yours. In your state a thought to be realized must always be followed by effort directed towards conquering obstructions and inertia—that is the nature of the material world. But in our condition no such obstruction exists. When I think of you or you of me I am at your side. Music directly transports us. When I think of a garment, it is on me. In our world there is such a fine response for thought. When I come to you I prepare myself every time as befits the occasion. I come to meet my lord and I dress myself as befits the occasion. I think of the subtlest perfume and it already pervades my being; and I think of the garment that will most please you: the wedding saree, shimmering purple woven with gold, I have on me at this very moment. You think you saw it in that trunk, how can it be here? What you have seen is its counterpart, the real part of the thing is that which is in thought, and it can never be lost or destroyed or put away." (p. 149)

During the times when the communication with his wife fails to be particularly convincing, Krishna's earlier depression returns. Once again he feels desolate; he begins to loathe his work. He tells us he hates food, work, and friends. It is his teaching, however, that especially bothers him. When a student asks him a question about a specific literary work, Krishna replies, " 'Don't worry so much about these things—they are trash, we are obliged to go through and pretend that we like them, but all the time the problem of living and dying is crushing us...' " (p. 170). Shortly thereafter he begins to look at his teaching as so much "literary garbage" (p. 171). The culmination of this crisis is Krishna's contemplation of suicide—both to get away from his job and to be with his wife: "It [death by suicide] seemed to be the greatest aspiration one could have" (p. 172). Soon after this, in one of their dialogues through the medium, Susila tells him not to contemplate such matters.

The third variation on death—concerning Leela's headmaster—has slowly been developing parallel to these other two. The headmaster's unorthodox school presents another contrast to Krishna's own educational background—once again highlighting the East/West conflict. The headmaster himself is a haunting character who almost overshadows Krishna by the end of the narrative. He tells Krishna a number of times, " 'it [is] very difficult for me to manage in an adult society' " (p. 159). Krishna thinks of him as "a man who had strayed into a wrong world" (p. 167). Later the headmaster reveals to him the knowledge of his own imminent death: " 'I know exactly when I am going to die. An astrologer, who has noted down every minute detail of my life, has fixed that for me. I know the exact hour ...' " (p. 168).

What provides such a contrast here is the headmaster's attitude about death compared to Krishna's. He fully expects to die on the predicted date, and, consequently, asks Krishna to take over the direction of his school for him. He approaches death stoically, telling Krishna, " 'The only reality I recognize is death. To me it is nothing more than a full-stop. I have trained myself to view it with calm,' " (p. 187) to which he adds, " 'I'm to be born in a Cochin village to Brahmin parents ...' " (p. 187). When the day arrives, however, it does not bring about physical death but liberation. The reincarnation he has anticipated ironically becomes a more literal rebirth, since he decides to leave his termagant wife and wild children and devote all of his time to the children at his school. When Krishna sees him the day following his expected death, "He looked rejuvenated" (p. 189). As he tells Krishna, " 'I'm going to treat myself as dead and my life as a new birth .... I have ceased to be my old self, and so don't belong to that home in Anderson Street .... It is all over. This school is my house hereafter. I will settle here ...' " (pp. 190–191). He has been freed of the old restrictions that have prohibited him from fulfilling his life's intentions—devoting himself fully to the children at his school. From the possibility of death he has made something positive.

It is the rebirth that Krishna witnesses in the headmaster that makes it possible for him to gather the necessary strength to change his own life. Krishna's metamorphosis is total, but first he has to cast aside all of the aspects of his old way of life that have plagued him. He reflects,

> "Wife, child, brothers, parents, friends ....We come together only to go apart again. It is one continuous movement. They move away from us as we move away from them. The law of life can't be avoided. The law comes into operation the moment we detach ourselves from our mother's womb. All struggle and misery in life is due to our attempt to arrest this law or get away from it or in allowing ourselves to be hurt by it. The fact must be recognized. A profound unmitigated loneliness is the only truth of life. All else is false." (p. 203)

Krishna begins to spend as much time as possible with his daughter, and he notices that his loneliness begins to disappear when he is around the children at her school. "When I sat there at the threshold of his [the headmaster's] hut and watched the children, all sense of loneliness ceased to oppress, and I felt a deep joy and contentment stirring within me" (pp. 203–204).

The denouement of the novel, after Krishna's decision to join the headmaster at his school, comes quickly. Krishna resigns from the college, informing his colleagues, " 'I'm seeking a great inner peace. I find I can't attain it unless I withdraw from the adult world and adult work into the world of children. And there, let me assure you, is a vast storehouse of peace and harmony' " (p. 211). These realizations grow out of Krishna's final rejection not only of the adult world, but of Western education. Initially, he intends to send Mr. Brown a bitter letter of resignation.

> I would send in a letter which would be a classic in its own way, and which would singe the fingers of whoever touched it. In it I was going to attack a whole century of false education. I was going to explain why I could no longer stuff Shakespeare and Elizabethan metre and Romantic poetry for the hundredth time into young minds and feed them on the dead mutton of literary analysis and theories and histories, while what they needed was lessons in the fullest use of the mind. This education had reduced us to a nation of morons; we were strangers to our own culture and camp followers of another culture, feeding on leavings and garbage. (p. 205)

This is the strongest attack on Western education in the novel and, at the same time, one of the most emphatic statements on the need for cultural restoration, that cultural independence from the colonial power is as important as political independence. By rejecting Western education, Krishna has rejected the Western intellectual edifice.

These harsh statements and other related thoughts are not included in the resignation letter that Krishna eventually sends to Mr. Brown but are important instead because they connect the two major themes of the novel: education and death. Western education has been a kind of slow death for Krishna. In these final revelations that he experiences, the reader understands the importance of the title Narayan originally gave to his novel, *The English Teacher*. One of Krishna's last thoughts at the time of his resignation from the college is particularly revealing: " 'I am up against the system, the whole method and approach of a system of education which makes us morons, cultural morons, but efficient clerks for all your business and administrative offices' " (p. 206). It is necessary for Krishna to cease being the English teacher of the novel's original title (changed by his American publishers), necessary for him to rid himself of those aspects of Western education that have encumbered him before he can have his final revelation about death—since the two, after all, have become irrevocably locked together.

It should be apparent that *The English Teacher* is a more appropriate title than *Grateful to Life and Death*. There is a pattern in many of Narayan's novels of the main character's having to renounce what he believes he is. Krishna must become something other than an English teacher since it is not only his profession but the source of much of his dissatisfaction. The same is true of *The Bachelor of Arts* (1937), *The Financial Expert* (1952) and *The Vendor of Sweets* (1967)—the characters in these works are not free until they escape what the title proclaims they are. In Krishna's case, re-education has thus become the pathway for his final psychic development.

The night after he leaves the Albert Mission College for the last time his re-education is completed. Sitting at home, his mind suddenly tranquil for the first time in months, flooded by memories of the past few days, he calls to his wife:

> I softly called "Susila! Susila, my wife . . ." with all my being. It sounded as if it were a hypnotic melody. "My wife . . . my wife, my wife . . . ." My mind trembled with this rhythm, I forgot myself and my own existence. I fell into a drowse, whispering, "My wife, wife." How long? How could I say? When I opened my eyes again she was sitting on my bed looking at me with an extraordinary smile in her eyes.
> "Susila! Susila!" I cried. "You here!" "Yes, I'm here, have always been here." (p. 212)

And the novel concludes, "We stood at the window, gazing on a slender, red streak over the eastern rim of the earth. A cool breeze lapped our faces. The boundaries of our personalities suddenly dissolved. It was a moment of rare, immutable joy—a moment for which one feels grateful to Life and Death" (p. 213).

Krishna has discovered that the Western education and culture that he has considered all his life to be the final end of knowledge and wisdom is in fact hollow when he confronts the mystery of personal death. He has found true meaning by returning to the sources, to the traditional concepts of death, which make communication with the dead possible. He has moved outside of time, stepped aside from his old life; the discovery of a mystical world annihilates any interest in life's other occupations—education, politics, even revolution.

Krishna has passed over the bridge between life and death and achieved a oneness with the spirit world. The stages of this transformation have been arduous. He has had to reject his life of worldly possessions, the security of a well-paid college teaching position. He has had to learn the proper ways of meditation, of purification—to reduce his condition to a state of passivity and peacefulness in order for his spiritual development to proceed. The supernatural experience that results is the culminating state in his re-education, a rebirth similar to the headmaster's.

The theme of rebirth here is not limited solely to the process of re-education but extends also to the role that children play in this novel. I mention this because, for the most part, the novels we have looked at have tended to be childless, though it is true that in three of them (*The Crocodile, In the Castle of My Skin,* and *Two Virgins*) the main character is first seen as a child or an adolescent. In *Grateful to Life and Death* on the other hand, children are depicted as holding the key to existence, to life itself. Subconsciously, Krishna begins to realize this after his wife's death when he begins to spend more time with his daughter, but it takes the example of Leela's teacher before he can understand the role that he himself must play. Earlier, however, before the headmaster enters the narrative, Krishna's wife tells him during one of their sessions with the medium, " 'Children are keener sighted by nature [than adults]. She sees me, and perhaps takes it naturally, since children spontaneously see only the souls of persons' " (p. 135). For Leela, her mother is not dead. Susila's explanation continues, " 'And don't you agree that there is a certain peace about her, which elders lack, although I was no less important to her than to anyone else?' " (pp. 135–136).

These ideas are reiterated the first time that Krishna talks to the headmaster: " 'We can learn a great deal watching [children] and playing with them. When we are qualified we can enter their life . . . . When I watch them, I get a glimpse of some purpose in existence and creation' " (p. 141). Leela's teacher has suggested that he is not a teacher at all; the educational process, if it should not be reversed, should at least be reciprocal. The child learns from the adult, but the adult must learn from the child also. At the headmaster's school, the educational process is based on this reciprocity. As he tells Krishna another time—indirectly attacking Western education—his idea for his school grew out of memories of his own childhood:

> "Most of us forget that grand period. But with me it has always been there. A time at which the colours of things are different, their depths greater, their magnitude greater, a most balanced and joyous condition of life; there was a natural state of joy over nothing in particular. And then our own schooling which put blinkers on to us; which persistently ruined this vision of things and made us into adults. It has always seemed to me that our teachers helped us to take a wrong turn." (pp. 167–168)

The Leave Alone system of education (as he calls it) is the only way one can escape "the curse of adulthood" (p. 168). One is reminded of Wordsworth's "Intimations of Immortality": for both the headmaster and Krishna, life has been a sleep and a forgetting; their formal education has taken them away from the culture of their births. Adulthood has become a kind of dream, as Krishna eventually understands it, shortly before he relinquishes his teaching at the college for the primary school: " 'How little do we know what a dream is, how little do we understand!' " (p. 194).

By the conclusion of the narrative, Krishna's questionings have brought him peace and happiness. He has undertaken a kind of archetypal quest, a spiritual journey triggered by his questioning the basic precepts of his life—beginning with that initial question, "What was wrong with me?" and resulting in his metamorphosis. His re-education has been possible because he has dared to confront the fundamental beliefs of his life. From a restless and unhappy person he has evolved to a heightened consciousness aware of a deeper meaning to life. We have seen a move toward the singular consciousness, for it is through Krishna's eyes that we observe all of these events; but in the end, it is also a move toward others—the children at the school—a return once again to one's cultural origins. Narayan's achievement is to have shown us that the introspection we call private history often moves the individual back into the mainstream of public history. Krishna's final state of selflessness is a merging of the two. I can think of few other novels that present this fusion as effectively as *Grateful to Life and Death*. Clearly, this novel is Narayan's masterpiece.

Private history also merges with public history in Bessie Head's *A Question of Power*, though the road toward recovery is much more chaotic than in Narayan's *Grateful to Life and Death*. There is room for speculation that both of these novels have drawn heavily on autobiographical materials. Narayan describes the death of his young wife and his interest in spiritualism in his autobiography, *My Days: A Memoir* (1974):

> Within a hundred days of her arrival, Rajam had departed from this world. She caught typhoid in early May and collapsed in the first week of June 1939. Looking back it seems as if she had had a premonition of her end, and had wanted to stay back with her parents and sister. I have described this part of my experience of her sickness and death in *The English Teacher* so fully that I do not, and perhaps cannot, go over it again. More than any other book, *The English Teacher* is autobiographical in content, very little part of it being fiction.... The dedication of the book to the memory of my wife should to some extent give the reader a clue that the book may not be all fiction; still, most readers resist, naturally, as one always does, the transition from life to death and beyond.[2]

Bessie Head's own life shares a number of similarities with that of her heroine, named Elizabeth (Bessie?). Ms. Head was born in South

Africa of racially mixed parentage, which relegated her to the apartheid "Coloured" classification. Eleven years ago she fled South Africa (because of political activities, in part) for Botswana where as a stateless person she taught school for a time before becoming a gardener in a private commune. Two earlier novels, *When Rain Clouds Gather* and *Maru*, were published in 1968 and 1971, but they are of minor importance when placed next to *A Question of Power*.

Novels by African women are still a fairly rare occurrence, an event to be greeted with more than passing interest.[3] Introspective novels by African writers tend to be equally rare in large part because the situational novel tends to be concerned with external events instead of internal states of mind.[4] Bessie Head's *A Question of Power* is important not solely because it is an introspective novel by an African woman but because the topics of her concern are also, for the most part, foreign to African fiction as a sub-division of the novel in the Third World: madness, sexuality, guilt. In its concern with these ideas, *A Question of Power* bears closer affinity to the works by two Caucasian writers from southern Africa—Doris Lessing and Nadine Gordimer—than to those of Ms. Head's African contemporaries.

Although *A Question of Power* is told in the third person, the point of view is always Elizabeth's. The reader understands the events in the story the same way that Elizabeth does, which is to say that when she is confused (which is often) he is confused. The extended passages of introspection are depicted primarily through the use of the internal monologue; the chronology of the narrative is often associative. The achievement is another intellectual puzzle, like *Cane*, though the content here is radically different. The reader has to keep reading to find out what is going on, to learn what has already happened. The story has to be constructed in the reader's mind from bits and pieces, often contradictory ones, somewhat in the manner of a Robbe-Grillet novel.

From the beginning, Elizabeth's life is one of exile and alienation. She teaches in a school in a village called Motabeng, cut off from the people around her, and only slowly realizes that she has found no lasting peace in Botswana because she has failed to come to grips with the problems that forced her to fled South Africa in the first place. She simply brings them along with her, and in Motabeng they threaten to take control of her. Ms. Head dramatizes these problems through Elizabeth's elaborate fantasies, rooted in multiple layers of guilt. Of Elizabeth herself we know only the scantiest information, in part because the facts of her childhood were concealed from her by her foster parents until she was thirteen. At that time she was placed in a mission school and informed that her mother (an English woman) killed herself in an insane asylum when Elizabeth was six years old. Her father was African. The principal warns her, " 'We have a full docket on you. You must be very careful. Your mother was insane. If you're not careful you'll get insane just like your mother. Your mother was a white woman. They had to lock her up, as she was having a child by the stable boy, who was a native.' "[5]

Elizabeth's origins, then, are rooted in forbidden passion—her mother's breaking of the Immorality Act.[6] But perhaps more damaging to her psyche is the classification as a Coloured—including hints that she has been re-classified after originally having been classified as a white. As a child she was sent to a nursing home from which, as her foster mother tells her much later, "A day later you were returned because you did not look white" (p. 17). Reflecting upon this event much later in her life, Elizabeth thinks of the futility of "filial ties in a country where people were not people at all" (p. 17). After she left the mission, she "married a gangster just out of jail" (p. 18). This is the second major event in her life that contributes to her eventual insanity in Botswana. The marriage is a dead-end: a month later she discovers that her Coloured husband is a promiscuous bisexual. A year later, she walks out of the house with her child, a boy, and leaves for Botswana on an exit permit—that is, a visa that makes re-entry into the country of her birth impossible.

Most of the guilt that Elizabeth develops originates from these early events in her life: her Coloured classification, her orphan status at the mission, and her short-lived marriage. All of these factors are direct results of the South African policy of apartheid which treats people as something other than human beings. If there were no Immorality Act, Elizabeth could have lived with her mother—and would not have had to bear the stigma of being classified as a Coloured—a race to which neither of her parents belongs. The implication is that Elizabeth's mother was not insane at all, but the government felt it had to punish her in some way because she had broken the Immorality Act; it was probably easier for them to place her in a mental hospital than in a jail. Elizabeth's marriage to a bisexual is also a commentary on South Africa's racist practices. Much later in her life, Elizabeth reflects,

> She had lived for a time in a part of South Africa where nearly all the Coloured men were homosexuals and openly paraded down the street dressed in women's clothes. They tied turbans round their heads, wore lipstick, fluttered their eyes and hands and talked in high, falsetto voices. It was so widespread, so common to so many men in this town that they felt no shame at all. They and people in general accepted it as a disease one had to live with. No one commented at these strange men dressed in women's clothes. Sometimes people laughed when they were kissing each other in the street.
>
> An African man gave her the most reasonable explanation: "How can a man be a man when he is called boy? I can barely retain my

own manhood. I was walking down the road the other day with my girl, and the Boer policeman said to me: 'Hey, boy, where's your pass?' Am I a man to my girl or a boy? Another man addresses me as boy. How do you think I feel?" (pp. 44–45)

At its very base, then, *A Question of Power*—like all of the other works we have examined—is concerned with the power play between the West (the white South Africans) and the Third World. There are the ubiquitous problems of racism that we have already seen in many novels—the relationship between subjugators and the subjugated. Elizabeth thinks of her classification as follows: "In South Africa she had been rigidly classified Coloured. There was no escape from it to the simple joy of being a human being with a personality. There wasn't any escape like that for anyone in South Africa. They were races, not people" (p. 44). The scars of her childhood have never completely healed. As a child she had often wondered "why white people . . . had to go out of their way to hate you and loathe you" (p. 19). The basis of the story, then, is racial; it is the development of the narrative that is so unusual, though there are novels of South African life in which neuroses abound. As Elizabeth is later told by an Afrikaner who is also living in exile in Botswana, " 'A lot of refugees have nervous breakdowns' " (p. 52). Elizabeth extends this observation so that it becomes more directly a comment on apartheid: "South Africans usually suffered from some form of mental aberration . . ." (p. 58).

The layers of guilt that develop out of the early situations of Elizabeth's life are often embellished with her sexual fantasies. These fantasies and her several stages of insanity are in large part triggered by two men who live in Motabeng, Sello and Dan, though these fantasies become much more real to Elizabeth than the men do. Often the things Elizabeth believes they say to her relate back to her early life. She is disturbed about her physical appearance, for example. She fears that men are not physically attracted to her. "She would never have earned a second glance from a man like Dan. She was not his type—Miss Glamour, Miss Beauty Queen, Miss Legs, Miss Buttocks . . ." (p. 14). Later she thinks, " 'I shouldn't mind if anyone told me I'm ugly because I know it's true' " (p. 48). One of her demons tells her, " 'You're too fat' " (p. 61). Not only does she feel that men are not sexually attracted to her but that she holds only an intellectual interest for them: "she was the sort of woman men never said foolish, tender things to. Men just didn' get that close . . ." (p. 119).

The failure of her marriage also contributes to her guilt, for Elizabeth feels that if she were more attractive, her husband would not have turned to other women (and men) to fulfill his sexual desires. As her guilt intensifies, she wonders if she is not responsible for turning the men around her into homosexuals. In one of her fantasies "as she closed her eyes all these Coloured man lay down on their backs, their penes in the air, and began to die slowly" (p. 45). Even Sello and Dan—men who enter her fantasies initially because of their masculinity—eventually become associated with the Coloured South African homosexuals. In one of the last scenes in the novel, they bugger each other and molest young children. Elizabeth thinks of Sello's control over her mind: "He was saying he had the potential to be evil, and he was saying awful things about molesting children. He couldn't be trusted to be alone with children else he'd do awful things to them. And he was saying awful things about Dan. Dan was a child-molester too, but much worse still, he went for other men like mad" (p. 116). Although Elizabeth comes to believe that Dan has seduced one of his own daughters, it is easy to understand her greater fear—that one of these men will molest her own son.

All of these aspects of sexual guilt are related to Elizabeth's racial origins and the issues of exile and alienation. Initially, she feels estranged in Botswana because she is a "foreigner": "Motabeng was a village of relatives who married relatives, and nearly everyone had about six hundred relatives" (p. 20). Elizabeth soon realizes that she, too, is racially prejudiced. She looks down at Africans. A voice tells her, " 'You have never really made an identification with the poor and humble... the poor of Africa' " (p. 31). By leaving South Africa, she has simply been running away—trying to avoid the realities of life: "So many people ran away from South Africa to forget it or throw it off" (p. 47). Exile itself, then, becomes another source of her guilt, just as it has in the works of many South African writers who have fled their homeland.[7]

As these feelings of exile and alienation become intensified, Elizabeth comes to realize that almost every aspect of the life around her reminds her of her guilt. She does not know any African languages; she has to communicate with the people of Motabeng solely in English—like the Europeans do. Her hair is not like the Africans'; it is more like her mother's; her physical features are more Caucasian than African. She thinks of herself as a "half-breed," (p. 104), a "mixed breed" (p. 147), "not genuinely African" (p. 159). She answers one of the voices in her fantasies:

> "It wasn't my fault.... I am not a tribal African. If I had been, I would have known the exact truth about Sello, whether he was good or bad. There aren't any secrets among tribal Africans. I was shut out from the everyday affairs of this world. Dan knew and traded on my ignorance. He did more. He struck me such terrible blows, the pain made me lose my mind." (p. 145)

She has developed a love/hate relationship with the Africans around her. On the one hand she wants to be one of them; on the other, she hates them, believing they are inferior. To that extent the apartheid indoctrination she has undergone has been successful.

The accumulation of these guilt feelings—the substance of her erotic fantasies and her frequent nightmares—eventually breaks through into her consciousness when Elizabeth realizes that by implication Dan and Sello are saying that she is sexually frigid because of her white blood. Dan tells her of Miss Sewing Machine who "can go with a man the whole night and feel no ill-effects the next day, provided you stimulate her properly" (p. 127). By contrast, Dan says, "you are inferior as a Coloured. You haven't got what that girl has got" (p. 127). Elizabeth begins to think of herself as "the Coloured dog" (p. 129). As the sexual hysteria continues, she watches Dan make love to seventy-one women. One of them, Miss Body Beautiful, "had an orgasm right on top of Elizabeth" (p. 164). Another one, Miss Squelch Squelch "exposed a spotless vagina right in Elizabeth's face" (p. 165). Another time in the cinema of her mind she sees Dan in "a demonstration of sexual stamina with five local women, this time with the lights on" (p. 148). Her mind has become a movie screen, cluttered with images of sexual perversions.

Perhaps the most interesting aspect of Elizabeth's multiple sexual fantasies is that she is never a participant in them. Rather, she is a voyeur, watching the others in a kind of fascinated way but not involving herself. There is more than an implication of wish fulfillment here, though Elizabeth thinks that "normal" sex is dirty because it leads to abnormal perversions. Of almost equal importance is the fact that Elizabeth's fantasies involve two men (Sello and Dan) she does not actually know—not the men with whom she has some sort of frequent contact, such as Tom, the American, and Eugene, the head of the co-operative she joins. Yet Sello and Dan dominate most of the novel, and their names are used as titles for the two halves of the book. Of Sello, the reader learns only a handful of facts—presumably no more than Elizabeth herself knows: he is married to a Motswana woman; he is a crop farmer and cattle breeder, and "a wonderful family man" (p. 29), according to a nurse at the Motabeng hospital. Elizabeth saw him only once, as she turned the corner of a building and came face to face with him: "She stopped and stared straight at him. He slowly averted his face. She glanced at his companion [Dan], briefly. He had pretty eyes, large, luminous, black, with a thick cluster of lashes. His eyes gave his face a wonderful expression of innocence and friendliness. He immediately bowed his head to Elizabeth in silent greeting" (p. 27). Everything else Elizabeth "knew of the living man was by hearsay" (p. 137). Elizabeth's first-hand knowledge of Dan is equally limited. The facts of his life are mentioned only once:

> He was one of the very few cattle millionaires of the country. He ordered a fantastic array of suits from somewhere, and he was short,

black and handsome. He was the friend of Sello, so people said. Someone told her he was also greatly admired for being an African nationalist in a country where people were only concerned about tribal affairs. Otherwise the circle of people he moved amongst were so removed from the sorts of people she associated with as to make his way of life a total mystery. (p.104)

The fantasies involving these two men dominate Elizabeth's life for three years. She loses her job for making a spectacle of herself in a public office, screaming and cursing the people around her. A short spell in a local hospital is followed by her joining the Motabeng Secondary Project, where she works as a gardener. Her fantasies become increasingly populated with Sello and Dan's cohorts: Medusa, Osiris, Isis, Al Capone, Caligula, Buddha, Bathsheba—plus Dan's seventy-one erotic girls. In the course of the narrative, Sello and Dan themselves undergo a number of metamorphoses. Eventually Elizabeth is placed in a mental institution for seven months during which time she contemplates suicide and infanticide.

Elizabeth's "recovery" in the insane asylum is intended to be more than ironic; it is hardly the result of the medicine or the treatment she receives. Rather, the asylum brings out the strongest of her aversions, and she is forced to acknowledge them for the first time. From the beginning, she is as out of place there as she had been in Motabeng for the past two years: "It was strictly for poor, illiterate Batswana, who were treated like animals. They seemed to be the only people who went insane in Botswana . . ." (p. 180). Her color and her education make her different, forcing her racialism to the surface. Elizabeth shouts at one of the attendants: " 'I'm not an African. Don't you see? I never want to be an African. You bloody well, damn well leave me alone' " (p. 181). It is the European psychiatrist—the only one in the country—who makes her fully cognizant of her racial feelings. Elizabeth develops an immediate affinity to him when she realizes that he treats her better than the other patients because she is not an African, that he hates his black patients. "The shock of being thought of as a comrade racialist had abruptly restored a portion of her sanity" (p. 184).

Besides her race prejudice, the European doctor helps Elizabeth discover an equally destructive prejudice she has harbored during her years in Botswana: intellectual superiority, pride. She has, in fact, willingly isolated herself from the people around her, because she has always considered herself above them. The clues have been apparent throughout the entire narrative. As she tells Eugene, the director of the cooperative, the first time she meets him, " 'I don't care whether people like me or not. I am used to isolation' " (p. 56). She has never made any attempt to understand the people around her, just like the Europeans who come to Botswana as part of various aid projects. Months before her entry into the mental hospital, Elizabeth remarks to Kenosi, " 'I have no friends' " (p. 90). She has, in fact, often fought those friendships that would have been most helpful to her. She has been guilty of refusing to believe in the brotherhood of man.

Though far from completely recovered, Elizabeth is released from the mental institution after seven months. As she begins to articulate what has happened to her, she understands some of the darker aspects of her personality:

> I seem to have taken a strange journey into hell and darkness. I could not grasp the darkness because at the same time I saw the light. That captured and riveted my attention. It was Sello. It seemed to me that his job was religion itself, because he moved towards me like that, then right in front of my eyes did a slow, spiritual strip-tease act. He half showed me that the source of human suffering was God itself, personalities in possession of powers or energies of the soul. (p. 190)

Eventually Elizabeth seeks solace in the land, returning to the garden, and the village co-operative of which she had earlier been a part. From Kenosi, an African woman, she learns to respect the soil and the people of Botswana. Her error has been her inability to comprehend the African sense of humanity—she fled those people who would harbor her:

> There was no direct push against those rigid, false social systems of class and caste. She had fallen from the very beginning into the warm embrace of the brotherhood of man, because when a people wanted everyone to be ordinary it was just another way of saying man loved man. (p. 206)

The journey of the singular consciousness has once again ended in the collective consciousness, the brotherhood of man.

The question of power in the title of Bessie Head's novel is as many-layered as the multiple fears and guilts from which Elizabeth has been fleeing for much of her adult life. Initially, Ms. Head speaks of this as one's personal power and the way it operates in relationships with others: "It was harder to disclose the subtle balances of powers between people—how easy it was for people with soft shuffling, loosely-knit personalities to be preyed upon by dominant, powerful persons" (p. 12). To this Ms. Head adds a whole list of extraterrestrial powers: "energies, stars, planets, universes and all kinds of swirling magic and mystery ..." (p. 35)—forces over which the individual has little control. (There are hints throughout the novel of the importance of witchcraft in Botswana life.) In her nightmares, Elizabeth sees traditional African society as powerful enough to cut all non-Africans out: "The wild-eyed Medusa was expressing the surface reality of African society. It was shut in and exclusive. It had a strong theme of power-worship running through it, and power people needed small, narrow, shut-in worlds" (p. 38).

As these ideas embellish the narrative of Elizabeth's own struggles for personal power to pull her life together, they take on a quasi-religious framework of spiritual power—the struggle between God and man. At first Elizabeth sees them as inseparable: "God is the totality of all great souls and their achievements" (p. 54). If God is here, everything is safely in its place. In the depths of her struggle with good and evil, however, she begins to doubt the validity of a God-centered universe, eventually concluding, *"If the things of the soul are really a question of power, then anyone in possession of power of the spirit could be Lucifer"* (p. 199), that is, Sello and Dan. Any man who wields power blindly over others becomes a devil. Spiritual power must be man-oriented, not God-oriented:

> the basic error seemed to be a relegation of all things holy to some unseen Being in the sky. Since man was not holy to man, he could be tortured for his complexion, he could be misused, degraded and killed. If there were any revelation whatsoever in her own suffering it seemed to be quite the reverse of Mohammed's dramatic statement. He had said: There is only one God and his name is Allah. And Mohammed is his prophet.
> She said: There is only one God and his name is Man. And Elizabeth is his prophet. (pp. 205–206)

Finally, then, spiritual power becomes personal power—the power of the individual to resist evil, to pull his life together. In this context, a remark made by Roberta Rubenstein about *A Question of Power* is particularly illuminating, because it takes us back to the novel's concern with insanity: "The most important kind of power implied in the novel is, finally, the power of the human spirit to overcome its own movement toward annihilation.[8]

Political power is, as we have already noted, a given throughout the entire work: the South African apartheid policies start Elizabeth on her road to madness. If she had remained in South Africa, her life would always have been politically controlled by the Europeans. As a Coloured, she will be a kind of outsider no matter where she goes in Africa—though Botswana, an enclave dependent on South Africa in so many ways, is a particularly ironic choice to flee to. The European psychiatrist confronts Elizabeth with this idea, though she is already well aware of the fact: "He let fly about the country. It was full of South African spies. They needn't think they could do a thing with *their* independence. The country was really run by the South African government" (p. 184).

In the final analysis, Bessie Head wants us to consider all of these variations of power as the evils that thwart each individual's desire to be part of the human race, part of the brotherhood of man. The facts of one's race, color, religion, education—these should not be considered prerequisites for membership in the human race. This is the supreme reality of *A Question of Power*, expressed in the first two sentences of the novel, before Elizabeth becomes insane: "It seemed almost incidental that he [Sello] was African. So vast had his inner perceptions grown over the years that he preferred an *identification with mankind* to an identification with a particular environment" (p. 11; italics mine). The idea is reiterated in a discussion Elizabeth has with Tom about black power in the United States. She tells him, " 'I've got my concentration elsewhere.... It's on mankind in general, and black people fit in there, not as special freaks and oddities outside the scheme of things, with labels like Black Power or any other rubbish of that kind' " (p. 133).

The private consciousness is the lonely consciousness; the pathway is uncertain, the goals often elusive. Art—in the West—breeds, we say, on frustration and alienation. The novelist's life is the loneliest of all. He writes his books in privacy; they are intended to be read by others in privacy. In the Third World these precepts of the artist have not always been applicable—function often replaces art for art's sake; the poet (the artificer of words) is a part of the whole, strongly rooted at the center of the communal stage. How strange these aspects seem then in the face of R. K. Narayan's *Grateful to Life and Death* and Bessie Head's *A Question of Power*. The private agony is something we would not have expected here. Or, again as Roberta Rubenstein has written, we have been conditioned to think of the "topography of madness" as a unique by-product of Western living.[9]

For these reasons *Grateful to Life and Death* and *A Question of Power* come as unexpected surprises to us. We are not used to reading fiction from the Third World that is so familiar to us or so closely based on the agony of the writer's own personal life. We have forgotten that the inward turning of the novel in the West grew out of similar social and historical conditions. Artistic freedom, like political freedom, shifts its ground from externals to internals. The artist, as Bessie Head has written of herself, faces the same struggle as the nation state—he wants to be a human being.

# Conclusion

Although my intention in this study has been to concentrate on ten novels from half a dozen disparate cultures of the Third World and to treat them as representative of the greater bodies of writing from which they have been singled out, I am aware at the same time of the uniqueness of many of these works—some of them still defy classification as Western or as Third World novels. Should René Maran's *Batouala* be regarded as representative of subsequent African fiction? Or of West Indian writing? How is it possible to regard Jean Tommer's *Cane* as typical of the vast totality of Afro-American novels? One might conclude that the novels treated here often share more similarities with each other than they do with the bodies of writing from which they have come. The fact that I accept such a possibility as a given has, of course, played a large part in my decision to include each one of these works in this study.

Examining these novels as a group, we can identify a marked evolutionary pattern—from the collective consciousness to the individual consciousness. This pattern is as follows:

—communal consciousness
  (little or no introspection)

—individual consciousness
  (introspection)

—group focus
  (no main character)

—individual focus
  (main character)

| | |
|---|---|
| —situational plot (conflict usually triggered by outside events—exposure to another culture) | —plot is secondary to character development (conflict triggered by personal problems) |
| —use of cultural materials (anthropological background, etc.) | —development of individual states of mind—of differing emotional states (the furniture of the mind) |

The novels that belong exclusively in the first column are *Batouala, Bound to Violence,* and *Seven Arrows*—where the emphasis is upon the communal consciousness or what might more accurately be called the "cultural consciousness." These novels are immediately concerned with the threat of cultural death, and they tend to rely heavily on anthropological or culturally related materials. In the last three novels examined in this study (*Two Virgins, Grateful to Life and Death,* and *A Question of Power*) the focus has shifted to the individual character, becoming highly introspective in the process. The writer is no longer concerned primarily with cultural matters or even with defending the past traditions, but, rather, concerned with the individual consciousness. The interceding novels generally share traits from both columns. There is a parallel evolution, of course, in the confrontation with the West, from the earliest stages of exposure to the final stages of rebellion and independence.

The rebellion is far off in the distance in *Batouala*, yet Maran, as we have already seen, paved the way for later black writers (African, West Indian, Afro-American) to write about those topics they felt were long overlooked, ignored by the Western world. In a sense, it is possible to look at Maran's novel as one of the earliest examples of protest fiction by a writer from the Third World who wanted to be objective (except perhaps in the introduction) and present traditional life as it was —through a black man's eyes, unromanticized. In this regard, Maran was the first of many subsequent African writers—Chinua Achebe, James Ngugi, Ayi Kwei Armah, Wole Soyinka, Kofi Awoonor, Bessie Head, and numerous others—who have set their works in an African setting, unglamorized, objective. In *Bound to Violence* Ouologuem attempts to do much the same thing that Maran did in *Batouala*—namely, to destroy the myth of a romanticized African past and replace it by one of "factual" truth. Although literary influences are difficult to prove, I suspect that Ouologuem was quite familiar with *Batouala* and that Maran's work played an important part in his own writing.

George Lamming's *In the Castle of My Skin* is perhaps the easiest book upon which to make a case for representativeness. The situation is archetypal—the growing awareness of one's racial consciousness, a theme that permeates a vast amount of Third World writing whether that be fiction, poetry, or drama. Lamming's genius is his ability to orchestrate his narrative with the use of multiple points of view (the composite image of the community) and the autobiographical overtones of the work (the individual consciousness). The latter characteristic relates it to any number of other black autobiographies—those of Richard Wright, Peter Abrahams, Claude Brown, Arnold Apple, Maya Angelou, to mention only a few, or a whole host of autobiographical novels that have similarly depicted the child's or young adult's growing awareness of his racial origins: Langston Hughes' *Not without Laughter* (1930), Peter Abrahams' *Mine Boy* (1946), James Baldwin's *Go Tell It on the Mountain* (1953), William Demby's *Beetlecreek* (1950), Michael Anthony's *The Year in San Fernando* (1965), Gwendolyn Brooks' *Maud Martha* (1953), Owen Dodson's *Boy at the Window* (1951), Toni Morrison's *Sula* (1974). The list could go on and on.

Jean Toomer's *Cane* is not so atypical, either, except for its form. The novel's central theme—the belief that an acceptance of the past is necessary for an understanding of one's cultural traditions—is, after all, a subject that concerned many of the other novelists of the Harlem Renaissance: Claude McKay (especially in *Banana Bottom*, 1933), Nella Larsen (in *Quicksand*, 1928, and in *Passing*, 1929), Countee Cullen (in *One Way to Heaven*, 1932). Certainly the Harlem Renaissance poets (Countee Cullen, Claude McKay, Sterling Brown, and Langston Hughes) were similarly concerned with this theme of the past, although they did, in fact, often treat it in a more romanticized fashion. Toomer's *Cane* should also be regarded as a backlash against those earlier Afro-American novelists like Charles Chesnutt and Paul Laurence Dunbar who had not been able to accept their pasts or the black man's collective history in the New World. For this reason alone, I think we have to agree with Arna Bontemps' statement that almost all subsequent Afro-American fiction is indebted to *Cane*.

The Indo-Anglian novels by Raja Rao, R. K. Narayan, and Kamala Markandaya are all representative of the greater whole from which they have been selected. We have already noted the frequency of Indo-Anglian novels dealing with Mahatma Gandhi and his ideas—as Raja Rao's *Kanthapura* so powerfully does. Nor are R. K. Narayan's *Grateful to Life and Death* and Kamala Markandaya's *Two Virgins* so unusual in their treatment of the Western/Third World conflict, except that they treat this theme with more subtlety than many other Indo-Anglian novelists have done. Perhaps, too, one finds even more of an affinity between these three novels and the rest of the Anglophone Indian fiction because the list of such novels is not as extensive as their African or Afro-American counterparts.

With the fiction by Native Americans and South Sea Islanders we encounter an opposing factor: so little fiction has appeared from these peoples that it is difficult to make any generalizations about the shape of that writing. Hyemeyohsts Storm's *Seven Arrows* shares only a few superficial similarities with N. Scott Momaday's *House Made of Dawn* (1967) or James Welch's *Winter in the Blood* (1974), for example. This does not mean, however, that it is impossible to draw a number of parallels between Native American novels and works by other Third World writers. The reader may already have recalled an Afro-American novel that bears a striking similarity to Storm's *Seven Arrows:* Ernest J. Gaines' *The Autobiography of Miss Jane Pittman.* The time factor is roughly the same; only the character focus is different. Storm shows the repetition of violent events by the use of multiple characters; Gaines shows the same repetition (of violence), using one main character.

Vincent Eri's *The Crocodile* provides an even stronger reason for not making speculations about future writing from the South Sea Islands. One might surmise that subsequent writing from this area would also illustrate a lack of concern with cause and effect or with time as part of an evolving historical perspective, but this hardly seems to be the case at all, as two other recent works clearly illustrate. Eri's *The Crocodile* was the first published novel by a Papuan. Since I began working on this book, several other novels by South Sea Islanders have been published: *Tangi* (1973) and *Whanau* (1974), by Witi Ihimaera, a Maori, who has lived most of his life in New Zealand; *Sons for the Return Home* (1973), by Albert Wendt, a Samoan (with a touch of German blood) who has also lived part of his life in New Zealand; and *Aimbe, The Challenger* (1974), by Paulias Matane, another writer from Papua New Guinea. Two of these works (*Tangi* and *Sons for the Return Home*) are as different from Eri's *The Crocodile* as one could imagine—especially in their treatment of causal events, time, and history. Yet both novels are technically innovative (as I would say Eri's is) in a cultural manner, weaving their themes and structural devices out of the raw materials of each writer's traditional heritage. Placed together with Eri's novel, these three works illustrate the complications that may arise when literary classifications are based solely on geography. Inevitably they will be thought of as "typical" South Sea Island novels—an assumption that all writing from a geographical area must be the same—while in fact they should be thought of (if typical at all) as Papuan, or Samoan, or Maori. Similarly, there is no African novel that is typical of *all* African novels, no Afro-American novel typical of *all* Afro-American novels, and so on.

The title of Ihimaera's first novel *Tangi,* literally means the mourning time, and the story itself centers on the death of the main character's father. In many ways, *Tangi* might be regarded as a simple tale—like Kamala Markandaya's *Two Virgins.* The narrative itself is structured by two events—an air flight home and a train ride back to the city—during which there are flashbacks of the narrator's youth and flashforwards describing the funeral ceremony. The treatment of the death itself is unlike anything that I have ever seen before—fictively presented in such a manner that the reader feels he is participating in a several-day-long Maori funerary rite. It is a loving tribute to the main character's father—poetic, haunting, mythic in its origins, as the following brief passage will illustrate:

My mother was the Earth.

My father was the Sky.

They were Rangitane and Papatuanuku, the first parents, who clasped each other so tightly that there was no day. Their children were born into darkness. They lived among the shadows of their mother's breasts and thighs and groped in blindness among the long black strands of her hair.

Until the time of separation and the dawning of the first day.[1]

The novel itself defies classification. One thing, however, is certain—it is almost impossible not to become emotionally involved with the story that unfolds. By any standards, it is a good read.

All of these comments have been by way of concluding that the novel in the Third World is still a very recent event and there is no reason to expect that subsequent writing from any of these areas will necessarily conform to the patterns I have identified in this study. I hope, in fact, that it will not, just as I hope that our own literature will continue to take on new forms and permutations with the passage of time. Yet the novelist in the Third World often does not have the choices that our own writers in the West have had. There are rarely enough publishers to encourage writing of a serious nature—in all of tropical Africa there are only a handful of publishers capable of producing printed books for the general mass market audience. In recent years, many of us have become aware of the remarks made by Afro-American writers about white publishing houses and the difficulties they have encountered there. Almost all Third World novelists feel they are fenced in by publishers, critics, and readers who do not understand their works. Perhaps it is only apocryphal, but there is an old story of an African novelist whose manuscript was returned from a British publisher with a cover letter saying "Not African Enough."

"Not African Enough" is, of course, the literary prison from which these writers have been trying to escape. Unfortunately, little progress has been made in the last ten or fifteen years. Reviewers who should know better by now are still treating Third World writing as so much exotica, refusing to admit that they can often learn something about the *form* of the novel from a writer whose culture is different from their own. The implications appear to be as follows: we read these works to learn something about another culture, not to learn something about literature itself. Hence, a recent unsigned review of Witi Ihimaera's *Tangi* in *The Times Literary Supplement* concludes rather typically:

> But most of the time there is too heavy a reliance on the reciting of strings of exotic names (Aunt Ruihi, Uncle Pita, Rangitane and Papatuanuku), the rehearsing of strange beliefs, and the charting of, to us, uncustomary religious customs involving Earth Mothers and Sky Fathers and many another Frazerian trapping. Even a Maori novel needs to be bulked out with something other than dollops of native lingo, endlessly reiterated.[2]

I doubt if a Maori reader would agree with this at all. Once again, a Western reviewer has ignored the problem of the dual audience that confronts almost every Third World writer. So debilitating can this be that the Third World writer often loses both of his audiences, for if he is true to his own culture, his work is often rejected by readers and critics from outside. If he tries to do something "typically" Western, his work is often rejected by his own people.*

The novelist in the Third World walks a lonely pathway. In spite of what appears to be a flowering of Third World fiction, in most cases the writer in the Third World still has to overcome almost insurmountable obstacles in order to become known. Problems of literacy and the dilemma of which language to write in, coupled with the prohibitive cost of books (for peoples in too many areas of the world) have often drastically curtailed the writer's availability for his own people. The lack of sufficient literary outlets (not just publishing houses for books, but other channels such as scholarly magazines and journals) has resulted in a situation in which most Third World writers have little control over what they publish, in which many of them have no choice except to publish their works *outside* of their own culture.

Misunderstood, often by their own people as well as those who have tried to dictate what they should write, Third World writers often find themselves caught in a kind of cultural limbo—exiled to a world they are not of or for. René Maran was self-exiled in France as is Yambo

---

*This is, in fact, part of the gist of Yambo Ouologuem's defense of himself in regard to the sexual passages in *Bound to Violence*. In another portion of the article in *Le Figaro Littéraire*, he says, "It is obvious that if the facts I raised had been the product of my own imagination, my racial brothers would not have been likely to pardon me of having sullied the Black race."

Similarly, I suspect that many an African reader (and some Western readers also) will find Bessie Head's *A Question of Power* too obscure for their tastes, just as Ayi Kwei Armah lost many readers (for similar reasons) when his fourth novel, *Two Thousand Seasons* (1973) was serialized in a Ghanaian newspaper prior to its publication in book form.

Ouologuem at this time. George Lamming and Kamala Markandaya live in London. Raja Rao lives in the United States. Bessie Head is in exile in Botswana. Jean Toomer passed for white. Hyemeyohsts Storm has been renounced by the Northern Cheyenne for, in so many words, "not being Indian enough." Only Vincent Eri and R. K. Narayan live within the cultures that nurtured them. Nevertheless, in spite of enormous complications, there is little doubt that the novelist from the Third World will be heard—even if his words come to us as the voice of a lonely exile.

# FOOTNOTES

## Introduction

[1]See my earlier book, *The Emergence of African Fiction* (Bloomington: Indiana Univ. Press, 1972), Chapter One.

[2]For a discussion of some of the earlier West Indian novels, see G. R. Coulthard, *Race and Color in Caribbean Literature* (Oxford Univ. Press, 1962) and Kenneth Ramchand, *The West Indian Novel and Its Background* (London: Faber and Faber, 1970).

[3]For a discussion of the Afro-American novel, see Robert Bone, *The Negro Novel in America* (New Haven: Yale Univ. Press, 1965), Edward Margolies, *Native Sons* (Philadelphia: J. B. Lippincott, 1968), and Roger Rosenblatt, *Black Fiction* (Cambridge, Mass.: Harvard University Press, 1974).

[4]For further discussion, see Meenakshi Mukherjee, *The Twice Born Fiction* (New Delhi: Heinemann, 1971).

[5]See *American Indian and Eskimo Authors: A Comprehensive Bibliography*, Compiled by Arlene B. Hirshfelder. (New York: Association on American Indian Affairs, 1973).

[6]For a limited discussion of this see, K. O. Arvidson, "The Emergence of a Polynesian Literature," *World Literature Written in English,* XII (April 1975), pp. 91-115.

[7]See Gerald Moore, ed., *African Literature and the Universities* (Ibadan Univ. Press, 1965); Chinua Achebe, "English and the African Writer," *Transition* 18, 1965; Gerald Moore, *The Chosen Tongue* (London: Longmans, 1969); and Joseph Jones, *Terranglia* (New York: Twayne Publishers, 1965).

[8]New York: New Directions, 1963, p. vii.

## Chapter 1: The Death of a Culture—René Maran's *Batouala*

[1]Donald E. Herdeck, "René Maran's *Batouala*: Polemic, Scandal, Metaphor, and Myth," Unpublished, n.d., pp. 1–2.
[2]Mercer Cook, *Five French Negro Authors* (Washington, D.C.: The Associated Publishers, Inc., 1943), pp. 123–148.
[3]Brian Weinstein, *Eboué* (Oxford Univ. Press, 1972), p. 81.
[4]Herdeck, p. 10.
[5]Mercer Cook, "The Last Laugh," in *Africa from the Point of View of American Negro Scholars* (Paris: Présençe Africaine, 1958), p. 204.
[6]Ibid., pp. 204–205.
[7]Herdeck, pp. 4–5.
[8]Nicolas Godian, "*Batouala* Reassessed," *West Africa* (Sept. 3, 1973), p. 1230.
[9]Ibid.
[10]Ibid.
[11]Ibid., p. 1231.
[12]Ibid.
[13]Herdeck, p. 2.
[14]*Whispers from a Continent* (New York: Random House, 1969), p. 84.
[15]New York: Collier Books, 1971, p. 48; Paris: Librairie Plon, 1954, p. 37.
[16]Ibid.
[17]"The Roots of Négritude," *Africa Report* (May 1966), p. 61.
[18]Mircea Eliade, *Cosmos and History* (New York: Harper Torchbooks, 1959), p. 86.
[19]Ibid., p. 85.
[20]Ibid., pp. 20–21.
[21]Ibid., p. 86.
[22]New York: Simon and Schuster, 1972, p. 289.
[23]Ibid.
[24]Godian, p. 1230.
[25]New York: Farrar, Straus & Giroux, Inc., 1974, p. 107.
[26]Ibid., p. 64.

## Chapter 2: History Without Time—Yambo Ouologuem's *Bound to Violence* and Vincent Eri's *The Crocodile*

[1]Yambo Ouologuem, *Bound to Violence* (New York: Harcourt Brace Jovanovich, 1971), from the dust jacket.
[2]See my earlier work, *The Emergence of African Fiction* (Bloomington: Indiana Univ. Press, 1972), especially Chapter One.
[3]Eric Sellin, "Ouologuem's Blueprint for *Le devoir de violence*," *Research in African Literatures*, II (Fall 1971), pp. 117–120.
[4]Ibid., p. 118.
[5]*The Times Literary Supplement* (May 5, 1972), p. 525.
[6]Ibid.
[7]Ibid.
[8]"Novel is Likened to Greene's Book," The New York *Times* (May 5, 1972), p. 34, col. 1.

[9] Ibid.

[10] Paul Flamand, "Letter to the Editor," *The Times Literary Supplement* (May 19, 1972), p. 576.

[11] Robert McDonald, *"Bound to Violence*: A Case of Plagiarism," *Transition*, No. 41 (1972), pp. 64–68.

[12] Ibid., p. 67.

[13] Ibid., p. 68.

[14] Yambo Ouologuem, "Le devoir de violence," *Le Figaro Littéraire* (June 10, 1972), p. 17.

[15] Eric Sellin, Letter, Dec. 5, 1973.

[16] Kaye Whiteman, "In Defence of Yambo Ouologuem," *West Africa* (July 21, 1972), p. 941.

[17] Ibid.

[18] Ibid.

[19] Ibid.

[20] Ibid.

[21] Rosemary Daughton, Letter, Jan. 23, 1974.

[22] T. G. Rosenthal, Letter, Feb. 4, 1974.

[23] Yambo Ouologuem, *Bound to Violence* (London: Heinemann Educational Books, 1971).

[24] Helen Wolff, Letter, Jan. 24, 1974.

[25] André Schwarz-Bart, *The Last of the Just* (New York: Bantam Books, 1961), p. 3. *Les Dernier des Justes* (Paris: Éditions du Seuil, 1959), p. 11. Subsequent page numbers for these editions will appear in the text.

[26] New York: Collier Books, 1971, p. 82; Paris: Librairie Plon, 1954, p. 72.

[27] James Olney, *Tell Me Africa* (Princeton Univ. Press, 1973), p. 208.

[28] Ibid., p. 234.

[29] Vincent Eri, *The Crocodile* (Queenstown: The Jacaranda Press, 1970), p. 24. Subsequent page numbers will appear in the text.


# Chapter 3: Survival of a Culture—Hyemeyohsts Storm's *Seven Arrows*


[1] Other significant works by Native Americans include the following: D'Arcy McNickle, *The Surrounded* (New York: Dodd, Mead & Co., 1936); D. Chief Eagle, *Winter Count* (Colorado Springs, Colorado: Dentan-Berkeland Printing Co., Inc., 1967); N. Scott Momaday, *House Made of Dawn* (New York: Harper & Row, 1968); James Welch, *Winter in the Blood* (New York: Harper & Row, 1974).

[2] Hyemeyohsts Storm, *Seven Arrows* (New York: Harper & Row, 1972), p. 1. Subsequent page numbers will appear in the text.

[3] Passages from *Seven Arrows* that are in italics (to indicate sign language) are indicated by an "I" following the page number.

[4] Faith Gabelnick, "Identity within the Melting Pot: A Critical Reading of Seven Arrows," unpublished, n.d., p. 13.

## Chapter 4: Toward a Sense of the Community—George Lamming's
### *In the Castle of My Skin*

[1]George Lamming, *In the Castle of My Skin* (New York: Collier Books, 1970), p. v. Subsequent page numbers will appear in the text.

[2]Ayi Kwei Armah, *The Beautyful Ones Are Not Yet Born* (New York: Collier Books, 1969), p. 91.

## Chapter 5: Return to the Past—Jean Toomer's *Cane*

[1]Arna Bontemps, "Introduction" to Jean Toomer's *Cane* (New York: Harper and Row, 1969), p. viii.

[2]Ibid., p. xiii.

[3]James Weldon Johnson, *The Autobiography of an Ex-Colored Man* in *Three Negro Classics,* ed. John Hope Franklin (New York: Avon Books, 1965), p. 499.

[4]Bontemps, p. x.

[5]Darwin T. Turner, *In a Minor Chord* (Carbondale: Southern Illinois Univ. Press, 1971), p. 14.

[6]Ibid., p. 2.

[7]See especially Todd Lieber, "Design and Movement in *Cane,*" *CLA Journal,* XIII (Sept. 1969), pp. 35-50 and Donald G. Ackley, "Theme and Vision in Jean Toomer's *Cane,*" *Studies in Black Literature,* I (1970), pp. 45-65. I am indebted to both of these articles—especially for their commentry about imagery in Toomer's novel.

[8]Jean Toomer, *Cane* (New York: Harper and Row, 1969), p. 1. Subsequent page numbers will appear in the text. All earlier editions of *Cane* have the same pagination.

[9]Nancy Carter Goodley, "How the White Folks Made the Bible Lie," unpublished ms., n.d., p. 3.

[10]Bontemps, p. xii.

[11]Turner, p. 32.

[12]Ibid., p. 30.

[13]Ibid., p. 37.

[14]Nathan Irvin Huggins, *Harlem Renaissance* (Oxford Univ. Press, 1971), p. 189.

[15]Turner, p. 59.

[16]W. E. B. DuBois, *The Souls of Black Folks* in *Three Negro Classics,* ed. John Hope Franklin (New York: Avon Books, 1965), p. 221.

# Chapter 6: Revolt and Rebirth, Cultural Renewal—Rajo Rao's *Kanthapura* and Kamala Markandaya's *Two Virgins*

[1]Washington, D.C.: Black Orpheus Press, 1973.

[2]Toni Morrison, Gayle Jones, and Maya Angelou, though the latter has written only autobiographies. Two black female poets should be cited here too: Nikki Giovanni and the "new" Gwendolyn Brooks.

[3]Kamala Markandaya, Anita Desai, R. Prawer Jhabvala (Polish by birth, but usually included among Indo-Anglian writers), Bharati Mukerjee, and Nayantara Sahgal.

[4]Raja Rao, *Kanthapura* (New York: New Directions, 1967), p. 1. Subsequent page numbers will appear in the text.

[5]M.A. Naik, *Raja Rao* (New York: Twayne Publishers, Inc., 1973), p. 76.

[6]Kamala Markandaya, *Two Virgins* (New York: John Day, 1973), p. 11. Subsequent page numbers will appear in the text.

# Chapter 7: The Singular Consciousness—R. K. Narayan's *Grateful to Life and Death* and Bessie Head's *A Question of Power*

[1]R. K. Narayan, *Grateful to Life and Death* (East Lansing: Michigan State College Press, 1953), p.1. Subsequent page numbers will appear in the text.

[2]New York: The Viking Press, 1974, pp. 134–135.

[3]Other female African novelists include Flora Nwapa, Grace Ogot, Adsora Lily Ulasi, and Buchi Emecheta.

[4]The most introspective African novelists to date have been Wole Soyinka, Ayi Kwei Armah, and Kofi Awoonor.

[5]Bessie Head, *A Question of Power* (London: Davis-Poynter, 1973; New York, Pantheon Books, 1973; and London: Heinemann Educational Books, 1974), p. 16. All three editions have the same pagination. Subsequent page numbers will appear in the text.

[6]The original South African Immorality Act was passed in 1927, prohibiting sexual relations between Europeans and Africans. In 1950, it was amended to further prohibit carnal intercourse between whites and all non-whites, that is, Africans, Coloureds and Asians. Apparently still not strong enough, in 1957 the penalties for all such activities were increased. Source: Brian Bunting, *The Rise of the South African Reich* (Middlesex: Penguin Books, 1964).

[7]See especially the works of Dennis Brutis, Ezekiel Mphahlele, and Arthur Nortje.

[8]Roberta Rubenstein, Review of *A Question of Power*, *The New Republic*, LCXX (May 27, 1974), p. 31.

[9]Ibid., p. 30.

# Conclusion—The Novel in the Third World

[1]Witi Ihimaera, *Tangi* (Auckland: Heinemann, 1973), p. 26.

[2]"Maori-go-round," *The Times Literary Supplement* (July 12, 1974), p. 741.

# Bibliography

This bibliography is limited to the Third World writers who are mentioned in the text and the footnotes of this book. To these I have added the various critical and related works also mentioned in the text and the footnotes. In the case of primary works, an attempt has been made to list reprint editions currently in print. (The original date of publication is listed after the title of the work.)

Abbas, Khwaja Ahmed. *Inquilab*. Bombay: Jaico Publications, 1955.

Abrahams, Peter. *Mine Boy* (1946). New York: Collier Books, 1970.

———. *Tell Freedom* (1954). New York: Collier Books, 1970.

Achebe, Chinua. *Things Fall Apart* (1958). Greenwich, Conn.: Fawcett, 1969

———. *No Longer at Ease* (1960). Greenwich, Conn.: Fawcett, 1969.

———. *Arrow of God* (1964). New York: Doubleday, 1969.

———. *A Man of the People* (1966). New York: Doubleday, 1967.

———. *Girls at War and Other Stories* (1972). New York: Doubleday, 1973.

———. "English and the African Writer." *Transition*, No. 18 (1965), pp. 27–30.

Ackley, Donald G. "Theme and Vision in Jean Toomer's *Cane*." *Studies in Black Literature*, 1 (1970), 45–65.

Aidoo, Ama Ata. *The Dilemma of a Ghost* (1965). New York; Collier Books, 1971.

Anand, Mulk Raj. *Untouchable* (1935). New Delhi: Hind Pocket Books, 1970.

———. *The Sword and the Sickle* (1942). Bombay: Kutub-Publishers, 1955.

———. *The Old Woman and the Cow*. Bombay: Kutub-Popular, 1960.

Angelou, Maya. *I Know Why the Caged Bird Sings* (1970). New York: Bantam Books, 1971.

Anthony, Michael. *The Year in San Fernando* (1965). London: Heinemann, 1970.

Apple, Arnold. *Son of Guyana*. Oxford Univ. Press, 1973.

Armah, Ayi Kwei. *The Beautyful Ones Are Not Yet Born* (1968). New York: Collier Books, 1969.
————. *Fragments* (1969). New York: Collier Books, 1971.
————. *Why Are We So Blest?* New York: Doubleday, 1972.
————. *Two Thousand Seasons.* Nairobi: East African Publishing House, 1973.
Attaway, William. *Blood on the Forge* (1941). New York: Collier Books, 1970.
Baldwin, James. *Go Tell It on the Mountain* (1953). New York: Dell, 1965.
Bone, Robert. *The Negro Novel in America.* New Haven: Yale Univ. Press, 1965.
Brooks, Gwendolyn. *Maud Martha.* New York: Harper & Row, 1953.
Brown, Claude. *Manchild in the Promised Land.* New York: Macmillan, 1965.
Brown, William Wells. *Clotel* (1851). New York: Collier Books, 1970.
Cartey, Winfred. *Whispers from a Continent.* New York: Random House, 1969.
Chesnutt, Charles. *The House Behind the Cedars* (1900). New York: Collier Books, 1969.
————. *The Marrow of Tradition.* Boston: Houghton Mifflin, 1901.
————. *The Colonel's Dream.* New York: Doubleday Page, 1905.
Cook, Mercer. *Five French Negro Authors.* Washington, D.C.: The Associated Publishers, 1943.
————. "The Last Laugh" in *Africa from the Point of View of American Negro Scholars.* Paris: Présence Africaine, 1958.
Costo, Rupert. " 'Seven Arrows' Desecrates Cheyenne." *The Indian Historian,* 5 (1972), 41–42.
Coulthard, G. R. *Race and Color in Caribbean Literature.* Oxford Univ. Press, 1962.
Cullen, Countee. *One Way to Heaven.* New York: Harper & Brothers, 1932.
Demby, William. *Beetlecreek* (1950). New York: Avon, 1967.
Desai, Anita. *Cry, the Peacock.* London: Peter Owen, 1963.
Dodson, Owen. *Boy at the Window.* New York: Farrar, Straus & Co., 1951.
DuBois, W.E.B. *The Souls of Black Folks* (1903). In *Three Negro Classics,* ed. John Hope Franklin. New York: Avon, 1965.
————. *The Quest of the Silver Fleece.* Chicago: McClurg, 1911.
Dunbar, Paul Laurence. *The Uncalled.* New York: Dodd, Mead, 1898.
————. *The Love of Laudry.* New York: Dodd, Mead, 1900.
————. *The Fanatics.* New York: Dodd, Mead, 1901.
————. *The Sport of the Gods* (1902). New York: Collier Books, 1970.
Eagle, Dallas Chief. *Winter Count.* Colorado Springs, Colo.: Dentan-Berkeland Printing Co., 1967.
Ekwensi, Cyprian. *Jagua Nana* (1961). Greenwich, Conn.: Fawcett, 1969.
Eliade, Mircea. *Cosmos and History.* New York: Harper Torchbooks, 1959.
Ellison, Ralph. *Invisible Man* (1952). New York: Vintage Books, 1972.
Flamand, Paul. "Letter to the editor." *Times Literary Supplement.* 19 May 1972, p. 576.
Gabelnick, Faith. "Identity within the Melting Pot: A Critical Reading of *Seven Arrows.*" Unpublished, n.d.
Gaines, Ernest J. *The Autobiography of Miss Jane Pittman.* New York: Dial, 1971.
Godian, Nicolas. *"Batouala* Reassessed." *West Africa,* 3 Sept. 1973, pp. 1230–1231.
Goodley, Nancy Carter. "How the White Folks Made the Bible Lie." Unpublished, n.d.
Head, Bessie. *When Rain Clouds Gather.* New York: Simon and Schuster, 1968.
————. *Maru.* New York: McCall Pub. Co., 1971.
————. *A Question of Power.* London: Davis-Poynter, 1973 and Heinemann, 1974; New York: Pantheon, 1973.
Herdeck, Donald E. *African Authors: A Companion to Black African Writing* 1300–1973. Washington, D.C. Black Orpheus Press, 1973.
————. "René Maran's *Batouala:* Polemic, Scandal, Metaphor, and Myth." Unpublished, n.d.
Huggins, Nathan Irvin. *Harlem Renaissance.* New York: Oxford Univ. Press, 1971.
Hughes, Langston. *Not without Laughter* (1930). New York: Collier Books, 1969.

Ihimaera, Witi. *Pounamu, Pounamu*. Auckland: Heinemann, 1972.
————. *Tangi*. Auckland: Heinemann, 1973.
————. *Whanau*. Auckland: Heinemann, 1974.
Jhabvala, R. Prawer. *A New Dominion*. London: John Murray, 1972. (Published in the United States as *Travelers*. Harper & Row, 1973).
Johnson, James Weldon. *The Autobiography of an Ex-Colored Man* (1912). In *Three Negro Classics*, ed. John Hope Franklin. New York: Avon, 1965.
Jones, Joseph. *Terranglia*. New York: Twayne Publishers, 1965.
Kelley, William M. *A Different Drummer* (1962). New York: Doubleday Anchor, 1969.
————. *A Drop of Patience*. New York: Doubleday, 1965.
————. *dem* (1967). New York: Collier Books, 1969.
Kennedy, Ellen and Paulette J. Trout. "The Roots of Négritude." *Africa Report*, May 1966, pp. 61–62.
Lamming, George. *In the Castle of My Skin* (1953). New York: Collier Books, 1970.
————. *The Emigrants*. London: Michael Joseph, 1954.
————. *Of Age and Innocence*. London: Michael Joseph, 1958.
————. *Season of Adventure*. London: Michael Joseph, 1960.
————. *Water with Berries*. New York: Holt, Rinehart and Winston, 1971.
————. *Natives of My Person*. New York: Holt, Rinehart and Winston, 1972.
Larsen, Nella. *Quicksand* (1928). New York: Collier Books, 1971.
————. *Passing* (1929). New York: Collier Books, 1971.
Larson, Charles R. *The Emergence of African Fiction*. Bloomington: Indiana University Press, 1972.
————. "Heroic Ethnocentrism: The Idea of Universality in Literature." *The American Scholar*, XXXXII (Summer 1973), pp. 463–475.
Laye, Camara. *The Dark Child* (1953). London: Fontana Books, 1959; *L'enfant noir*. Paris: Librairie Plon, 1953.
————. *The Radiance of the King* (1954). New York: Collier Books, 1971; *Le regard du roi*. Paris: Librairie Plon, 1954.
————. *A Dream of Africa* (1966). New York: Collier Books, 1971; *Dramouss*. Paris: Librairie Plon, 1966.
Lieber, Todd. "Design and Movement in *Cane*." *CLA Journal*, 13 (1969), 35–50.
"Maori-go-round." *Times Literary Supplement*, 12 July 1974, p. 741.
Maran, René. *Batouala* (1921). Washington, D.C.: Black Orpheus Press, 1972 and London: Heinemann, 1973; Paris: Albin Michel, 1938. (Rev. ed.)
————. *Djouma, chien de brousse*. Paris: Albin Michel, 1927.
————. *Journal sans date*. Paris: Artheme Fayard et Cie., 1927.
————. *Le livre de la brousse*. Paris: Albin Michel, 1934.
————. *Un homme pareil aux autres*. Paris: Éditions Arc-en-ciel, 1947.
Margolies, Edward. *Native Sons*. Philadelphia: Lippincott, 1968.
Markandaya, Kamala. *Nectar in a Sieve* (1954). New York: New American Library, n.d.
————. *Some Inner Fury*. New York: John Day, 1956.
————. *A Silence of Desire*. New York: John Day, 1960.
————. *Possession*. New York: John Day, 1963.
————. *A Handful of Rice*. New York: John Day, 1966.
————. *The Coffer Dams*. New York: John Day, 1969.
————. *The Nowhere Man*. New York: John Day, 1972.
————. *Two Virgins*. New York: John Day, 1973.
Matane, Paulias. *Aimbe, The Challenger*. Port Moresby: Niugini Press, 1974.
McDonald, Robert. "*Bound to Violence*: A Case of Plagiarism." *Transition*, No. 41 (1972), pp. 64–68.
McKay, Claude. *Banana Bottom*. New York: Harper, 1933.
McNickle, D'Arcy. *The Surrounded*. New York: Dodd, Mead & Company, 1936.
Momaday, N. Scott. *House Made of Dawn* (1967). New York: New American Library, 1969.

Moore, Gerald, ed. *African Literature and the Universities.* Ibadan Univ. Press, 1965.
————. *The Chosen Tongue.* London: Longmans, 1969.
Moravia, Alberto. *Which Tribe Do You Belong To?* New York: Farrar, Straus & Giroux, 1974.
Morrison, Toni. *Sula.* New York: Knopf, 1974.
Mphahlele, Ezekiel. *The Wanderers.* New York: Macmillan, 1971.
Mukerjee, Bharati. *The Tiger's Daughter.* Boston: Houghton Mifflin, 1972.
Mukerjee, Meenakshi. *The Twice Born Fiction.* New Delhi: Heinemann, 1971.
Nagarajan, K. *Chronicles of Kedaram.* Bombay: Asia Pub. House, 1961.
Naik, M.A. *Raja Rao.* New York: Twayne Publishers, 1973.
Naipaul, V.S. *The Suffrage of Elvira.* London: Andre Deutsch, 1958.
————. *A House for Mr. Biswas.* London: Andre Deutsch, 1961.
————. *The Mimic Men.* London: Andre Deutsch, 1967.
Narayan, R. K. *Swami and Friends* (1935). New York: Fawcett, 1970.
————. *The Bachelor of Arts* (1937). East Lansing: Michigan State College Press, 1954.
————. *The English Teacher* (1945). East Lansing: Michigan State College Press, 1953. (Published under the title *Grateful to Life and Death.*)
————. *The Financial Expert* (1952). New York: Noonday Press, 1959.
————. *Waiting for the Mahatma* (1955). East Lansing: Michigan State College Press, 1955.
————. *The Guide.* New York: Viking, 1958.
————. *The Sweet-Vendor* (1967). New York: Avon, 1971. (Published under the title *The Vendor of Sweets.*)
————. *My Days: A Memoir.* New York: Viking, 1974.
Ngugi, James. *Weep Not, Child* (1964). New York: Collier Books, 1969.
————. *The River Between.* London: Heinemann, 1965.
————. *A Grain of Wheat.* London: Heinemann, 1967.
"Novel is Likened to Greene's Book." The New York *Times,* 17 May 1972, p. 34, col. 1.
Olney, James. *Tell Me Africa.* Princeton Univ. Press, 1973.
Ouologuem, Yambo. *Bound to Violence* (1968). New York: Harcourt Brace Jovanovich, 1971 and London: Heinemann, 1971; *Le devoir de violence.* Paris: Éditions du Seuil, 1968.
————. "Le devoir de violence." *Le Figaro Littéraire,* June 1972.
————. *Les mille et une bibles du sexe.* Paris: Éditions du Dauphin, 1969. (Published under the pseudonym of Utto Rodolph.)
Ousmane, Sembene. *God's Bits of Wood* (1960). New York: Doubleday Anchor, 1970; *Les bouts de bois de Dieu.* Paris: Le Livre contemporain, 1960.
Raja Rao. *Kanthapura* (1938). New York: New Directions, 1967.
————. *The Serpent and the Rope.* London: John Murray, 1960.
————. *The Cat and Shakespeare.* New York: Macmillan, 1965.
Ramchand, Kenneth. *The West Indian Novel and Its Background.* London: Faber and Faber, 1970.
Roumain, Jacques. *Masters of the Dew* (1944). New York: Collier Books, 1971; *Gouveneurs de la Rosée.* Paris: Les Editeurs francais réunis, 1944.
Schwarz-Bart, André. *The Last of the Just* (1959). New York: Bantam Books, 1961; *Les Dernier des Justes.* (Paris: Éditions du Seuil, 1959.)
————. *A Woman Named Solitude.* New York: Atheneum, 1973; *La mulâtresse Solitude.* Paris: Éditions du Seuil, 1972.
Schwarz-Bart, Simone. *The Bridge of Beyond* (1972). New York: Atheneum, 1974; *Pluie et rent sur Télumée.* Paris: Éditions du Seuil, 1972.
Sellin, Eric. "Ouologuem's Blueprint for *Le devoir de violence.*" *Research in African Literatures,* 2 (1971), 117–120.
"Something *New* Out of Africa." *Times Literary Supplement,* 5 May 1972, p. 525.
Soyinka, Wole. *The Interpreters* (1965). New York: Collier Books, 1970.

————. *Season of Anomy*. London: Rex Collings, 1973.

Storm, Hyemeyohsts. *Seven Arrows*. New York: Harper & Row, 1972.

Toomer, Jean. *Cane* (1923). New York: Harper & Row, 1969.

————. *Essentials*. Chicago: The Lakeside Press, 1931.

Turnbull, Colin. *The Mountain People*. New York: Simon and Schuster, 1972.

Turner, Darwin T. *In a Minor Chord*. Carbondale: Southern Illinois Univ. Press, 1971.

Tutuola, Amos. *The Palm-Wine Drinkard* (1952). New York: Grove Press, 1953.

Walsh, William. *R. K. Narayan*. London: The British Council, 1971.

Weinsten, Brian. *Eboué*. Oxford Univ. Press, 1972.

Welch, James. *Winter in the Blood*. New York: Harper & Row, 1974.

Wendt, Albert. *Sons for the Return Home*. Auckland: Longman Paul, 1973.

Whiteman, Kaye. "In Defence of Yambo Ouologuem." *West Africa*, 21 July 1972, pp. 939–941.

Wright, Richard. *Black Boy* (1945). New York: Harper & Row, 1966.

# INDEX